LEJEUNE

John Archer Lejeune by Joseph Cummings Chase, 1919. Courtesy of the Smithsonian Institution and the Marine Corps Historical Center.

LEJEUNE:

A MARINE'S LIFE, 1867–1942

BY MERRILL L. BARTLETT

UNIVERSITY OF SOUTH CAROLINA PRESS

Library of Congress Cataloging-in-Publication Data

Bartlett, Merrill L.
   Lejeune : a marine's life, 1867–1942 / by Merrill L. Bartlett.
     p. cm.
   Includes bibliographical references and index.
   ISBN 0–87249–771–2 (hardcover : acid-free)
   1. Lejeune, John Archer, 1867–1942. 2. United States. Marine
Corps—Biography. 3. Generals—United States—Biography.
4. World War, 1914–1918—Campaigns—France. I. Title.
VE25.L45B37   1991
359.9′6′092—dc20
[B]   91-21551

To Blythe

CONTENTS

ILLUSTRATIONS

PHOTOGRAPHS

John Archer Lejeune by Joseph Cummings Chase   *frontispiece*

MAPS

FOREWORD

To all Marines interested in the history of our Corps, and all others dedicated to researching and writing that history, a study of the nine-year commandancy of our 13th Commandant of the Marine Corps, Major General John A. Lejeune, will provide many insights into the changing character of our country and the changing mission of the Marine Corps. When World War I began, the United States was not quite yet a world power, even though it had interests in China, the Philippines, and Latin America. With its participation in and influence on the course of the war in Europe, America truly became an international force.

Participation in the fighting in France had a great impact on the Marine Corps, also. First, the Corps expanded fivefold to 79,524 Marines, including 269 women reservists dubbed "Marinettes." For the first time in their history, Marines in France fought and served together in the largest Marine combat formation to date, the 4th Marine Brigade. Another Marine Corps first occurred when Major General John A. Lejeune, the brigade commander, became Commanding General of the 2d Infantry Division, the first time in history that a Marine general officer commanded so large a unit.

When he assumed the commandancy in 1920, General Lejeune headed a Corps numbering approximately 17,400 men, a considerable reduction from what it had been in World War I. He envisioned a Marine Corps whose success depended on two factors: "first, an efficient performance of all the duties to which its officers and men may be assigned; second, promptly bringing this efficiency to the attention of the proper officials of the government and the American people." General Lejeune saw that his Marine Corps faced at least three major internal problems. First, there was the issue of educating officers for broader and more complex and technical duties than those to which they had been assigned theretofore. At the same time, the Corps had to attract to its ranks a smarter, younger, and more easily motivated type of recruit who would be able to fit into a changing Marine Corps. Finally, General Lejeune had to seek for the Marine Corps an appropriate role in the defense of the country and a mission which it alone could fill.

He looked to the future of the Corps and instinctively knew that the Corps could not revert to its prewar role and outlook. As the noted Marine Corps historian, Colonel Robert D. Heinl Jr., observed: "Lejeune understood this fact well, even though many other Marines did not. General Lejeune was not only a field soldier of high ability, and a beloved leader, but also a Marine of prescient, active intelligence."

After reviewing the prewar missions of the Marine Corps and how they were accomplished, the Commandant and his advisors correctly concluded that readiness was the standard which inevitably ensured the success of any mission to which Marines were assigned. He then took several steps to guarantee that the Corps would be ready. One was to establish the Marine Corps Schools at Quantico, where his officers would be educated in their profession. As a corollary, General Lejeune encouraged his officers to attend the excellent schools run by the Army at that time. As a result, many of those who attained senior officer rank in World War II were those who had attended and graduated from the Fort Benning Infantry School, or the Command and General Staff Course at Fort Leavenworth, or the Fort Sill Artillery Course, among others, as well as from Navy and foreign military institutions. For enlisted Marines, there was the Marine Corps

Institute, established during the commandancy of General Lejeune's predecessor, Major General George Barnett, but nurtured and supported by Lejeune.

A major achievement attained during General Lejeune's tenure was the realignment of the Marine Corps into the East and West Coast Expeditionary Forces, leading to the establishment of the Fleet Marine Force in 1933, which, in turn, compelled the Corps to develop amphibious warfare doctrine and techniques.

We Marines today are the heirs of General Lejeune's legacy, which he enunciated so well in Article 38 of the 1921 edition of the *United States Marine Corps Manual:*

> In every battle and skirmish since the birth of our Corps, Marines have acquitted themselves with great distinction, winning new honors on each occasion until the term Marine has come to signify all that is highest in military efficiency and soldierly virtue.
>
> This high name of distinction and soldierly repute, we, who are Marines today, have received from those who preceded us in the Corps. With it we also received from them the eternal spirit which has animated our Corps from generation to generation and has been the distinguishing mark of the Marines in every age. So long as that spirit continues to flourish, Marines will be found equal to every emergency in the future, as they have been in the past, and the men of our Nation will regard us as worthy successors to the long line of illustrious men who have served as "Soldiers of the Sea" since the founding of the Corps.

These words of General Lejeune are as valid today as they were when he first wrote them. And succeeding generations of Marines will find them as timely as well.

A. M. GRAY
General, U.S. Marine Corps (Retired)
Commandant of the Marine Corps (1987–1991)

ACKNOWLEDGMENTS

The undertaking of a serious, scholarly endeavor presupposes the stimulus of valued teachers and professors. At Washington State University, Professor Melvin R. Gibson challenged me to seek new and broader horizons. During the studies for my M.A. at San Diego State University, Professor Alvin D. Coox honed my skills as a scholar and convinced me to research and write history seriously; in the process, he transferred his passion for the historical pursuit to me. At the University of Maryland, College Park, Professor Keith Olson sharpened my proficiency as a historian and an author during studies at the doctoral level.

The intellectual impetus for the undertaking of this project began during my tenure in the Department of History, United States Naval Academy, 1977–82. While my superiors and colleagues alike urged me to research and write for publication, my good friend Associate Professor Jack Sweetman offered unflagging encouragement and advice when it appeared that my efforts might flounder. Jack shared his special insights into the history of the Naval Academy during Lejeune's era, and he also read earlier versions of the manuscript, offering inestimable criticism. The staff of Nimitz Library at the academy proved invaluable in the quest for out-of-print manuscripts, with computer searches of the literature, and by funding the microfilming of the Lejeune Papers held by the Manuscripts Division, Library of Congress. The Naval Academy Research Council (NARC) provided generous grants, which allowed me to spend two summers researching and writing the life of a Lejeune contemporary, Major General Commandant George Barnett.

Acknowledgments

Anyone researching and writing on a subject germane to the United States Marine Corps knows that the first and last stops must be at the Marine Corps Historical Center (MCHC) in the Washington Navy Yard. Brigadier General Edwin H. Simmons, USMC (Retired), Director of Marine Corps History and Museums, provided invaluable advice and encouragement; he also read an earlier version of my manuscript. At the MCHC, I was assisted by Evelyn A. Englander in the library; Danny Crawford, Ann A. Ferrante, and Robert V. Aquilina in the reference section; first Charles A. Wood and then J. Michael Miller, personal papers; and Benis M. Frank in oral histories. Regina Strother and Jack Dyer aided in the location of Lejeune-related photographs. My good friend in the histories section, Jack Shulimson, shared invaluable materials from his extensive research into the Marine Corps in the Age of Mahan. The Marine Corps Historical Foundation provided a generous grant to support my organization of the Lejeune papers and the preparation of a register. Across the street, two directors of the Naval Historical Center, Ronald Spector and Dean C. Allard, offered their full resources for the navy side of the Lejeune story.

Elsewhere in Washington, at the National Archives (NA), Timothy K. Nenninger assisted me in locating obscure or misplaced documents. His contribution to my researches into the records of the American Expeditionary Forces (AEF) (Record Group 120) added immeasurably to my understanding of Lejeune's place in the history of the AEF. Richard A. von Doenhoff, Military Reference Branch, aided me in researching both navy and Marine Corps records germane to Lejeune's professional life. In the Manuscripts Division, Library of Congress, first Paul T. Heffron and then James J. Hutson and their staffs guided me in my researches into the large number of manuscript collections cited in this study.

Outside the Washington area, Gertrude M. Beauford, secretary, Louisiana Historical Society, provided useful materials on Lejeune's boyhood in Louisiana; Ms. Beauford even traveled to Pointe Coupee Parish to photograph the tombstones of Lejeune's ancestors buried in the churchyard of St. Stephen's so as to ensure the accuracy of published dates of births and deaths. Colonel John E. Greenwood, USMC (Ret.), editor, *Marine Corps Gazette*, made the full resources of the Marine Corps Association available and shared his extensive knowledge of the early years of the Naval Academy with me. Also at Quantico, Lieutenant Colonel Donald F. Bittner, USMCR (Ret.), Professor of Military History, Marine Corps Command and Staff College, offered useful observations and insights about the interwar Marine Corps.

Captain Edward L. Beach, USN (Ret.), kindly allowed me to read his father's unpublished memoir, an important document because the elder Beach was Lejeune's Naval Academy roommate. Lelia Gordon Lucas, Major General George Barnett's surviving stepdaughter, shared her mother's personal papers and unpublished memoirs with me along with a scintillating day of reminiscences of the early interwar years. At the Virginia Military Institute, Julia Smith Martin, Assistant Public Information Officer, opened the archives of the institution to me and provided a wealth of unusual information with regard to Lejeune's tenure as superintendent. My good friend Professor Allan R. Millett, Mershon Institute, The Ohio State University, contributed countless bits of advice and wisdom from his seemingly endless storehouse of information on World War I and Marine Corps history in general.

At the University of South Carolina Press, Warren Slesinger, Acquisitions Manager, guided my manuscript from initial proposal to first submission and ultimately to the finished product; his encouragement and counsel has kept the production of this volume on track throughout. In all of my research and writing on the naval history of the Age of Mahan, and especially the years of Barnett and Lejeune, my family has endured numerous distractions far too often. My children, Blythe and Brendan, displayed remarkable forbearance as their father immersed himself in his historical efforts. My wife, Blythe W. Bartlett, provided the atmosphere and environment at home that are the envy of scholars everywhere. Moreover, she read and re-read countless versions of Lejeune-related manuscripts, as well as other essays and monographs intended for publication. Her editorial eye and critical analyses kept me on task and prevented my study of John Archer Lejeune from going astray; to her, this volume is affectionately dedicated.

CHRONOLOGY OF THE LIFE OF
JOHN ARCHER LEJEUNE

31 August 1820: Ovide Lejeune born.

6 December 1840: Laura Archer Turpin born.

14 June 1859: Laura Archer Turpin and Ovide Lejeune married.

22 March 1860: Augustine Lejeune born.

19 January 1867: John Archer Lejeune born.

September 1881–April 1884: Louisiana State University.

15 May 1884–8 June 1888: naval cadet, U.S. Naval Academy.

8 June 1888: graduated, U.S. Naval Academy.

7 September 1888–14 January 1889: midshipman in the *Mohican*.

19 January–23 March 1889: midshipman in the *Vandalia*.

16 December 1889: Ovide Lejeune dies.

27 April 1889–15 March 1890: midshipman in the *Adams*.

6 April–19 June 1990: postcruise examinations, Annapolis.

25 July 1990: commissioned second lieutenant, U.S. Marine Corps.

1 September 1890: reported to Marine Barracks, New York.

3 November 1890: reported to Marine Barracks, Portsmouth, Virginia.

1 October 1891–28 July 1893: Marine Detachment in the *Bennington*.

11 April 1892: promoted to first lieutenant.

August 1893–August 1897: Marine Barracks, Norfolk.

23 October 1895: Ellie Harrison Murdaugh and John A. Lejeune married.

18 August 1896: Ellie Murdaugh Lejeune born.

2 August 1897–17 February 1899: Marine Detachment in the *Cincinnati.*

18 February–10 May 1899: Marine Detachment in the *Massachusetts.*

2 January 1899: Laura Archer Lejeune dies.

3 March 1899: promoted to captain.

3 July–10 November 1900: officer in charge, Marine Corps Recruiting Station, New York.

1 December 1900–6 January 1903: commanding officer, Marine Barracks, Pensacola.

9 June 1902: Laura Turpin Lejeune born.

November 1902: hospitalized, Union Protestant Infirmary, Baltimore.

3 March 1903: promoted to major.

May–July 1903: officer in charge, Marine Corps Recruiting Station, New York.

8 August–25 October 1903: commanding officer, Marine Corps battalion on the *Panther.*

26 October 1903–31 December 1904: commanding officer, Marine Corps battalion on the *Dixie.*

14 February 1904: Eugenia Dickson Lejeune born.

January 1905–March 1907: commanding officer, Marine Barracks, Washington.

May–July 1906: commanding officer, marine battalion, Panama.

April 1907–May 1909: commanding officer, Marine Barracks, Cavite.

---

13 May 1909: promoted to lieutenant colonel.

September 1909–September 1910: student, Army War College.

November 1910–November 1914: commanding officer, Marine Barracks, New York.

26 May–2 August 1912: commanding officer, marine battalion, 1st Provisional Regiment, Cuba.

20 February–2 May 1913: advance base force maneuvers, Culebra.

25 February 1914: promoted to colonel.

22 April–15 November 1914: commanding officer, 1st Provisional Regiment, Vera Cruz.

January 1915–August 1917: assistant to the commandant.

29 August 1916: promoted to brigadier general.

27 September 1917–17 May 1918: commanding general, Marine Corps base, Quantico.

19 June–4 July 1918: 35th Division, AEF, for observation.

5 July 1918: commanding general, 64th Brigade, 35th Division, AEF.

15 July 1918: commanding general, 4th Brigade (Marine), Second Division, AEF.

28 July 1918: commanding general, Second Division, AEF.

31 July 1918: promoted to major general.

27 October 1919–29 June 1920: commanding general, Quantico.

30 June 1920–5 March 1929: commandant of the Marine Corps.

12 November 1929: retired from the Marine Corps.

23 March 1929–1 October 1937: Superintendent, Virginia Military Institute.

14 December 1935: Augustine Lejeune dies.

8 April 1942: promoted to lieutenant general on the retired list.

20 November 1942: John Archer Lejeune dies.

23 November 1942: memorial service and burial, Washington and Arlington National Cemetery.

DECORATIONS:

    Distinguished Service Medal (navy)
    Distinguished Service Medal (army)
    Sampson Medal
    Marine Corps Expeditionary Medal (with three stars)
    Mexican Service Medal
    Victory Medal, World War I (with clasps for St. Mihiel, Meuse-Argonne, and Defensive Sector)
    Second Nicaraguan Campaign Medal
    Legion d'Honneur (commander)
    Croix de guerre (bronze palm)

LEJEUNE

INTRODUCTION

Near the end of the first century of its existence, the United States Marine Corps appeared increasingly to be an anachronism. Founded in 1798 on the pattern of the British Royal Marines, the Marines Corps (whose members are sometimes referred to as leathernecks because of leather collars worn during the age of sail as a protective device) served mostly as small security forces in the ships of the Republic and at naval stations ashore. Periodically, marines aboard ship joined larger units of sailors in brief expeditions. There, such as at Qualla Battoo in 1832, bluejackets carrying pistols and cutlasses and leathernecks armed with muskets and bayonets stormed ashore to protect American interests. Occasionally, such as in the Seminole Indian uprisings (1836–42) or in the Mexican War (1846–48), larger bodies of marines participated with troops of the U.S. Army.

A small armed force with a rather dubious status as a separate service within the Department of the Navy, the Marine Corps was often vulnerable to both congressional critics and opponents from its sister services. During its first hundred years, the corps survived several spirited assaults. The most famous and influential head of the small force in its first century, Brigadier General Commandant Archibald Henderson, secured passage of legislation guaranteeing the existence of the Marine Corps on 30 June 1834. This led Henderson and his senior officers to believe that the leathernecks had a secure niche in America's naval establishment.

The smell of gunpowder from the Civil War still hung over the Capitol when a resolution appeared in Congress calling for the

1

transfer of the Marine Corps to the army. Only a spirited offensive by the corps' senior officers and a few loyal navy officers prevented passage. The lackluster performance of the Marine Corps during the Civil War doubtless contributed to the effort by critics to eliminate it as a separate service. In less than a century of service, the Marine Corps weathered numerous such attempts to have it absorbed by a sister service or disbanded altogether.[1]

In the two decades following the Civil War, the Marine Corps (numbering only 92 officers and 1,871 enlisted men in 1876) undertook the most intense reforms since its founding. Plagued with desertions and morale problems with the corps' largely foreign-born enlisted force, and buffeted by demands from some navy officers for the removal of leathernecks from the ships of the fleet, Colonel Commandant Charles G. McCawley sought to improve the professional starch of the corps. Commissioning better-educated officers became an important part of the reform effort; one critic of the corps' junior officers suggested that USMC meant "useless sons made comfortable." Between 1883 and 1897, all of the 51 new second lieutenants for the Marine Corps came from the graduating classes of the U.S. Naval Academy. Most of the midshipmen accepted by the Marine Corps stood too low academically to be commissioned in the navy and thus faced either discharge to civilian life or commissions as second lieutenants. Nonetheless, the Marine Corps profited from this influx of new officers with superior intelligence and more inclination to accept the smaller of the naval services for a full career.[2]

When the class of 1888 returned to Annapolis in the late spring of 1890 from its postgraduation cruise, most midshipmen had already made up their minds as to service selection: navy line or engineering, or the Marine Corps. Although he ranked thirteenth in his class, John Archer Lejeune raised his standing for the purposes of service selection to sixth following a spectacular performance on the postcruise examinations. Thus, senior navy officers were understandably bemused and nonplussed when the feisty Louisianan requested assignment to the Marine Corps. At first rebuffed by navy superiors, one of whom admonished him by exclaiming, "Frankly, Mister Lejeune, you have altogether too many brains to be lost in the Marine Corps," he persisted and obtained a second lieutenant's commission only after the intervention of his senator.[3]

For the first two decades of his service in the Marine Corps, Lejeune's assignments reflected what had become routine for junior officers since 1798—sea or foreign duty alternating with stints at naval stations in the United States. Unlike most of his contemporaries, however, he chose marriage at a young age and began a family. Many of his peers adopted life-styles of hard-drinking womanizers or dandies, claiming that the lengthy periods at sea or abroad forced them to remain perpetual bachelors. As he matured, Lejeune became increasingly devout and moralistic.[4]

A chance assignment as a student at the Army War College in 1909–10 opened new vistas. He probably began his quest for the commandancy then at the urging of the president of the college, who relayed rumors that the helm of the Marine Corps might pass to a staff officer due to the lack of distinguished applicants. Although Lejeune was too junior to be considered seriously for the corps' highest post, either in 1910 or 1913–14, the idea that he might one day head the Marine Corps never disappeared. Following a superlative performance as a regimental commander during the landing at Veracruz in 1914—although he failed to receive one of the several specious awards of the Medal of Honor— Lejeune became the assistant to the commandant, Major General George Barnett. By then, Lejeune had captured the eye and respect of Secretary of the Navy Josephus Daniels. They became fast friends and Daniels sought to include Lejeune in his intraservice political intrigues. More than two decades later, Daniels exclaimed unabashedly: "Our deep friendship formed in the days when we were both in the Navy together is permanent and lasting on both sides. You know that nowhere outside your own kin have you friends who hold you in more affectionate esteem."[5]

Almost from the beginning of America's declaration of war in

1917, Lejeune pressed for orders to join the American Expeditionary Forces (AEF) in France. As a brigadier general, he assumed
that he would be given command of a brigade of infantry. Because
of wartime expansion, Congress authorized the promotion of an
additional major general for the Marine Corps. Daniels involved
himself directly in the selection process and insisted that the
promotion go to his good friend. Lejeune received a second star
in the summer of 1918. Surprising both army and navy observers,
General John J. Pershing gave Lejeune command of the Second
Division, AEF.

Lejeune believed that he received the coveted assignment
because of his superlative performance at the Army War College;
many of his former classmates and instructors served in the highest councils of the AEF. But his appointment may well have
reflected Pershing's strong desire to end the meddling of the
Department of the Navy in AEF affairs. From the outset of the
token deployment of marines in France, senior officers of the
AEF had bridled over the repeated queries from Washington with
regard to employment of leathernecks. Major General Commandant George Barnett hoped to field an entire division of marines
in France, a proposal anathema to higher-ranking army officers.
By giving Lejeune command of a division, Pershing may have
sought to put a damper on leatherneck aggrandizement. Lejeune
led the Second Division, AEF, during the offensives of St. Mihiel,
Blanc Mont, and the Meuse-Argonne and during its deployment as an occupation force along the Rhine. Lejeune became
the first Marine Corps officer to command an entire division,
despite mixed reviews of his performance by army superiors.[6]

A year after Lejeune's return from Europe in 1919, Secretary
Daniels—the appointee of a Democratic administration—stunned
Washington naval and political circles by ousting Major General
Commandant Barnett. The appointment of Lejeune, well known
for his support for the Democrats, produced considerable controversy. Barnett's Republican backers attempted to prevent Lejeune's
confirmation as the thirteenth commandant of the Marine Corps

but failed. For almost a decade, rumors of Lejeune's participation in a cabal to discredit Barnett swirled around him. When Barnett died in 1929, his widow charged Lejeune with hastening her husband's death! Later, she threatened to go public with information linking Lejeune with an alleged conspiracy.

To bring about the change in the corps' highest post, Daniels had sought the support of the controversial and mercurial Brigadier General Smedley D. Butler, an outspoken critic of bureaucrats in uniform and Naval Academy graduates. Butler's father sat on the powerful House Naval Affairs Committee and often intervened at his son's behest in Marine Corps matters. In this instance, the elder Bulter encouraged a change in the commandancy. Although Lejeune and the younger Butler appeared to be close friends, hindsight suggests the relationship existed only to foster their respective career goals. When Congressman Butler died in 1928, Lejeune distanced himself quickly from the sometimes embarrassing Butler. He even declined an invitation to attend Butler's retirement ceremony in 1931, claiming to be pressed by his new duties as superintendent of the Virginia Military Institute.

Although Lejeune received his appointment as commandant of the Marine Corps in an atmosphere rife with acrimony and recrimination, he provided the soothing balm to alleviate the pain and outrage felt by the ousted incumbent and his Republican supporters. Whereas Secretary Daniels continued to humiliate Barnett and exacerbate the controversy, Lejeune, a canny political infighter, whose down-home Louisiana charm masked his shrewdness, suggested the solution that put the difficulty to rest. He alone seemed to understand that Barnett's bruised ego, as well as the embarrassment of his socially prominent and wealthy wife, had to be assuaged. A promotion to major general for Barnett—he had been demoted to brigadier general as a result of his ouster from the commandancy—served to put much of the rancor aside.

The nine years that Lejeune held the reins of the corps remain the least known and appreciated. During these lean years of America's military and naval retrenchment, he redirected the focus of Headquarters Marine Corps (HQMC) from its traditional concerns over manpower and budgetary matters toward operational planning. Seizing on the prophesy of War Plan Orange—envisioning a conflict with Japan—he directed his subordinates to begin operational planning so as to prepare for the employment of amphibious forces in the event of a naval war in the Pacific.

While the genesis of modern amphibious doctrine is rightly attributed to the visionaries of the 1930s, Lejeune's stewardship during the lean years of the Harding-Coolidge retrenchment of the 1920s set the stage. Although plagued with congressional requests for personnel and budgetary reductions, and despite a continuation of traditional commitments overseas or in support of the fleet, Lejeune managed to steer a steady course for the Marine Corps through a period of intense and unrealistic cuts. Only with the election of another Republican in 1929 did Lejeune opt for retirement. Disappointed with Herbert C. Hoover, Lejeune elected to step down; had he requested reappointment to the commandancy, a fourth term at the helm of the Marine Corps could have been his.

Lejeune's Louisiana charm worked wonders on almost everyone whom he encountered, even navy superiors who often came to loggerheads with him over peccadillos of service custom and seniority or army officers who bridled over his unwillingness to adopt a style of leadership based on intimidation and threat. An aide-de-camp recalled Lejeune admonishing a young soldier for an unbuttoned blouse: "Son, General Pershing would give me hell if I went around with my blouse unbuttoned." Sitting on a promotion board, Lejeune and the other members heard a young officer describe his duties as a guard officer. One board member professed ignorance as to the meaning of "gahd," to which Lejeune replied: "Mister Vandegrift is from the south; he spells 'gahd' correctly as 'g-u-a-r-d' but pronounces it correctly as 'gahd'."[7]

Before an accident in 1932 affected his ability to articulate, Lejeune gained a fair amount of respect and admiration for his strong and stirring extemporaneous speeches. After more than four decades in uniform—military cadet at Louisiana State University, naval cadet at the U.S. Naval Academy, midshipman in the fleet, and an officer in the Marine Corps—Lejeune had acquired fixed ideas about citizenship, morality, duty to corps and country, and the high standards expected of a Marine Corps officer. Even before the advent of Prohibition, Lejeune had taken the pledge of temperance.

Of the officers who have held the corps' highest post, two stand out: Archibald Henderson, because he returned the Marine Corps to respectability after a court-martial found his predecessor guilty of public drunkenness and whoring; and Lejeune, who established the basis for the orderly genesis of a modern amphibious doctrine for the Marine Corps. In the process, he maintained the friendship and allegiance of three secretaries of the navy—one of whom was his Naval Academy classmate—and the senior officers of the navy and the Marine Corps. Sustaining the loyalties of his own officers proved to be the most difficult task for Lejeune. While maintaining a friendship with such colorful bushwhackers as Littleton W. T. Waller and Butler; intellectuals and visionaries such as Eli K. Cole, Robert H. Dunlap, John H. Russell, and Dion Williams; and veterans from the AEF like Wendell C. Neville and Harry Lee, Lejeune aligned himself with no particular professional clique.

By the 1920s, the ranks of the officer corps had become badly split. One group, led by the frenetic Butler, wanted a Marine Corps led not by the intellectuals from Annapolis or the war colleges but by seasoned campaigners with tropical sweat stains and powder burns on their uniforms. Another faction, festooned with decorations earned on the battlefields of France, demanded recognition and preferential treatment for their heroic service. A third clique sought a Marine Corps led by officers with intellect and vision to prepare for its assault mission in support of the fleet.

This last coterie—composed largely of Annapolitans—sought the transformation of the Marine Corps from a rather colorful and quaint light infantry corps d'elite into a modern amphibious force. Intellectually and professionally, Lejeune sided with the visionaries. Yet he took pains to not appear to belong to any faction, because the ideological dispute had the potential to engulf the officer ranks in disruptive acrimony. The political debris resulting from the abrupt ouster of Barnett in 1920 still hung heavy over the Marine Corps. Lejeune and his senior officers could not likely weather another public inquiry into the machinations of its leaders—however popular, professional, or colorful.

Identification with and support from each group in the ideological dispute among Marine Corps officers during the 1920s was paramount. As the thirteenth commandant, Lejeune represented the interests of all divisions in the professional disagreements that raged and often threatened to consume the Marine Corps during the interwar years. Each faction, in turn, thought Lejeune represented it and the corps' best interests. Butler in particular appeared to believe that Lejeune sided with him in his polemic. However, the speed with which Lejeune distanced himself from the volatile bushwhacker following Congressman Butler's death in 1928 is remarkable, given their purported friendship. Sadly, Lejeune appears to have used Smedley's important political connection for his own purposes, a phenomenon that was not lost on at least one senior officer. Disappointed in the appointment of Ben H. Fuller to the commandancy in 1930 and in Lejeune's failure to support either Butler or himself for the post, Major General Logan Feland shared his outrage with a close friend: "He [Lejeune] works in an underhanded way always. Probably he worked for Butler for a time, then double-crossed him and went in for Fuller to beat me. I know him like a book and there is nothing too low for him to do." A few weeks later, Feland continued his diatribe: "I have known [Lejeune] and have endured for a long time the results of his malice and underhanded methods."[8]

Lejeune's career encompassed what many naval historians, such as Allan R. Millett and Jack Shulimson, consider to be an important and overlooked era in the history of the U.S. Marine Corps.

As the new American navy embraced the technology of the twentieth century, leatherneck participation in modernization became tenuous at best. Clinging to the traditional task of providing ships' guards and small landing parties no longer justified the existence of a separate naval service. The colonial infantry mission, believed to be the raison d'être of the corps by senior officers such as Waller and Butler, passed quickly into the dustbin of history. Although when Lejeune became commandant in 1920, large forces of marines remained in Santo Domingo and Haiti, both Capitol Hill and the White House sought increasingly to end America's troublesome naval presence in the region. While the Good Neighbor policy of President Franklin D. Roosevelt resulted in eventual removal of leathernecks from the troubled nations of Latin America, the stimulus for this retrenchment had its origins in the 1920s. Lejeune, along with most senior Marine Corps officers, realized that the era of bushwhacking had ended. Butler, on the other hand, failed to perceive the changes in America's naval and military requirements. In an angry letter to President Roosevelt, written just two years after Butler's stormy retirement, the corps' enfant terrible lashed out at the class of officers he believed to be the ruination of his beloved Marine Corps: the "class of Marines *fast passing out* [not Naval Academy graduates] [is] almost entirely responsible for the proud record of the Marines."[9]

Butler may have had a point, but he missed its significance; his generation of bushwhackers had become an anachronism. Lejeune, who possessed some of the same trappings as the colorful campaigner, also had the intellect and vision to realize that the Marine Corps' future remained with the fleet. The era of colonial infantry assignments for his beloved leathernecks, along with Waller and Butler, slipped into the marines' colorful history. When the Joint Army and Navy Board gave the amphibious assault mission to the Marine Corps during Lejeune's commandancy, it marked the end of the colonial infantry era for the corps and the beginning of the golden age of amphibious warfare.

Lejeune's yeoman tenure at the helm of the Marine Corps established the basis for the commandants of the 1930s to complete the codification of a modern naval mission. Lejeune's professional life encompassed the far-reaching changes of this important era and linked his name with the evolution of a modern Marine Corps. Not since the lengthy tenure of Archibald Henderson has a commandant had such an impact on the Marine Corps.

Notes

1. Robert D. Heinl, Jr., "The Cat with More Than Nine Lives," *U.S. Naval Institute Proceedings* (hereafter, *USNIP*) 80 (June 1954): 659–71.
2. Jack Shulimson, "The Transitional Commandancy: Colonel Charles G. McCawley and Uneven Reform, 1876–1891," *Marine Corps Gazette* (hereafter, MCG) 72 (October 1988): 70–77. Although the Marine Corps was authorized to accept fifty-one second lieutenants from among the graduates of the Naval Academy, ultimately only fifty served as leathernecks. Walter Ball, class of 1892, accepted a commission in the Marine Corps on 1 July 1894; however, when an appointment as an assistant engineer became available the following fall, he rejoined the navy. Cf. *Annual Reports of the Secretary of the Navy, 1883–1897* (Washington: GPO, 1883–1897), and *Register of Alumni, 1845–1982* (Annapolis, Md.: Naval Academy Alumni Association, 1982), pp. 180–189. For contemporary materials critical of Marine Corps performance, see: "The Marine Corps," *Army-Navy Journal* (hereafter, *ANJ*) 29 (21 November 1891): 218; "Desertion: Sailors' Dislike for a Man-of-War," *New York Times* (hereafter, *NYT*), 5 April 1885; "Foreigners in Crews," *NYT*, 9 December 1888; and "Marines' Duties, Training," *NYT*, 7 April 1889.
3. Edward C. Beach, "From Annapolis to Scapa Flow," unpublished memoir, p. 57, Beach MSS, privately held.
4. Cf. John A. Lejeune (hereafter, JAL) to Augustine Lejeune (hereafter, AL), 14 June 1895, reel 1, Lejeune MSS, Library of Congress; with George Barnett to the Class of 1881, 15 October 1885 and 15 February 1888, Reports of the Class of 1881, New York Public Library.
5. Josephus Daniels to JAL, 5 March 1941, reel 9, Lejeune MSS.
6. Cf. John A. Lejeune, *The Reminiscences of a Marine* (1930; reprint, Quantico: Marine Corps Association, 1979), pp. 257–86; and Allan R. Millett, *Semper Fidelis* (New York: Macmillan, 1980), pp. 292–311.
7. General Archer A. Vandegrift and Lieutenant General Edward A. Craig, oral histories, Marine Corps Historical Center (MCHC).
8. Logan Feland to James G. Harbord, 22 August 1930; and Feland to Harbord, 19 September 1930, "F" file, correspondence folders, Harbord MSS, New York Historical Society.
9. Smedley D. Butler to Franklin D. Roosevelt, 17 July 1933, file 18E, Roosevelt MSS, Presidential Library, Hyde Park, New York. (Emphasis added.)

1

GROWING UP

1867–1890

> We are splendidly looked after here—tell Mama not to worry
> herself about my wearing flannel, as every morning at
> breakfast, the officer of each division asks each man if he
> has on woolen underclothing. If not, seven demerits.
>
> *Naval Cadet John A. Lejeune to Augustine Lejeune*

The heat and humidity came early to Annapolis during the
late spring of 1884, making the young men arriving in hopes of a
naval career all the more uncomfortable. In endless long lines,
they filled out forms and signed ledgers in a ritual differing little
from that of the sister service academy to the north. On 15 May,
John A. Lejeune stepped up to the desk before the registrar of the
U.S. Naval Academy to fill out the book known as the "register
of candidates."

Besides his name and address, the form asked for information
on the prospective candidate's background. Lejeune took the
opportunity to read above his name to learn something about his
fellow applicants. Most potential naval cadets reported northern
addresses, and their fathers seemed to have more lofty occupa-
tions than farming. Many had attended private schools as well.
For the most part, applicants to the class of 1888 differed little
from those who had entered the Naval Academy since its founding in 1846: white, middle-class Protestants from the eastern
United States. Feeling somewhat inadequate, the young man
from the rural South took solace in the fact that a few of his
fellow applicants listed their fathers' occupation as "farmer." With

the long line fidgeting behind him, Lejeune wrote "planter" and gave his home as "Pointe Coupee Parish, Louisiana." Years later, Lejeune recalled that the unnerving experience caused him to reflect on his heritage for the first time.[1]

Lejeune's paternal ancestors traced their lineage to Jean Baptiste Lejeune and his two brothers, who migrated from their native Brittany in the 1730s to seek new lives and fortunes in France's Canadian colony of Nova Scotia. In 1758, when the Seven Years' War spread to the colonies, the Lejeune brothers fled their new home. Joining French forces in the defense of Quebec, only to see it fall to the British, they then traveled south across the Great Lakes and down the Mississippi to attempt a new start in Louisiana. In the Fausee River district, Jean Baptiste Lejeune found the peace and prosperity that he had sought in the new world. His son married Augustine Lemoine, daughter of an old and proud French family. Sad to note, the couple died when both were still young, leaving an orphan, Ovide Lejeune.

As a young man, Ovide claimed his inheritance and embarked upon a career as a sugar planter. In 1852, he purchased a small sugar plantation and the manor house that came with it. Located southeast of present-day Innis, "Old Hickory" lay one and one-half miles south of the old concourse of the Mississippi River and one-half mile north of the New Texas Landing in a pastoral setting surrounded by majestic live oaks and pecan trees. Ovide prospered and made the plantation pay. Considered a pillar of the community and one of its most eligible bachelors, Ovide caught the eye of a neighbor's lithesome niece. On the eve of the Civil War, Ovide became smitten by Laura Archer Turpin, then residing with her aunt and uncle at a nearby plantation. Laura's parents grew cotton across the river in Mississippi. The Turpins traced their lineage to French Huguenots who fled their native land during the persecution of the Protestants. Settling first in the English colony of Maryland, they had moved to the South a generation ago. Joseph A. Turpin married Laura Archer, also a native of Maryland, whose family emigrated from Londonderry, Northern Ireland, in 1710.

Rebuffed initially by Laura's aunt and uncle, the heavily bearded planter persisted. A determined suitor, Ovide attended Sunday services with the Archers at nearby St. Stephen's Episcopal Church and the romance blossomed. On 14 June 1859, the couple exchanged wedding vows and established their home at Old Hickory. But the war clouds threatening the Union hung heavily over their early married lives. Although opposed to secession, Ovide formed a troop of cavalry with his own funds. The men elected him their captain. For the first year of the war, he rode with Company I, First Louisiana Cavalry. Ovide applied for a discharge when, plagued with painful hemorrhoids, he could no longer endure the long marches on horseback. Returning home to Old Hickory after being discharged on 4 November 1862, Ovide tried to put the pieces of his plantation back together. The worsening economic conditions brought on by war and the defeat of the South resulted in financial ruin.[2]

The perilous economic times meant no capital to buy seed to plant cane or for machinery and firewood to process the sugar crop. In 1861, southern Louisiana supported 4,291 sugar houses; by 1865, the number had dropped to only 871. With no credit available because of the collapse of the southern economy and the worthless Confederate currency, Ovide and most of his fellow planters lost their land to creditors. Old Hickory passed to a wealthier neighbor, leaving Laura and Ovide with only the house and a few acres of land. Ovide obtained employment as manager of the larger Taylor Sugar Plantation but found it just as difficult to make a profit for its owners.

During these troubled times, Laura gave birth to their second child on 19 January 1867, John Archer, named after his physician uncle who delivered him. A sister, Augustine, had been born on 22 March 1860; there would be no other children from this union. Although his family was poor, John Archer Lejeune retained happy memories of his childhood. He and his father raised bees together and sold the honey to neighbors, providing the young boy an occasional purchase of penny candy at LeCour's General Store. Father and son enjoyed each other's company, and Ovide gave him a small bore rifle to hunt small game in the woods surrounding the diminished property.

As John grew to manhood, the problem of his education became increasingly troublesome. Because the local public schools had closed during the war, Laura Lejeune began an elementary school in her home. This proved inadequate for John Archer, and the Lejeunes enrolled him in his great uncle James Archer's boarding school near Nachez in January 1879. Like many youths before him, Lejeune endured the pain of homesickness: "The first time . . . I had been away from home, I suffered the keenest pangs of homesickness which were accentuated by my intense bashfulness or diffidence. To be with strangers was torture."[3]

During the summer of 1881, he and his parents opted for another change in schooling. It became apparent to the Lejeunes, in discussions with their son over the vacation months, that John Archer needed an education in an environment that would allow him to meet other young men of his age and otherwise broaden the sheltered youth's world. Thus, for the next three years, he was a military cadet at Louisiana State University (LSU).

Prospective candidates for admission to LSU took a superficial entrance examination, deposited two hundred dollars against their books and uniforms, and signed a statement promising not to marry while enrolled or to spend money from home in excess of the small allowance decreed in the cadet regulations. Entering cadets had a choice of three curricula, based in part on their performance on the entrance examinations. Lejeune chose the classical curriculum over agricultural or mechanical and began his first year in the preparatory program in September 1881. He performed well academically and enjoyed the daily military drills, dress parades, guard mounts, and battalion formations. Lejeune received the coveted rank of second lieutenant and appeared earmarked for success; however, continued economic problems in Pointe Coupee meant the end of his time at LSU.

The unstable economic conditions of post–Civil War Louisiana ate heavily into the diminishing resources of Lejeune's father. Although supported largely by state revenues, LSU still required its cadets to pay for their room and board. In young Lejeune's case, sixteen dollars a month exceeded what his family could afford, and they began to cast about for a less costly alternative to his education. Raised to revere the Confederate leadership of the Civil War, Lejeune could not fail to notice that many had attended the United States Military Academy. Unfortunately, no appointments were available at the moment. His senator, Judge E. T. Lewis, did have a vacancy for the U.S. Naval Academy. Taking an alternative less costly than his present situation, Lejeune resigned from LSU in April 1884 and spent a month of intensive study for the formidable entrance examinations waiting for him at Annapolis. Before he left home in May 1884, his father impressed upon him the obligation Lejeune was about to accept: "I was about to become an officer of the U.S. Government, that I would owe the government my undivided allegiance, and it would be my duty to serve it honorably and faithfully in peace, and to defend it loyally and courageously in war against all enemies."[4]

In Lejeune's day, a congressional appointment to the Naval Academy meant only that the recipient would be given the opportunity to take a series of difficult entrance examinations in mathematics, reading comprehension, geography, foreign languages, grammar and writing, and spelling. The academy did not welcome marginal scholars, as the following examination questions from Lejeune's era suggest:

A man buys twenty-one sheep for $144, and sells twelve of them at a loss of three per cent; at what price per head must he sell the remainder in order to make two and one-half per cent on the whole purchase?

Explain the use of the indicative mood, and of the tenses under it.

Making a coastal voyage from Savannah to Cayenne, name in
order the states or countries you pass and the waters you pass
through.

Spell: referred, vengeance, coincidence.[5]

With the academic background of his great uncle's preparatory
school in Nachez and studies at LSU, Lejeune experienced little
difficulty with the entrance examinations. When the results
appeared, Lejeune had scored 3.56 out of a possible 4.0, scoring
above 3.0 in every area except grammar and algebra. Seventy-
three young men took examinations with Lejeune in early June
1884, and another 72 made the attempt the following September.
While many failed completely and returned home to their parents,
others attempted the examinations again and gained entrance to
the academy. When classes began that fall, the class of 1888
numbered 90 out of 239 young men enrolled as naval cadets.
Before they began their studies, however, they had to learn to be
sailors.[6]

After Lejeune and his classmates were sworn in as naval cadets,
upperclassmen marched them to the *Santee,* an old sailing vessel
tied up at Annapolis. Wearing sailor's uniforms for the first time,
they learned the rudiments of their new vocation. Climbing the
shrouds and sliding down the backstays became an exhilarating
experience for a farm boy from Louisiana, barked shins, rope
burns, and bruises notwithstanding. Learning to sleep in a ham-
mock also offered unique challenges. The new naval cadets lived
aboard the *Santee* but marched to the new cadet quarters ashore
three times a day for meals. The heat and humidity typical of the
summer on Chesapeake Bay made their days long. After one
spirited seamanship drill, lasting more than two hours, he reported
home that he had gone below to the berthing deck almost
"wilted."[7]

Lejeune and the new plebes began to use the strange language
of the naval cadet, words alien to any other environment. A

cadet who succeeded in making a good recitation in class or who pleased an instructor had "frap'd it," while to receive a high mark from a professor indicated that the cadet had "knocked it." To study hard meant to have "boned," in order to know everything about a subject and become "savvy" and avoid being the lowest in class or the "wooden section." To a cadet, anything to be coveted or that was new and handsome earned the description of "sux."[8]

After a month of introductory training to a life at sea, Lejeune and more than a hundred naval cadets embarked in the *Constellation*, an old frigate used as a training vessel. The future naval officers cruised Chesapeake Bay and the waters off New England that summer, arriving back in Annapolis just before classes began in the fall. Aboard the *Constellation*, cadets existed in a Spartan environment, living on the berth deck below the water line without lights or ventilation. There, they studied, ate, and slept. Each evening, they washed in cold sea water.

Hard work and a hot, unrelenting sun dominated their days. Seasick cadets received no sympathy as they drilled from morning to night under the stern eyes of the captain and his officers: boat drill, small-arms instruction, fire drill, and reefing top sails; their leisure time was nil. Regulations specified that cadets be in their hammocks by eight, and reveille was at seven each morning; most cadets had to stand watch at night, either at midnight or at four o'clock. Often, the boatswain's mate roused the cadets out of their warm bedding to reef topsails, an event hated by all. Few would forget the cry in the night: "All hands reef top'ls; lively now, my hearties, show a leg there, tumble up, lads![9]

The food in the ship earned the constant criticism of the naval cadets. The fare consisted largely of salted meat. An enterprising black steward known only as "Pinckney" did his best to vary the simple menu: hard tack, hot water, and bacon baked in an oven became "lob-scouse." A dreadful concoction, the contents of which have been lost to history, is remembered only as "Pinckney's love." An entrepreneur, Pinckney purchased pies and cakes with his own funds when in port and sold them to cadets for exorbitant prices while the *Constellation* was at sea.

Only Sundays in the ship offered a change in the tedium of endless drills. On the Lord's day, the naval cadets received some leisure time before compulsory church services. Divine worship began with a reading of the "Articles for the Better Government of the Navy of the United States." A detailed inspection of each cadet and his personal possessions usually followed Sunday worship. Hot, humid days and the monotony of the drills made young Lejeune anxious for the classroom that fall: "On the first of October, the hard work begins. The first month will decide everything. I am determined to do my utmost [to succeed]" he told his sister.[10]

Plebe summer developed and toughened Lejeune, physically and mentally. More than four decades later, he still exuded pride for having survived the ordeal: "It was a hard, rough, three months' experience, an experience which the present-day midshipmen could not possibly visualize or comprehend . . . [it] developed us physically to such an extent that by the end of the plebe practice cruise we were hard as nails."[11]

Barely on a steady course, the institution that accepted Lejeune had been founded in 1846 through the bureaucratic legerdemain of Secretary of the Navy George Bancroft. Bancroft's detractors thought that naval officers should receive their training at sea, not in the classroom, and pointed critically at the country's other service academy at West Point. When Bancroft demonstrated that he could operate the school on the banks of the Severn at no more cost than the present system of employing civilian professors to teach midshipmen academic subjects at sea, Congress approved the establishment of the Naval Academy. But in less than two decades of progress, the Civil War disturbed its growth.

When the students and faculty returned to Annapolis in 1865, they found the original site in disarray. It required a superintendent of herculean qualities to restore the institution. Initially,

Admiral David Dixon Porter ordered new buildings constructed. Then, he ordered the curriculum changed so as to reflect an emphasis on professional subjects over academics. Discipline improved along with morale, and Porter inaugurated a seasonal series of dances that attracted the elite of Washington and Baltimore society. Athletic programs appeared as well. Subsequent superintendents sought to change the institution to reflect their own convictions on the substance of a naval officer's education. From admininstration to administration, the curriculum emphasis swung between academics and naval professionalism.[12]

More than one superintendent argued that learning the correct way to rig a sailing vessel was more important than integral calculus. During some regimes, sailing in Chesapeake Bay replaced liberty or free time for the cadets on Saturday afternoons. Lejeune's education at the academy reflected the continued controversy over curriculum. Progressives prophesied a revolution in naval warfare and believed that the institution should provide a diverse intellectual background. This faction argued that the duties of naval officers had become more complex and demanding, pointing toward the need for a liberal education.

Ranged against the progressives stood the older navy officers who never wavered from the belief that naval cadets needed a practical, professional education. Their attitudes resulted in the elimination of civilian professors until 1873, but even after that date and into Lejeune's tenure at the Naval Academy, their influence reflected the conclusion of the academy's Board of Visitors: "[It is not] the work of the Naval Academy to perfect the education of its pupils in literature or in theoretic science [but to supply] practical seamen, men who can navigate ships and fight their guns."[13]

Most cadets of Lejeune's era agreed with the old-navy types. They had signed on to sail to foreign waters, to find a life of adventure, and if necessary to fight. Conjugating verbs in French or comparing the political systems of medieval France and the

Holy Roman Empire seemed less important than steam engineering or gunnery. The following doggerel from *Fag Ends*, a student publication of Lejeune's day, reflects the naval cadet's view:

> Now we've had quite enough of antique ideas
> of those chaps who are nothing but sailors:
> They were well in their way, but this is the day
> of science, aesthetics, and tailors.
> Scarce one of all those who with Farragut fought
> or with Porter stood fire stout-hearted
> Is versed in keramics or thermodynamics,
> so the day of their use has departed.[14]

During Lejeune's time at the academy, the pendulum had swung once again to emphasize academics. Under the direction of Captain Francis M. Ramsay, the twelfth superintendent, classes ran from October to June and met five days a week and Saturday mornings. Reveille was at six o'clock with roll call and breakfast fifty minutes later. Classes began at 8:00, 9:00, 10:30, and 11:30, with dinner at 1:00 P.M. In the afternoons, classes began at 2:00 and 3:00, followed by infantry drill from 4:00 to 5:00. Supper was at 6:30, and study hours followed from 7:30 to 9:30. Taps or "lights out" came at 10:00; everyone was expected to be in bed asleep so as to be rested for another day of rigorous classroom work. Naval cadets like Lejeune who stayed up past taps to play cards usually found themselves on report.[15]

Freshman or plebe subjects included algebra, geometry, English, history, French, and Spanish. Lejeune's hard work and dedication to the academic regimen paid off. At the end of the year, he ranked high in his class in every area except deportment: second in history, English, French, and Spanish; twentieth in mathematics; and a dismal sixty-first in conduct, with a whopping 112 demerits for a variety of minor violations of the strict rules imposed on the cadets. This disregard for authority endured during Lejeune's years at the Naval Academy. In letters home, Lejeune suggested that it was the unbending and unrealistic system and not his attitude that resulted in his problems with the Conduct Roll of Cadets. "We get demerits for almost everything under the sun," he complained to his sister.[16]

Concern for grades, not deportment, dominated letters home. After failing a mathematics examination and performing poorly on a French quiz, he confided to his sister: "I feared that I would fall still more. Mr. Leroux, our [French] instructor, is a terror."[17] By the end of his fourth class year, Lejeune's hard work placed him third in a class of sixty-three cadets who had survived the rigors of the first year at Annapolis. Twenty-seven of his classmates saw their hopes of a naval career dashed because of academics or deportment, and an unfeeling administration sent them back to their parents.[18]

Despite the emphasis on academics during Lejeune's tenure at the academy, most naval cadets took a lighthearted approach to the regimen. Classmate Armin Hartrath composed the following poem for the amusement of the class of 1888, which it sang while marching to class:

> Exams they are a comin',
> Upon the same old plan;
> We'll bone [study] like Hell as usual,
> And bilge [fail] upon the semi-an [finals].[19]

Lejeune and his fellow cadets subsisted in a simple environment. They lived two to a small room measuring twelve feet square, with bunk beds, a wooden table and sturdy upright chairs for studying, iron wash stands, water buckets, and a mirror. Each cadet had his own wardrobe and could decorate the inside of the doors with photographs (usually of girl friends). Otherwise, the decor remained void of ornamentation or individuality. The administration enforced strict cleanliness, and an officer wearing white gloves inspected their rooms each day. Lejeune's roommate after his first year was Edward N. Beach.

They and most of their fellow naval cadets did not have to worry about gaining weight with the institution's uninspiring cuisine. Very quickly, the cadets found the diet to be bland and unvarying no matter how ravenous they might be at mealtime. Dessert appeared twice a week on the menu: six gingersnaps apiece on Wednesday and two halves of a canned peach on Sunday. For some strange reason, only upperclassmen could drink milk. Any variation in the dismal diet reflected an attempt by the medical officer to administer mass doses of a new medicine to the cadets, a ruse that rarely succeeded. At mealtime, the upperclassmen enforced good table manners rigorously and some-times ruthlessly, as a contemporary of Lejeune's remembered. When an upperclassman observed a rather backwoods plebe eat-ing peas with his table knife instead of a fork, one of the black stewards received instructions: "Heh is a fo'k fo' you suh, wid Mr. A's compliments." More forks followed, much to the youth's discomfort.[20]

Besides the rigorous academic routine and the bleak subsistence, plebes like Lejeune had to endure a certain measure of hazing. Most cadets of Lejeune's era earned nicknames. Not to have one suggested that his peers held the person in poor esteem. An upperclassman discovered that Lejeune's forefathers had been Arcadians and ordered him to learn the words to Longfellow's poem "Evangeline." His nickname, furthermore, was to be "Gabriel Lajeunesse" after Evangeline's lover, Gabriel. To the end of his days, he answered to the nickname "Gabe." A classmate, Curtis D. Wilbur, earned the nickname "Magic" because he had been instructed to recite the following litany upon request: "I am magical Mike, the untutored terror of the wild northwest, the blowing blizzard of the Great Desert. Please don't look at my feet."[21]

While recitations and nicknames presented no threat of bodily harm to the plebes, other aspects of hazing could be brutal. As in most military schools, hazing remained a fact of life despite rigor-ous attempts to put down the practice. At times, upperclassmen exposed plebes to potentially dangerous stunts such as being thrown through a transom or forced to drink ink or eat soap. Other hazing consisted of practices more tomfoolery in nature: imitating animals, conducting debates on unusual or absurd subjects, shaving with a blunt instrument, being thrown into the Severn River, "made into a sandwich," mustering in strange uniform combinations, and performing the manual of arms with brooms. Frequent parental complaints over hazing resulted finally in congressional action that made the practice a court-martial offense and empowered the superintendent with the authority to dismiss perpetrators of the practice. Three years before Lejeune arrived on the scene, the hazing problem reached the stage where a disgusted superintendent confined forty-eight first classmen for engaging in the practice.[22]

Lejeune's exposure to hazing came shortly after arriving at the academy. In his first few days during "plebe summer," Lejeune received a summons to report to the officer in charge of the plebe detail. The officer claimed to have observed several upperclassmen "running" or hazing Lejeune. He demanded that Lejeune verify the incident and name the perpetrators so that the officer could place them on report. Lejeune refused, simply because he did not know the names of the upperclassmen involved. Later that fall, a group of upperclassmen visited Lejeune's room intent on hazing him. One of the naval cadets remembered the incident of the previous summer: "This plebe saved me from being court-martialed; he is my friend and is exempt from hazing or running by any member of the Class of '86."[23]

The ritual of the daily routine for naval cadets seemed to be more important than its substance. They marched to their classes to endure periods of instruction designed more to prove that each naval cadet had mastered the assigned reading assignments for the day than to gain new knowledge. The academy's professors, officers or civilians, taught very little; instead, the cadets "manned the boards" to solve problems or outlined lessons under the watchful eye of the instructor, who would then assign a grade for the day. Rather than letter grades, cadets received numerical scores, with a minimum average of 2.5 required in a 4.0 system. The administration demanded and received total compliance, as a directive of the era suggested: "Any cadet who may fail to hand in a theme at a time specified by the instructor, shall be considered to have made a total failure, and shall be marked accordingly."[24]

Attempting to be placed on the sick list and remain in bed all day became a constant endeavor in Lejeune's era, despite the emphasis on a high level of personal honor. One enterprising cadet obtained a medical encyclopedia from which he and his friends mined a never-ending list of unusual ailments in order to "pull the list" or be "sick in quarters." A contemporary of Lejeune's recalled joining a rather large group of malingerers at sick call one morning to hear the unfeeling surgeon exclaim: "Sore eyes, eh? Sore ears, pain in the toe, back ache? My, my! What a sick looking lot of young gentlemen!" Then the physician added: "But cheer up my friends, I'll give you something that will fix all that!" The cadets received glasses of mineral salts, which made each of them genuinely ill.[25]

Despite his numerous transgressions of the institution's strict rules, Lejeune often criticized the moral tone of the academy. Near the end of his plebe year, he made a rather pithy observation to his sister on the morality of his school while commenting on the new plebe class beginning to report in: "They are taken as a whole a very poor lot—most of them are very small, and ought to have stayed home a couple of years more." Lejeune added that "little fellows try to be more manly and are easily corrupted—this place cannot be considered the most moral place in the world."[26] Another naval cadet of the era came down a bit harder on the academy: "There were but four Christians at the Naval Academy and they were all Japanese."[27]

Lejeune noted the shortage of fellow Louisianans at Annapolis. Although he remembered that four or five young men from his home state had arrived with him during the summer of 1884, only Leroy A. Stafford managed to graduate. Moreover, the register of alumni reveals that between 1848 and 1887, only fourteen young men from Louisiana graduated from the Naval Academy. Of that number, three resigned their commissions and another three "went South" during the Civil War. In a letter home, Lejeune commented again on the shortage of naval officers from his home state: "Louisiana is noted for its blockheads, [there] can't [be] but three or four naval officers, this fact owing to the laziness or wildness of those who enter the Naval Academy."[28]

When the superintendent canceled liberty for all naval cadets on Washington's birthday because of the obstreperous behavior of some of them, a disappointed Lejeune reported the incident home. Apparently the unseemingly conduct of the cadets during the previous holiday precipitated the edict, causing Lejeune to sputter: "Christmas comes but once a year . . . and nearly every upperclassman and a rather large number of fourth classmen try to get drunk on that day even if they never touch a drop during the whole remaining year."[29]

Despite the frequent lapses in gentlemanly conduct, the spiritual life of the naval cadets received the close attention of the administration. Everyone had to attend Sunday services and a chaplain said prayers at breakfast. The academy offered a choice of chapels and denominations, but most cadets of Lejeune's era opted for the Episcopalian services because of its closer location to the cadet dormitory. The naval cadets lined the sides of the church while the officers and their families sat in the center. A contemporary of Lejeune's recalled that the poverty-conditioned cadets rarely gave anything when the offering plates passed by. On one memorable occasion, an ingenious fellow obtained three hundred copper pennies, which he distributed to his friends in the church formation on Sunday morning. As the collection plates made their way up and down the rows of worshipers, it rained copper cents for ten minutes. Although the ringing sound of the falling coins amused the naval cadets, superiors fidgeted and looked aghast.

Sometimes in their seriousness, the chaplains' sermons or prayers seemed to be more amusing than inspiring. After four decades, Lejeune's roommate could still recall one comical prayer at breakfast: "Therefore I say unto you, do away with filthiness and the superfluity of naughtiness, and receive the engrafted word."[30] In addition to expecting morning prayers and attendance at Sunday services, academy officials required the cadets of Lejeune's era to stay in their rooms and meditate religiously from 2:00 to 3:00 P.M. on Sundays.

Besides monitoring the moral and intellectual growth of its students, the academy encouraged physical fitness with a variety of varsity sports that began with gymnastics, boxing, fencing, and sabre practice in 1867. English-style football appeared first on the academy grounds in 1879, and three years later the institution tried the American version of the sport against a college team from Baltimore. Lejeune turned out for football and reported home often on the successes of his team. They called themselves the "Hustlers." Years later, Lejeune referred to a photograph of himself along with fellow ballplayers Admiral Henry A. Wiley, Rear Admirals Ashley H. Robertson and Charles F. Hughes, and Brigadier General Theodore P. Kane, suggesting that they "were linked for life with rivets of steel." But when Lejeune served as the superintendent of the Virginia Military Institute after retiring from the Marine Corps, he admitted that perhaps his prowess on the gridiron had been overstated: "I confess here and now, that my only football experience was [as] an obscure player on the second team at the Naval Academy, which was organized for practice games against the first team."[31]

The rigorous exercise developed Lejeune into a strong and husky young man. His letters home never contained complaints of real sickness. Sometimes his correspondence revealed that he was maturing. Even as early as Lejeune's era, the academy had the reputation that it holds today as an attraction for young ladies drawn by a large group of young men—presumably gentlemen. Lejeune enjoyed the seasonal hops and balls and sent his dance programs home. During the early part of 1885, he seemed to have a bad case of spring fever: "You should see our Yard [academy grounds]. It is one of the prettiest places I think in the country . . . and just at this time of year [the yard is] covered with pretty girls."[32] While seeming to enjoy his encounters with young women, none that he met made a lasting impression. Lejeune played the field, hoping never to be seen with a "brick" (homely girl) or be called a "Red Mike" (a naval cadet who had nothing to do with girls). Meanwhile, another of his extracurricular activities got him into serious trouble with academy authorities.

Soon after arriving at the Naval Academy, Lejeune confessed to his sister that he had taken up cigarette smoking: "I have become a lover of the soothing weed," he noted in a letter home. Regulations permitted smoking by cadets but limited the practice to designated areas and then only on Saturdays and Sundays. Apparently, Lejeune would have none of these restrictions. At the beginning of his third class year, academy officials placed him on report three times in one day for unauthorized smoking. The third offense occurred when Lejeune heard the footsteps of the duty officer outside his quarters. He attempted to escape being put on report by throwing the smoldering cigarette into the corner of the room.[33]

The ruse failed to amuse the officer and Lejeune's name appeared on the report list again. Thinking that they had a recalcitrant naval cadet on their hands, the academy administration sentenced Lejeune to thirty days confinement in the *Santee*, the old training ship used as a brig for mischievous naval cadets during the academic year. In another letter home, Lejeune admitted that "it wasn't a very nice place." Feeling no repentance, he merely indicated that he would not be caught again.[34]

With most of the naval cadets, serious infractions of the rules occurred only infrequently. In such instances, the culprits usually received swift and sure justice. Beach's first roommate came to the gates of justice branded a thief and received a dismissal from the academy. Most deviations from the rules fell into a pattern

---

like those of Lejeune's—boyish pranks to test the determination of their navy superiors. The legendary Philo N. McGiffin of the class of 1882 dismantled a decorative pyramid of cannonballs and rolled them down the steps of the cadet quarters with predictable damage. Sentenced to the *Santee* for his mischief, he obtained six powder charges, which he fired upon his release from confinement. Lejeune and his classmates relished the memories of such youthful high jinks. At class reunions, they told these tales again and again, savoring them like fine wine. Academic performance counted for more than anything else, however. After two years, only forty-eight of the naval cadets who had begun with Lejeune remained; difficulties with grades or deportment took their toll.[35]

When his professors and instructors submitted their grades to the academy's academic board after the spring semester in 1885, Lejeune stood fourth in his class. He had performed well in every area except, as usual, in deportment. The notation "inattention to regulations" appears often after his name on the Conduct Roll of Cadets. Academics became increasingly more difficult as he progressed through the curriculum. Chemistry and physics, called "skinny" after the legendary and popular Professor Paul J. Dashiell, seemed to be the most difficult subjects for many naval cadets. Lejeune managed to survive skinny, while mathematics remained his most troublesome subject.

After studying for final examinations near the end of his third class year, Lejeune reported home that "I have never studied so hard for anything in my life." Even a diligent application to his studies sometimes failed to produce the results desired. In a letter the previous April, Lejeune reported that he had spent an entire Sunday preparing for an examination in mathematics only to score a dismal 1.72, or a "bust." Professor Dashiell reported twenty of Lejeune's classmates unsatisfactory in chemistry and physics. Academics became even more difficult, and Lejeune's high standing began to fall.[36]

By the end of Lejeune's second year in 1887, his class had been reduced to forty naval cadets. During the 1886–1887 school year,

Lejeune stood thirty-third in mechanical drawing; seventeenth in international law; fifteenth in calculus and mechanics; twentieth in sound, light, and heat; fourteenth in electricity and magnetism; and sixteenth in engineering. His conduct failed to improve, and he ranked sixteenth in the number of demerits received. Lejeune considered most of the regulations irksome and petty and the officers who enforced them mere martinets. Nevertheless, Lejeune stayed within the bounds of the rules of the institution suffi- ciently so that he could join his classmates on 8 June 1888 as they received their diplomas from Secretary of the Navy William C. Whitney.

Lejeune and his classmates had every reason to feel pride in their accomplishments. Of the ninety young men who began with them four years before, only thirty-two survived the rigorous program; Lejeune ranked thirteenth in the class of 1888. From a purely academic standpoint, Lejeune stood second in his class; however, the academic board of the era considered conduct in determining final standings, and Lejeune's sorry record of deport- ment brought him down.[37]

Although Lejeune retained an affection for many of his class- mates and friends, he did not seem to hold any deep feelings for the institution. Lejeune had the education that he and his family had sought for him. He packed his belongings to leave Annapolis with a sense of relief. Despite his letters emphasizing the rigorous academic program, Lejeune often found his life boring. In his plebe year, he confessed: "When there is nothing to do, I always turn in and read a lot. I always read the trashiest books I can find."[38]

With mixed emotions and a diploma in his hand in 1888, he left Annapolis. Reflecting on the experience four decades later, Lejeune had to admit that the harsh discipline and rigid aca- demic regimen toughened him mentally and physically. Yet he continued to be critical: "A defect in the conduct of the [Naval] Academy which I observed was the fact that it impressed me as being a great machine. I missed the human appeal."[39]

Four years at the Naval Academy and graduation did not mean
an immediate commission for the naval cadets of Lejeune's time.
Graduates went to sea as midshipmen for two years, then returned
to Annapolis for more examinations. After graduation, Lejeune
returned to Old Hickory for the summer to await his orders. At
first fearful that he would be assigned to a ship steaming "'round
the horn," he opened a telegram instructing him to join the
Mohican at Mare Island. Earlier, Lejeune and classmates Eli K.
Cole, Henry A. Wiley, and Leroy A. Stafford had requested
assignment to the ship after learning that it would likely remain
in dry dock until the end of 1888; thus, if assigned to the *Mohican*,
they could remain home until at least the fall.

Although he had obtained the orders he wanted, Lejeune
expressed to his father misgivings about a naval career. For Lejeune
and many of his classmates, there seemed to be few reasons to
pursue a career in the navy. Since the civil War, the U.S. Navy
had declined in numbers of qualified men and modern ships.
Most sailors came from the ranks of foreigners and constituted a
motley, obstreperous group constantly at odds with their officers
and often incapable of performing their duties. Like many graduates of the Naval Academy, Lejeune could see little promise for a
lifetime in such an organization. However, Ovide encouraged his
son to remain in the naval service rather than face a questionable future in the harsh economic climate of post-Civil War
Louisiana. Then, in a sad exchange, Ovide told his son that he
was ill and did not have long to live.

Midshipman Lejeune reported to the *Mohican* on 7 September
1888. A steam sloop-of-war, the *Mohican* lay up in the repair yard
while its crew lived in the receiving ship *Independence*. For the
remainder of the fall, Lejeune and most of the officers had few
professional duties to perform and enjoyed the social opportunities of the San Francisco Bay area: "I soon decided that Navy life
was more enjoyable than I had anticipated it would be during my
four long years at the Naval Academy."[40]

After the first of the year, Lejeune received orders that would result in an experience he would never forget. Some of the officers in the *Mohican*—including Midshipmen Lejeune, Stafford, and Wiley—were to report by 14 January 1889 to the screw sloop *Vandalia*, then being outfitted for a speedy run to an area of potential trouble in the South Pacific. By the late 1880s, the islands of Samoa remained the only major group in the region not under the control of a foreign power. While the United States eyed the seemingly unimportant islands as a potential coaling station, Germany saw an opportunity to expand its nascent colonial empire. American diplomats feared that the considerable German naval force in the waters off Samoa, coupled with the machinations of the German diplomatic mission in the islands, could result in their complete takeover for the kaiser. The British shared American uneasiness over the situation and demonstrated concern by maintaining their own naval presence in the region.

While the *Vandalia* sailed from San Francisco, the *Trenton* left Panama to meet her in Samoa. On 22 February, the *Vandalia* arrived on the potentially explosive scene. When the ship entered the harbor of Apia, it joined another American ship, *Nipsic*; a British cruiser, *Calliope*; and a German cruiser, *Olga*, accompanied by two gunboats. A few days later, the *Trenton* arrived with an admiral embarked. A potential military confrontation began to brew, as all sides attempted to involve themselves in local politics. Then nature intervened to diffuse the tense situation.

On 14 March 1889, the barometer began to fall, and the next afternoon a violent storm lashed the islands. Lejeune had the midwatch and he spent most of it lashed to the deck to keep from being washed overboard. As the fury of the storm increased, waves swept across the port bow and washed everyone about the forecastle off their feet. Rain came in blinding sheets, making it difficult to hold onto the ropes. Early on the morning of the fifteenth, the ship began to drag her anchor. The *Vandalia's* stern slammed into the reef and the crew took refuge in the rigging;

those who could not hold onto the rigging drowned. Survivors crawled along lifelines to the shore, assisted by Samoan natives. Lejeune watched the commander of the *Vandalia's* marines, Second Lieutenant Frank E. Sutton (USNA 1881) drown. The experience affected him deeply: "I saw him as he sank, lying face upwards, with his eyes turned towards the sky, and a look of peaceful resignation on his face."[41]

The wooden screw gunboat *Adams* arrived to replace the crippled *Vandalia*, and the survivors continued their mission in the region until the spring of 1890. Lejeune's letters home after the harrowing experience contain mostly news about trips ashore and tourism and very little about professional duties. Seamanship had lost its attraction for him, apparently. The evaluations of his performance for the remainder of the cruise reflect disinterest: while the fitness reports are complimentary, an unknown navy officer penned "B" and "C" in the margins. In the late spring of 1890, Lejeune left the *Adams* to return to Annapolis for the postcruise examinations, which would decide his future.[42]

The navy that most of the class of 1888 hoped to join had fallen on hard times. Although in 1865 the American navy could claim to be the largest in the world, demobilization after the Civil War took its toll. The decline continued into the 1870s. By the time Lejeune entered the Naval Academy, there seemed to be little room for new officers. Two years before his arrival in Annapolis, a befuddled secretary of the navy noted that he had 1,817 officers on his rolls to man only thirty-seven ships; the navy counted one Annapolis graduate for every four sailors![43]

As both congress and the navy wrestled with the problem, opposition from both within and outside the navy mounted. When progressive-minded officials suggested that the navy prune the deadwood from its upper ranks, congressional opposition struck quickly. On the heels of the Union victory, a grateful Congress decreed that navy officers who had served honorably in the Civil War could stay in uniform for forty years or until reaching age sixty-two. Other reformers urged the advancement of the more talented officers ahead of their contemporaries; however, no one could devise a fair and workable plan for such a program. Some members of Congress even suggested that perhaps the navy should reduce the size of the classes entering the Naval Academy. This last proposal could only be anathema to a navy that had fought so hard for the creation of the institution. With no apparent solution emanating from within the navy, Congress implemented a surgical solution to the problem.[44]

As a rider to the annual Naval Appropriations Bill for 1882, Congress decreed that there must be two vacancies in the officer ranks at the top of the lineal list before a new graduate from Annapolis could be commissioned. The academy's academic board established a preference system: an aggregate score based on a naval cadet's academic record, fitness reports from the post-graduation cruise, and the results of the postgraduation examinations. A minimum of ten midshipmen would receive commissions in the navy, and a few—characteristically, those low in the class—could fill vacancies in the Marine Corps. The remaining midshipmen would be given severance pay and discharges.[45]

Even before Lejeune returned to Annapolis for the postcruise examinations, he had most likely selected the Marine Corps over the navy. In his published memoirs, written from the vantage of an older man who had enjoyed a successful and distinguished career, Lejeune recalled that he had been attracted to the Marine Corps' style of leadership and had admired the way Sutton delegated authority to the marine sergeant in the *Vandalia*. When Lejeune graduated in 1888, he knew that his class standing did not guarantee him a commission in the navy once the ten names above him had been selected. Only a spectacular performance on the postcruise examinations could better his chances for an ensign's commission. Thus, for the two years spent at sea following graduation, he had to be considering other career options besides the navy. More important, he nurtured a growing dislike for life at sea and the navy in particular.

In all of his letters home, Lejeune never mentioned any love for the life of the sailor or discussed the possibility of a career in the navy. One letter did reflect an aversion to life at sea, however. During the hot and humid Annapolis summer of 1886, he trained in a ship tied up at the Naval Academy: "It is very dry and tiresome here now, nothing going on . . . I prefer this sort of life to the cruise where one has to work hard with very little sleep and very poor food."[46]

Other considerations may have entered his mind as well. The unusual pay system of the time benefited the second lieutenants over the ensigns. An ensign received a thousand dollars per annum while an assistant engineer earned seventeen hundred dollars. If either spent time ashore waiting for a vacancy in a ship, they received a substantial reduction in pay. In contrast, a second lieutenant earned fourteen hundred dollars a year, whether at sea or ashore. Thus, for a variety of reasons, Lejeune had apparently opted for the Marine Corps by the time he returned to Annapolis. Diligent application on the postcruise examinations raised him to a position of sixth in his class for the purpose of service selection. Thus, he assumed that his choice was secure. A classmate trumpeted the bad news: "Gabe, the Academic Board has recommended your assignment to the [navy] engineers."[47]

Notes

1. Entry 62, Register of Candidates, 1 April–1 September 1884, Records of the U.S. Naval Academy, RG 405, National Archives (hereafter NA); see also Peter Karsten, *The Naval Aristocracy: The Golden Age of Annapolis and the Emergence of Modern American Navalism* (New York: Macmillan, 1980), pp. 1–17.

2. Lejeune's genealogy can be found in JAL, *The Reminiscences of a Marine* (1930; reprint, Quantico: Marine Corps Association, 1979), pp. 15–21; Joe Simon, "Lieutenant General John A. Lejeune, U.S. Marine Corps" (M.A. thesis, Louisiana State University, 1967), pp. 1–12; and Judy Riffel, ed., *Point Coupee Parish History* (Baton Rouge, La.: Le Comite des Archives de la Louisiana, 1983), p. 192. Ovide's brief military record is on MF 107, roll 4, Civil War Military Records, NA. For an appreciation of the threatening economic conditions of Lejeune's youth, see Joe Gray Taylor, *Louisiana Reconstructed, 1863–1877* (Baton Rouge: Louisiana State University Press, 1974).

3. JAL, *Reminiscences of a Marine*, p. 29.

4. Ibid., p. 34.

5. JAL's entrance examination is not extant; however, the examination administered in 1878 is thought to be similar. RG 405.

6. Register of grades received by candidates for appointment at entrance examinations, May–September 1884, entry 71, RG 405, NA; and *Annual Report of the United States Naval Academy, 1884–1885* (Washington: GPO, 1885), pp. 29, 43; however, the *Register of Alumni* (Annapolis, Md.: Naval Academy Alumni Association, 1980) p. 181, lists eighty-six naval cadets in the class of 1888. See also Carol H. Foster, "The Requirements for Admission to the Naval Academy," *USNIP* 44 (February 1918): 339–53.

7. *Annual Report of the Naval Academy, 1883–1884* (Washington: GPO, 1884), pp. 16–17, 29.

8. Michael P. Parker, ed., "Good Gouge: An Investigation into the Origins of Naval Academy Slang" (unpublished essay, Department of English, U.S. Naval Academy, 1982); and Cyrus T. Brady, *Under Tops'ls and Tents* (New York: Scribner's Sons, 1901), pp. 13–14.

9. Brady, *Under Tops'ls and Tents*, p. 73. Cyrus T. Brady graduated with the class of 1883.

10. JAL to AL, 9 September 1884, reel 1, Lejeune MSS, Library of Congress.

11. JAL, *Reminiscences of a Marine*, pp. 41–42.

12. Jack Sweetman, *The U.S. Naval Academy: An Illustrated History* (Annapolis, Md.: Naval Institute Press, 1979), pp. 1–126.

13. "Education at the Naval Academy," *Nation* 26 (20 June 1878): 400–401.

14. Quoted in Park Benjamin, *The United States Naval Academy* (New York: Putnam's Sons, 1900), p. 308. Benjamin graduated with the class of 1867.

15. Edward C. Beach, "From Annapolis to Scapa Flow," unpublished memoir, pp. 26–27, Beach MSS, privately held.

16. JAL to AL, 29 December 1884, reel 1, Lejeune MSS.

17. Ibid.

18. Monthly class reports, 1865–1904, Records of the U.S. Naval Academy, entry 93, RG 405, NA.

19. Beach, "From Annapolis To Scapa Flow," p. 45.

20. Brady, *Under Tops'ls and Tents*, pp. 52–53.

21. Beach, "From Annapolis to Scapa Flow," p. 45; for an explanation of the importance of the nicknames, see Brady, *Under Tops'ls and Tents*, p. 14.

22. Robert E. Coontz, *From the Mississippi to the Sea* (Philadelphia: Dorrance, 1930), pp. 57–60.

23. JAL, *Reminiscences of a Marine*, p. 38.

24. Superintendent's special order no. 10, 28 February 1882, RG 1, Naval Academy Archives, Nimitz Library.

25. Brady, *Under Tops'ls and Tents*, p. 6.

26. JAL to AL, 24 May 1885, reel 1, Lejeune MSS.

27. Brady, *Under Tops'ls and Tents*, pp. 9–10. According to Brady, the author of this pungent comment was Philo N. McGiffin.

28. JAL to AL, 24 May 1885, reel 1, Lejeune MSS.

29. JAL to AL, 24 February 1885, reel 1, Lejeune MSS.

30. Beach, "From Annapolis to Scapa Flow," p. 35.

31. Dedication Program, Lejeune Hall, U.S. Naval Academy, 28 April 1982, p. 26. See also Walter Arnold, "Naval Academy Athletics, 1845–1945" *USNIP* 72 (April 1946): 105–117.

32. JAL to AL, 27 April 1885, reel 1, Lejeune MSS.

33. Concern over nicotine and alcohol abuse prompted Congress to request the teaching of a new course in physiology at the Naval Academy. JAL to AL, 16 January 1887, reel 1, Lejeune MSS.

34. JAL to AL, 18 October 1885, reel 1, Lejeune MSS. See also JAL to AL, 6 December 1885, reel 1, Lejeune MSS.

35. The expulsion of Beach's first roommate is treated in fiction. See Edward N. Beach, *Ralph Osborne: Mid'n at Annapolis* (Boston: Wilder, 1909); for a sample of Lejeune's sorry deportment, see the Conduct Roll of Cadets, pp. 175 and 239, entry 84, RG 405.

36. JAL to AL, 4 June 1886, reel 1, Lejeune MSS; and *Annual Report of the Naval Academy, 1885–1886* (Washington: GPO, 1886), pp. 28–29.

37. *Annual Report of the United States Naval Academy, 1887–1888* (Washington: GPO, 1888), pp. 9, 16, 22–23, 63; and Monthly Class Reports, 1865–1904, Records of the U.S. Naval Academy, entry 93, RG 405, NA.

38. JAL to AL, 15 March 1885, reel 1, Lejeune MSS.

39. JAL, *Reminiscences of a Marine*, p. 48; for a contrasting view of a contemporary, see George Barnett, "Soldier and Sailor Too," unpublished memoir, Barnett MSS, Marine Corps Historical Center (MCHC).

40. JAL, *Reminiscences of a Marine*, p. 56.

41. Ibid., p. 77; see also "Trenton, Vandalia, and Nipsic Wrecked at Samoa," *NYT*, 30 March 1889.

42. E. T. Woodward and [?] Hunken to the Secretary of the Navy, 12 October 1899, and 28 February 1890, reel 3, JAL MSS. See also JAL to AL, 12 September 1899, reel 1, Lejeune MSS; and log of the *Adams*, 22 April 1889–31 July 1890, RG 24, NA. For an interpretation of the scores earned on the postgraduation cruise, see the minutes of the academic board, 13 July 1891, RG 405.

43. "Navy Report to Senate," *ANJ* 19 (24 December 1881): 321, 450.

44. Walter R. Herrick, "William E. Chandler," and Edwin H. Hall, "Samuel Lewis Southard," in Paolo E. Coletta, ed. *American Secretaries of the Navy*, 2 vols. (Annapolis, Md.: Naval Institute Press, 1980), 1:133–34, 401.

45. Peter Karsten, "Armed Progressives," in Karsten, ed., *The Military in America* (New York: Macmillan, 1980), pp. 229–46.

46. JAL to AL, 30 July 1886, reel 1, Lejeune MSS. But early in his days in Annapolis, Lejeune may have been concerned with regard to service selection. In an undated note to his sister, he exclaimed: "I hope to stay among the first ten." JAL to AL, reel 1, Lejeune MSS. Even as his standing dropped in 1888, he still considered himself a viable candidate for an ensign's vacancy; see JAL to AL, 19 February 1888, reel 1, Lejeune MSS.

47. JAL, *Reminiscences of a Marine*, p. 93. The academic board recommended only eighteen midshipmen for commissioning as ensigns and another four graduates to become assistant engineers (including Lejeune and Beach). *Annual Report of the Secretary of the Navy, 1890* (hereafter, ARSN), p. 142. See also Bureau of Navigation to the Superintendent, U.S. Naval Academy, 30 June 1890, RG 405; and Minutes of the Academic Board, 21 June 1890, Records of the U.S. Naval Academy, RG 405, NA.

2

AT SEA AND ASHORE

1890–1914

The politicians who are stationed at headquarters are the least important part of the Marine Corps.

John A. Lejeune to Augustine Lejeune

Lejeune could feel only outrage. After six years of hard work and raising himself to near the top of his class, his wishes had been ignored. Lejeune appealed to the academic board and ultimately to the superintendent, but to no avail. Earlier that spring, the chief of the Bureau of Engineering had requested a share of the top graduates from the academy to fill his depleted ranks. Among those high-ranking scholars, only Lejeune selected the Marine Corps over the navy. Thus, senior navy officers determined that he and they would be better served if Lejeune received a service assignment in their ranks. Lejeune's response to the series of curt dismissals and inadequate explanations came quickly and decisively. While he pondered his dilemma, Lejeune received a cordial letter from Louisiana senator Randall L. Gibson that lauded his performance as a naval cadet and added, "I will always be glad to see you at my home in Washington."[1]

Lejeune called on Senator Gibson, who introduced his constituent to the chairman of the Senate Naval Affairs Committee. This courtesy led to a meeting with the secretary of the navy, who overruled Lejeune's navy superiors. But in an unpublished and relatively unknown memoir of the class of 1888, Lejeune's roommate remembers the events of June 1890 differently. According to Beach, he and Lejeune journeyed to Washington to seek an audience with the chief of the Bureau of Navigation—then responsible for personnel matters. Like academy officials, he rebuffed Lejeune's request; unless the commandant of the Marine Corps asked for him specifically, no change would occur. As Lejeune pressed his case, the exasperated officer responded sarcastically: "You have altogether too many brains to be lost in the Marine Corps." When Lejeune and Beach reported the caustic rejoinder to the commandant, he flew predictably into a rage and requested Lejeune by name.[2]

Which version is the correct account is unimportant. Lejeune's persistence had overcome an arbitrary and perhaps capricious decision on the part of his navy superiors. He left Annapolis and returned home to spend the summer visiting relatives. Ovide had succumbed to pneumonia the previous winter and his absence cast a gloom over Lejeune's homecoming. Shortly after arriving in Pointe Coupee, his commission as a second lieutenant arrived in the mail. The letter from Headquarters Marine Corps included orders to report to Marine Barracks, New York, by 1 September 1890. Lejeune's Marine Corps career was about to begin. Lejeune and the other new second lieutenants trained under the watchful eyes of Major Robert W. Huntington, the commander of the old barracks in Brooklyn. Huntington and his staff provided occasional classroom instruction, but mostly the new officers learned by experience. As officers of the barracks' guard, they inspected the sentries—including the disagreeable requirement to examine the guards once each evening after midnight. Huntington attempted to teach the young officers something about the Marine Corps and its unique role as the lesser of the naval services. Lejeune could not help but notice that his branch of the sea services was held in low esteem by both navy officers and educated civilians.[3]

Many navy officers considered the assignment of a marine guard in the warships of the fleet as nothing more than an anachronism dating from the age of sail. Because leatherneck officers stood no watches at sea, some navy officers held them in low regard.

Worse, many of the Marine Corps officers had gained their commissions after flunking out of West Point or Annapolis, or simply through political patronage. Navy officers, riding the tide of reform during the 1880s, found little positive to say about their sister service. The barracks that Lejeune joined contained no formal organization such as companies or battalions and numbered barely over a hundred enlisted men. The excessive guard duty attracted few quality recruits, and they for the most part were recent immigrants. Journalists took occasional swipes at the rough exteriors of the enlisted force and found the social whirl of many leatherneck officers a convenient and amusing subject of ridicule. Perhaps a bit tongue in cheek, a reporter described the Marine Corps in somewhat hyperbolic terms just four years before Lejeune accepted his commission: "The Marine Corps is the oldest, the smallest, the best uniformed and equipped and most artistically drilled branch of the fighting wing of the government."[4]

As the navy appeared to be working its way out of the doldrums following the Civil War, so did the Marine Corps. During his commandancy, Colonel Charles G. McCawley (1876–1891) attempted to improve the sorry lot of his enlisted force. First, he asked to increase his numbers so as to reduce the number of hours an enlisted marine might spend on guard duty. Then, McCawley sought increased appropriations to provide such amenities as sheets and pillowcases and a substantially increased ration allowance. Finally, the commandant requested that all of his officers come from among the graduates of the Military Academy. Allowing the excess from Annapolis—rather than West Point—to fill his vacancies, as in Lejeune's case, provided the intellectual and professional stimulus that McCawley sought.[5]

Compared to his classmates who had been commissioned in the navy, Lejeune and the new second lieutenants lived on a much grander scale. Coincident with the arrival of the new officers at the barracks, a local journalist seized on the problem of the disparity of pay among recent graduates of Annapolis. In his account, he trumpeted the living conditions for the new second lieutenants in Brooklyn: "They have exclusive quarters in a spacious, three-story brick house . . . the house is sumptuously furnished . . . cook, janitor, and a uniformed sentry," adding that "[it] completes the attention which a provident government bestows upon its junior Marine officers."[6]

In late October, the young officers submitted their requests for permanent duty stations. Lejeune asked for Philadelphia, but McCawley and his staff ordered him instead to the small barracks in Portsmouth, Virginia. Reporting aboard on 3 November, he began his duties as a guard officer. Although each barracks was supposed to count at least three lieutenants, only two was the norm; thus, Lejeune usually had the duty every other day. The wretched condition of the old installation did little to improve his morale. While he thought that his living conditions in Annapolis had been Spartan, the sorry lot of the barracks' enlisted force filled him with remorse. Enlisted men slept on straw-filled mattresses stretched over double bunk beds and subsisted on a meager fare. More than four decades later, Lejeune still remembered a typical and unappetizing evening meal: bread, coffee, molasses, cheese, and a slice of bologna sausage.[7]

Quickly, Lejeune joined the social whirl of the naval officers in the Tidewater area. Evenings in the Ocean House Bar or at dances aboard one of the receiving ships provided a necessary respite from the boring grind of barracks duties. While visiting the *Atlanta*, he met Ellie Harrison Murdaugh, the stunning daughter of a Portsmouth judge. Before long, the couple became a social fixture as Lejeune pursued her determinedly. He recalled a frustrating courtship: "Miss Ellie was a most elusive lady, a carefree, laughing, bewitching damsel who seemed not to esteem one admirer more than another. Many were the heart pangs I suffered, and often was I visited by the green-eyed monster, jealousy." Ellie's obvious beauty and charm, however, did not prevent Lejeune from requesting orders to the new School of Application for junior officers. Lejeune's correspondence probably reminded some-one at headquarters that he was due for his obligatory stint of duty at sea and he received orders to the *Bennington*. Before he departed Portsmouth, Lejeune took Ellie for a buggy ride and told her of his undying love and admiration. He left to join his ship in the fall of 1891, hopeful that she would be waiting when he returned.[8]

Commissioned just that June, the *Bennington* weighed seven-teen tons, mounted six 6-inch breechloading naval rifles, and could steam at eighteen knots. Lejeune's marines numbered 28 out of a crew of 192, and he was one of ten officers. The vessel steamed south in company with the *Atlantic* and the *Chicago* to take up station in the south Atlantic. When diplomatic tempers flared between the United States and Chile as a result of the Chilean civil war, the United States maintained a squadron oper-ating between Montevideo and Buenos Aires. Lejeune found his duties to be more boring than demanding. Each day, he took the small detachment ashore for drills; otherwise, he had little to occupy his time except to socialize in port or write moody, dreamy letters to Ellie.[9]

Lejeune's lackluster performance and apparent disinterest in his duties brought him to the attention of his commanding officer. A strict disciplinarian and somewhat of a martinet, Commander Royal B. Bradford reported Lejeune's alleged shortcomings to the commandant. Heywood responded with a scathing letter of admo-nition to the young officer: "Sir: I have received a report . . . on your fitness as an officer, which has occasioned much regret on my part. In this report, your 'attention to duty' is stated as 'not good' . . . This report has greatly disappointed me both as regards you, and the fact that the Corps has been so poorly represented on board the *Bennington*, and your record as an officer will be greatly affected unless you pay closer attention to your duties."[10]

Although he smarted under the contents of the commandant's letter, Lejeune chose not to contest the negative report. In midsummer, the *Bennington* left the south Atlantic for the Mediterranean. For the remainder of the year, she showed the flag in company with the battleship *New York*. While in dry dock at Caddiz, Bradford left the ship and Lejeune took the opportunity to vent his spleen in a letter to Augustine: "All of us that remain will be delighted to see him leave as he is heartily despised by every man and officer aboard."[11]

Assigned to the barracks at Norfolk, Lejeune resumed his courtship of Ellie. On 23 October 1895, the couple exchanged marriage vows in the parlor of her home. Given the doubtful future for naval officers of the era and the typical life-style of many of the Marine Corps' lieutenants, Judge Claudius W. Murdaugh most likely did not think much of his daughter's choice for a husband.[12]

The Marine Corps that Lejeune joined five years earlier had changed little. While the commissioning of officers from the Naval Academy and the establishment of the School of Application promised better-trained junior officers, the training of recruits continued in a haphazard manner according to the whims of the various barracks commanders. Congressional appropriations remained consistently low. Advancements for leatherneck officers came at an agonizingly slow pace, based on vacancy and strict seniority. Lejeune appeared to face a bleak future in a rather quaint, antiquarian military service. The uncertain, dismal economic climate of rural Louisiana kept him in uniform simply because he had nowhere else to turn for employment. Lengthy tours of duty at sea did little to encourage marriage at a young age, but Lejeune was in love and could not wait: "It is better for a young man to fall in love early in life, as it makes him a much better man, and gives him an object to strive for," he confided to his sister. This dedication to home and family increased as he grew older, and such an attitude appears in marked contrast to that of many of his contemporaries.[13]

For most of 1896, the couple settled into a style of living that became commonplace for the next decade—residence in a boardinghouse near Lejeune's barracks or ship. That summer, their first

Lejeune as a military cadet, Louisiana State University, probably photographed in 1883. Courtesy of the Naval Academy Archives.

Lejeune as a plebe at the United States Naval Academy, 1884.
Courtesy of the Naval Academy Archives.

The class of 1888, United States Naval Academy, posing around the statue of Tecumseh. Lejeune is at the far right in the second row of naval cadets. Courtesy of the Naval Academy Archives.

The *Bennington*, in which Lejeune served, 1891–1893. Courtesy of the Naval Historical Center.

Lejeune as a major. Courtesy of the Naval Academy Archives.

Officers and NCOs, Marine Battalion, Cavite, Philippines, 1908. Lejeune is second from left in the front row. Courtesy of the Marine Corps Historical Center.

Inspection of the Marine Barracks, New York, 1913. The commandant's representative, Colonel Charles H. Lauchheimer, is on the left; Lieutenant Colonel Lejeune is in the center; and Lejeune's executive officer, Captain R. C. Dewey, is on the right. Courtesy of the Marine Corps Historical Center.

The brigade commander and his principal officers, Veracruz, 1914. Front row, left to right: Lieutenant Colonel Wendell C. Neville, Colonel John A. Lejeune, Colonel Littleton W. T. Waller, Major Smedley D. Butler, and Major Randolph C. Berkeley. Courtesy of the Marine Corps Historical Center.

child, Ellie Murdaugh Lejeune, was born. A year later, Lejeune reported to the *Cincinnati* for another tour at sea. The ship displaced over three thousand tons and could steam at nineteen knots with an impressive array of weaponry: ten 5-inch rapid-fire cannon, one 6-inch naval gun, eight 6-pounders, and two 1-pounders. Soon after reporting aboard, Lejeune requested that his marines be assigned to gunnery duties when the ship went to general quarters. In a sharp exchange, the *Cincinnati*'s executive officer dismissed the notion, perhaps reflecting the opinion of many navy officers of the era who argued for the removal of leathernecks from the ships of the fleet.

Determined, Lejeune appealed directly to Captain Colby M. Chester, and he granted the request: marines would man all of the 6-inch guns. The acrimonious exchange only foreshadowed a much more ominous bureaucratic struggle that would culminate in an executive order in 1908 to remove all marines from American warships. Writing from hindsight, Lejeune believed that his request for assignment of the *Cincinnati*'s marines to gunnery duties might deflect navy criticism of seagoing leathernecks: "The best way to defeat advocates of that policy was to build up and maintain the efficiency of the Corps and to make it of such great usefulness to the Navy as to cause far-seeing and broad-minded naval officers to oppose its abolition and to favor its growth and development."[14]

The *Cincinnati* steamed for the south Atlantic and operated just like the *Bennington* of Lejeune's earlier tour at sea. But now that he was a happily married man and a father, he had no interest in socializing in port. Between his second wedding anniversary and the Christmas holidays, Lejeune's morale plummeted and he shared his feelings in letters to his mother and Augustine: "As I grow older, I feel more deeply the sorrow of separation . . . married two years today, what a sad way to spend one's anniversary . . . My life is not to be envied, and as I grow older, and the ties that bind me increase in number, I feel more and more mournful at the prospect of many similar Christmas days."[15]

As the threat of war with Spain appeared, the *Cincinnati* joined other American warships in the sea lane between Cuba and Florida. Mostly, the ship provided fire support for landings in Cuba and Puerto Rico. In his only opportunity to earn some powder burns on his uniforms, Lejeune led a landing party from the *Cincinnati* and *Amphitrite* ashore at Fajardo. By then, however, the Spanish had retreated. Finding no defenders, Lejeune ordered a flag raised over the lighthouse, and the small force returned to its ships. Later in Key West, he received the shocking news that his mother had fallen and Augustine did not expect her to live. Returning to Louisiana, Lejeune learned that his mother had been buried beside Ovide in the churchyard of St. Stephen's the week before. Theirs was a close relationship; his mother affected him deeply, and a fair share of his noble character and worldview can be attributed to her. On the first anniversary of his mother's death, Lejeune waxed maudlin: "At this time, the thought of the last days on earth of our sainted mother fills our hearts and we turn to her grave as to a shrine of holiness. We can indeed thank God for having given us such a noble and beautiful character as a mother . . . her character and life were filled with mercy and love for the whole world."[16]

When the *Cincinnati* received orders to be decommissioned, the commandant ordered Lejeune to the *Massachusetts* for the completion of his tour at sea. Lejeune's marines manned the battleship's secondary battery of 6-inch guns and 1-pounders. Although his responsibilities had increased markedly, the assignment proved to be routine. Except for one brief run to the Caribbean in April, the *Massachusetts* operated with the North Atlantic Squadron in the waters off New England. On 10 May 1899, Lejeune left the ship to take up recruiting duties in Boston.[17]

The tour proved to be short-lived, however. Because of little Ellie's ill health, Heywood agreed to transfer Lejeune to an assignment in a warmer climate. For the next two years, he commanded the small barracks at Pensacola. While there, a second daughter, Laura Turpin Lejeune, was born. Then, Lejeune's own ill health

brought the pleasant assignment to an end. Suffering from appendicitis, he traveled north for surgery in Baltimore. While on
convalescent leave, a chance assignment at Headquarters Marine
Corps forced Lejeune to examine his career and make an important decision.

Following the Spanish-American War, Congress authorized significant increases in the size of the Marine Corps. As a result,
additional openings now existed in the staff. The secretary of the
navy directed Colonel George C. Reid—acting as commandant
because Heywood was out of town on an inspection trip—to effect
the new appointments to the staff without delay. Lejeune's duties
involved an examination of the commandant's files to determine
if Heywood had indicated any preference for the appointments or
if there were other officers who should be selected. Word of the
anticipated appointments spread quickly throughout the Marine
Corps. Not only did promotions come with the appointments,
but also expeditionary or sea duty seldom required a member of
the staff. Lejeune recalled later that several future senior officers
applied for the vacancies, including Franklin J. Moses, Wendell
C. Neville, and Dion Williams. Then, much to his surprise,
Reid offered an appointment as an adjutant and inspector—with
an immediate promotion to major—to him.[18]

This unexpected turn of events caused Lejeune to reflect on his
career and personal goals. For more than a decade, his duties at
sea and in barracks had failed to stimulate him. But with a
growing family and limited skills to apply to the civilian job
market, Lejeune remained a leatherneck. Accepting Colonel
Reid's offer meant the end of onerous assignments at sea or
overseas, with the likelihood of a comfortable position in Washington for the remainder of his career. But expansion following
the Spanish-American War resulted in the Marine Corps increasing in strength from 116 officers, and 4,700 enlisted men to 187
officers and 5,520 enlistees. As a result, the stagnation of the
officers' lineal list might end. Lejeune sought the counsel of
Colonel Reid, an officer whom he admired and trusted: "My

ambition has always been to be appointed Commandant," Reid said, "but there is strong prejudice against staff officers being appointed which will be difficult if not impossible to overcome."[19]

Just as Colonel Reid predicted in his candid counseling, President Roosevelt selected George F. Elliott—a line officer—to succeed Heywood, despite the urging of several prominent political figures and the General Board of the Navy to have Reid succeed to the corps' highest post. By declining Colonel Reid's generous offer, Lejeune made a conscious decision to accept the alternating tours of expeditionary duty that accompanied the duties of a line officer. When Lejeune had fully recovered from his attack of appendicitis, the new commandant ordered him to report to the transport Panther in midsummer 1903 with a battalion of marines from the barracks at League Island. He became a major on 3 March 1903. Lejeune anticipated deployment to Cuba but dreaded the assignment because of his new commanding officer.

By then, the Panther and its captain, John C. Wilson, were well known throughout the Marine Corps. Wilson enjoyed the reputation as a notorious antagonist of marines who lent his vocal support to those officers who urged the removal of all leathernecks from the fleet. Worse, Wilson insisted that the embarked marines be kept under the control—both afloat and ashore—of either him or his officers, and not by the assigned marines. Before Lejeune became involved in an interservice squabble, however, the Panther received orders for an overhaul. Transferred to the Dixie, Lejeune found its commander more amenable to allowing Marine Corps officers to control marines.[20]

The Dixie steamed to the Caribbean and took on coal in Cuba. When Colombian officials balked at President Roosevelt's heavy-handed political maneuvering to obtain a cross-isthmus canal, the United States opted to force the issue by coming to the aid of Panamanian rebels. The cruiser Nashville arrived first on the explosive scene, disembarking fifty marines on 5 November 1903. The following day, the Dixie steamed into the area. Lejeune and his battalion marched ashore to reinforce the landing party from the *Nashville*. Another battalion was formed from among the marines serving in the ships of the fleet. As additional warships arrived, Lejeune quickly became caught up in the euphoric wave of American neocolonialism. In a note to Augustine, Lejeune described his adventures as "the busiest week of his life" and added that "there is no telling what will happen next with such a strenuous president in the chair. It keeps the Marine Corps busy at any rate."[21]

Lejeune's marines patrolled the streets of Colon and otherwise kept the peace. Officially, the American forces received orders to protect the railway line transiting the isthmus; no matter what transpired between the Colombian authorities and the Panamanian rebels, the United States demanded the right of neutral transit and intended to enforce that prerogative by armed force if necessary. When President Roosevelt opted for additional U.S. forces, Elliott informed the secretary of the navy that he could form another battalion of leathernecks for immediate embarkation; this time, the commandant would accompany the force to Panama and organize all of the marines deployed there into a brigade. Colonel William P. Biddle commanded the First Regiment and Colonel Littleton W. T. Waller the Second Regiment; Lejeune and his Naval Academy classmate Eli K. Cole each commanded battalions in Biddle's regiment. When most of the U.S. force departed in early 1904, Lejeune and his battalion remained—10 officers and 407 enlisted men.[22]

With the departure of Elliott and the more senior Marine Corps officers, Lejeune found himself at loggerheads with the navy over the question of command and seniority. With the exodus of the commandant, Rear Admiral Charles D. Sigsbee ordered the command structure ashore changed to reflect what had become typical during the age of sail: naval landing parties would be commanded by a navy officer. Sigsbee passed command of all forces ashore to Lieutenant Commander Lucien Young. But when the command went subsequently to Lieutenant Commander Hilary P. Jones—an officer junior to Lejeune by lineal precedence—

the feisty leatherneck protested the decision. Incensed at Lejeune's temerity, Admiral Sigsbee rebuked him for his strong language and reminded the determined marine that juniors do not "protest" to their seniors but instead should "appeal" or "request reconsideration." In any event, Sigsbee took more than four months to reply to Lejeune's correspondence, leaving him to smart under Jones's command. In the close-knit naval fraternity, Lejeune's reputation for being argumentative in such matters continued to grow. [23]

Much to Lejeune's disappointment, he remained deployed while his third daughter was born. The proud parents named her Eugenia Dickson Lejeune. Anxious to see the newest member of his family, Lejeune nevertheless applied himself to the tedium of tropical soldiering. He directed that each of his marines carry a full canteen of water whenever leaving camp because of the variety of water-borne diseases endemic to the region. In addition, Lejeune required every man to sleep under a mosquito net because of the prevalence of malaria and yellow fever. He restricted liberty hours and placed the bordellos along the railway lines off limits. Demanding that every marine pay particular attention to personal hygiene, Lejeune and his officers inspected the battalion three times a week. Although he professed later to have thrived on his full load of duties, he grumbled repeatedly in letters home: "Pleasure down here—there is none," he sputtered on one occasion. [24]

Finally on 10 December 1904, Lejeune and his weary battalion embarked on the aged transport *Yankee* to return home. Pleased with Lejeune's performance, Elliott assigned him to command the corps' oldest post, Marine Barracks, Washington. Supposedly, the location had been selected by President Thomas Jefferson and Lieutenant Colonel Commandant Franklin Wharton because the former insisted that the marines be quartered within marching distance of the Capitol. By the time Lejeune arrived on the scene, the purpose and the physical plant of the historic post had

changed considerably. Shortly after the turn of the century, Headquarters Marine Corps and the office of the commandant occupied
offices in downtown Washington near the secretary of the navy.
When Lejeune assumed command, only the barracks for the
garrison and band, the officers' "Center House," and the historic
home of the commandant remained. The barracks mainly served
to support the office of the commandant and Headquarters Marine
Corps.

Several times during the two years that Lejeune served at "Eighth
and Eye," he found himself detailed to various boards of inquiry
or courts-martial, or simply to perform administrative duties. At
one point, he received instructions from Elliott to prepare a
recommendation on legislation that would affect the officer promotion system. Lejeune thought that the officer corps should
consist of the major general commandant, 3 brigadier generals
(there were none at the time), 9 colonels, 9 lieutenant colonels,
27 majors, 100 captains, and 150 lieutenants. More important,
his report called for the retirement of older and infirm officers.
Lejeune's conclusions on this subject did not change over the
next fifteen years and are consistent with the officer personnel
legislation that he so assiduously pursued—but failed to achieve—
while serving as commandant. Most officers of the era, like
Lejeune, kept current on the lineal precedence of their contemporaries, correcting the lineal list in pen and ink when someone
retired or died on active service. Public laws controlled the number of officers in each grade, causing ambitious young men like
Lejeune to chafe impatiently.[25]

In the spring of 1906, he received orders to form a battalion to
again embark for Panama. As had been the custom, the marines
to serve in the expeditionary force came from every barracks and
post on the east coast. Such requirements arrived with increasing
frequency following the Spanish-American War. Nevertheless,
expeditionary units of leathernecks continued to be formed in a
haphazard manner. Lejeune assembled his battalion at the barracks in Philadelphia. Eventually numbering 298 men, it embarked

on the transport *Columbia*. Major Charles G. Long commanded the other battalion, with both units under Lieutenant Colonel James E. Mahoney as regimental commander. Ostensibly, the force was to quell the rash of local disturbances in Panama.[26]

On 29 May 1906, the marines marched ashore and moved to Bas Obispo by rail. To Lejeune's dismay, he learned that the governor of the Canal Zone wanted them quartered in a swamp near Panama City. Predictably, within a week most of the regiment had malaria. When the force returned home the following summer, additional medical officers accompanied it. Nevertheless, when the ship docked in Boston, Lejeune and many of his marines still suffered from disease. After treatment at Chelsea Naval Hospital, Lejeune returned to Washington. With a wife and three daughters, he began to find the deployments increasingly troublesome. At home, he spent more time with his family.

Family dinners, especially on Sunday, became traditional times of fellowship. Each gathering began with prayers as Lejeune became increasingly religious. A devout Episcopalian, he and his family became members of a local church no matter where his duties took him. When Lejeune received orders to the Philippines early in 1907, the assignment—although expected—troubled him, and he expressed an unusual sadness with his sister: "The children are well and happy, and are the greatest joys of our lives. I feel sad to think of my next absence from home . . . I shrink from [the thought] of two and one-half years out there alone."[27]

Most Marine Corps officers accepted the lengthy tours of duty overseas without their families as a necessary but unpleasant aspect of their profession. Because adequate housing and Western-style amenities were not customarily available, Lejeune's contemporaries usually opted to endure their overseas tours alone. This time, however, he decided against leaving his young family at home. Taking advantage of army transport, Lejeune traveled with his family from San Francisco to Honolulu and eventually to Cavite. Arriving in April, then the hottest and most uncomfortable time of the year, he found a home outside the old Spanish naval arsenal and employed native servants.

The harsh climate and primitive living taxed Lejeune's determination to have his family with him. Few of the navy officers and none of the marines had brought their dependents. Quiet dinners at home became increasingly the staple of their social life. An occasional trip to Manila for more exciting entertainment meant returning by boat long after midnight. "It is [tiring] seeking pleasure under such circumstances," he grumbled to his sister.[28]

While Lejeune commanded a battalion at Cavite, another similar Marine Corps force served to protect the navy station at Olongapo. Colonel Biddle commanded all the leathernecks in the Philippines from his headquarters in Manila. The marines were intended to provide security for the naval stations and as an expeditionary force to support the U.S. naval presence in East Asia. A much larger army contingent functioned in the islands during the era to chase down the last of the insurgent Filipinos resisting American rule.

The Lejeunes did their best to maintain morale in the harsh environment. Late that summer, Ellie came down with dengue fever; that fall, huge boils erupted on her face. The heavy rains in the summer kept the children confined indoors for much of the time, trying the patience of their native nurse. Whatever domestic tranquility they could manage became increasingly important. Colonel Biddle became a surrogate grandfather to the family and spent many of the holidays with them. That fall, he married Mrs. Martha Adger, and Lejeune served as his commanding officer's best man. But mostly the days and weeks drifted by in uncomfortable tedium and seemingly endless boredom. When Biddle returned home, Lejeune commuted daily to Manila to assume the duties of marine brigade commander in the Philippines. He expected a promotion to lieutenant colonel and orders home, but official mail from Washington mentioned neither.

Then, Lejeune read in an old issue of the *Army-Navy Journal* that orders had been issued to Colonel Karmany for duty in the

Philippines. He assumed, correctly, that the veteran campaigner and graduate of the Naval Academy, class of 1881, would be his relief in Manila. But Karmany failed to arrive as scheduled, leaving Lejeune fretful and anxious. An unnamed confidant revealed the reason for Karmany's delay. The previous fall, the hard-drinking Karmany became embroiled in a messy divorce case. Now, he had appealed directly to the commandant for a delay in the execution of his orders so as to settle his personal dilemma and make arrangements to bring his girlfriend to the islands with him. The news only added to Lejeune's discomfort and he vented his frustration to his sister in the next letter home: "General Elliott is so weak that whoever is ordered out as my relief can get all the delay he wants." Decades later, however, Lejeune could afford to be more charitable towards Elliott, describing him in his memoirs as "a splendidly frank and courageous officer, and a kindly, though impulsive, and gallant gentleman."[29]

When Ellie contracted dengue fever again, the admiral commanding the station granted Lejeune leave to visit Japan in hopes of finding a healthier climate. Taking passage on the army transport to Nagasaki, Lejeune assumed that he could find passage home for his family while he returned to the Philippines alone. During the visit to Japan, however, Karmany arrived and Lejeune received orders to continue home. He had been promoted to lieutenant colonel, effective 13 May 1909. Lejeune reported to the commandant to discuss his next assignment. Normally, he could expect assignment as executive officer at one of the larger barracks or perhaps as commanding officer at a smaller station. With an eye for his future, however, Elliott had other plans.

Earlier, the acting chief of staff of the army, Major General Charles W. Wotherspoon, had spoken of the possibility of a qualified Marine Corps officer attending a course at the Army War College. The commandant asked Lejeune to call on Wotherspoon and discuss his possible attendance in the next course. Wotherspoon urged him to request the assignment, suggesting that completion of the demanding curriculum would prepare him for duties as a senior officer in the next war: "If you make good at the college, which I am sure you will do, your military future will be assured."[30]

The assignment proved to be a benchmark in Lejeune's career. At this juncture, he had a reputation as a steady but uninspiring performer. Considerably more intelligent than most of his contemporaries, he nevertheless lacked the panache and élan that characterized colorful leathernecks such as Littleton W. T. Waller and Smedley D. Butler. Others, like George Barnett and Charles H. Lauchheimer, appeared more adept at cultivating important political connections. Worse, Lejeune lacked the education and experience for such an assignment as a student at the war college. But his Naval Academy classmate Eli K. Cole, whose background differed little from that of Lejeune, completed the course with the class of 1907–1908.

College presidents insisted that all prospective students be sufficiently prepared to grasp the theoretical nature of the curriculum. Officers attending the course either attended the Command and General Staff College at Fort Leavenworth first or, as in Lejeune's case, undertook an abbreviated version at the war college prior to the term beginning. As Lejeune pored over his books during the early fall of 1909, Wotherspoon replaced Major General Tasker Bliss as the president of the college. With the change, the geographic focus of the curriculum shifted. Under Bliss, the tactical scenarios all emphasized the experience of European wars, especially the Franco-Prussian War, and stressed the superiorities of the German staff system. Wotherspoon insisted that the students apply themselves to potential military problems directly relevant to the interests of the United States. Lejeune's three research problems, "The Military Geography of Guam," "The Military Geography of Alaska," and "Japan's Military and Naval Organization and Resources," reflected this emphasis.[31]

When warm spring came to nearby Virginia in April 1910, Lejeune's class rode through the nearby Civil War battlefields on horseback. That fall, they traveled to Winchester, Antietam, and

Gettysburg. While in Pennsylvania, they operated as an ad hoc staff during the annual maneuvers of the National Guard. The war college experience proved of immense value to Lejeune's career, both in the near term and when he became a general officer. Besides gaining experience in the practice and planning necessary to field large military units in wartime, he earned a reputation amongst classmates and faculty as a scholar and dedicated professional. In less than a decade, promising army officers such as Malin Craig, Hunter Liggett, Fox Connor, Eli Helmlick, and Ebin Swift would influence his duties in France.[32]

As graduation drew near, Lejeune sought an audience with the commandant to determine his next posting. As a junior lieutenant colonel, his opportunities seemed slim. The Marine Corps of 1910 numbered only 328 officers and 9,232 enlisted men; of the officers, 115 served overseas or with the fleet. Internal problems at Headquarters Marine Corps added to the uncertainty of Lejeune's next assignment. The previous spring, the office of the commandant had been subjected to public ridicule as a result of a feud between Elliott and his staff. The issues seemed to rest on just who managed the affairs of the Marine Corps; worse, the press suggested that because the titular leader of the protagonists among the staff, Colonel Charles H. Lauchheimer, was Jewish, the sordid affair had anti-Semitic overtones. A board of investigation found fault with everyone involved and suggested shorter terms in office for the commandant and his principal staff officers. Elliott opted for retirement shortly thereafter and the principal participants in the controversy received letters of censure and transfers away from Washington.[33]

As the Marine Corps wrestled with this unsavory internal problem, Lejeune—still a lieutenant colonel—assumed command of Marine Barracks, New York, on 7 November 1910. Although he had earlier considered the barracks in Norfolk to be his first choice, he quickly decided that the old post in Brooklyn was better. Quarters on the grounds of the naval station were much nicer than anticipated. Lejeune decided to join the Church of the Messiah in a nearby neighborhood, and he encountered an old classmate who provided introductions to the right people. More financially secure, Lejeune found that he and his family could afford an occasional afternoon or evening in New York.

Command of the large barracks tested Lejeune's mettle as a leader. When he arrived, he found that its desertion rate numbered the highest in the Marine Corps. The strength of the barracks varied between four hundred and five hundred men, many of whom were recruits undergoing basic training; the remainder provided security for the naval station. Lejeune learned that most of the marines had liberty following the noon meal, unless assigned to guard duties. Alarmed by the scandalous desertion rate, he cracked down immediately.

Determining that the proliferation of saloons and bordellos in the neighborhoods outside the barracks contributed to the problem, he required all hands to appear in a formation at reveille. Following breakfast, physical training and drill appeared on the schedule. An inspection of the mess hall revealed the food to be bland and unappetizing and little improvement over what he had tasted as a second lieutenant in Portsmouth. Finally, Lejeune enjoined his officers to make the training interesting rather than perfunctory; as an example, he added athletics to the training schedule and required nonswimmers to take lessons at a nearby YMCA pool. Idleness or "bunk fatigue" plagued the command and he was determined to stop it.[34]

Almost immediately, his reforms bore fruit. When he assumed command in 1910, the desertion rate had reached 8.5 percent, but the following year, it dropped to 5.5 percent; and each year thereafter, the percentage dropped further. Although Lejeune's performance and that of his command pleased the commandant and his staff, his determined character ruffled navy feathers in Brooklyn. Soon after assuming command, Lejeune asked the commandant of the Navy Yard, Rear Admiral Eugene H. C. Leutze, for permission to fly the flag in front of the marine barracks. Leutze denied the request, opining that only one flag would be flown and that in front of his own headquarters. Lejeune notified Biddle, who in turn passed the matter on to the secretary of the navy. A ruling arrived in Brooklyn that overturned Leutze's edict, reinforcing Lejeune's reputation as a stickler for the details of service custom and not an officer appeased simply by seniority.[35]

Early in the spring of 1911, Lejeune received orders to prepare a large body of marines for deployment to Cuba. After supervising its movement to the Philadelphia Navy Yard for embarkation, Lejeune journeyed to Washington to seek a meeting with Biddle. He objected strongly to his omission from the troop list and indicated that in future deployments involving marines from his command, he expected to accompany them. Biddle seemed surprised by Lejeune's insistence, perhaps because senior officers of the era traditionally welcomed the opportunity to remain at their barracks. But in the following year when President Taft ordered a naval landing party ashore in Cuba to quell local disturbances, Lejeune commanded a regiment that landed with a brigade of leathernecks and bluejackets at Daiquiri. Although the American force was withdrawn by the end of the summer, Lejeune found himself back in the Caribbean a year later.[36]

Almost from its establishment in 1900 as a strategic planning body for the secretary of the navy, the General Board recommended the need to secure advance bases for the fleet. The troops to accomplish such a mission should come mostly from the Marine Corps. Initially, the General Board conceived a 400-man battalion of leathernecks dedicated to the new mission. By 1912, however, planners recommended an organization composed of two 1300-man regiments: a fixed defense regiment armed with large-caliber naval guns in temporary shore emplacements and a mobile defense regiment, consisting largely of an infantry force armed with machine guns to defend the advance base against an enemy assault. A year later, the General Board recommended that the concept be tested in full-scale maneuvers with the fleet.

Secretary of the Navy Josephus Daniels approved the proposed scenario, to take place on the Puerto Rican island of Culebra, on

20 October 1913. A European power—code-named Red for the purposes of the maneuvers but obviously Germany—declared war on the United States on 15 December. The Atlantic Fleet—code-named Blue—would sortie at Culebra to intercept the Red fleet in early January, then steam north to defend the east coast of the United States. The advance base force would remain in Culebra to defend the Blue fleet train, anticipating an attack by Red naval forces.

The mobile regiment, commanded by Lejeune, embarked on the ancient troopship *Prairie*. The fixed regiment, under Lieutenant Colonel Charles G. Long, loaded its equipment on the even more antiquated *Hancock*. Both ships sailed from Philadelphia on 27 November 1913, carrying with them Colonel George Barnett and the staff of the headquarters, advance base force. On 9 January 1914, the transports arrived off Culebra and disembarked the force. Lejeune's marines dug trenches and fields of fire under the fierce tropical sun. He placed one battalion on the southeast tip of Culebra to protect the flank of the harbor and ordered the other battalion along the west and northwest shores to cover the most likely landing area. Lejeune positioned the 3-inch landing gun company on a prominent hilltop to support the infantry.

Barnett had been ordered to prepare to defend the small island within six days. His leathernecks and bluejackets worked night and day in order to install the five 5-inch naval guns ashore, dragging them and much of their equipment through the jungle. At 3:00 A.M. on 18 January 1914, the ships and forces simulating an attacking enemy force arrived. An assault regiment attempted to come ashore three days later, but the chief umpire for the exercise, Captain William S. Sims, declared a victory for the defending force on the first morning of the assault. On 9 February, the ships returned and transported the advance base force north to Pensacola. Everyone seem pleased by the results of the exercise; the navy had the security for its fleet train and the Marine Corps had a mission consistent with that of the navy in the age of Mahan.[37]

Lejeune and his regiment's stay in Florida would be short-lived, however, because of a potentially explosive situation in Mexico. Since 1910, the United States had experienced troubled relations with its closest southern neighbor. When a group of conspirators murdered the president of Mexico and installed its leader as the chief executive, feelings north of the border cooled considerably. By this time, American investments in Mexico amounted to more than a billion dollars—exceeding the capital owned by native Mexicans. An estimated seventy thousand U.S. citizens lived and worked south of the border. Those with vested interests in Mexico demanded a more spirited American policy in the region. President Woodrow Wilson hoped to unseat the usurper through diplomatic and economic pressures, but over the circumstances of a seemingly trivial incident it appeared as if an opportunity to force a showdown had arrived.

When Mexican police in Tampico arrested a small party of American sailors loading supplies for the *Dolphin* in 1913, the naval commander on the scene demanded an apology and the firing of a twenty-one gun salute. Ultimatums flew back and forth between the two governments, with neither side willing to bend. Meanwhile, President Wilson dispatched warships and troops to the scene to force the issue. As diplomatic tempers flared between the two nations, important changes took place in the leadership of the Marine Corps.

In less than a year of service under the meddlesome scrutiny of Wilson's secretary of the navy, Josephus Daniels, the corpulent and lethargic Biddle opted for retirement. Although Waller appeared as the most likely candidate to succeed to the corps' highest post, Daniels bowed to political pressure from Senate Republicans and chose George Barnett to lead the corps. When the announcement was made public, Barnett asked Lejeune to accompany him to Washington as assistant to the commandant. But anticipating deployment of his regiment to Mexico, Lejeune requested and received permission for a delay in reporting to his new assignment. [38]

On 20 April 1914, President Wilson ordered the entire Atlantic Fleet to concentrate off Veracruz, the natural port of entry for a military advance on Mexico City. A day later, he ordered naval forces to intercept and seize a shipment of German-manufactured machine guns. Arriving off Veracruz two days later, Lejeune reported to Rear Admiral Charles J. Badger. By then, almost the entire U.S. fleet—including seven battleships—was in the area or under way. The day before Lejeune's arrival, a battalion of marines and sailors filed ashore. Then, two regiments of bluejackets and leathernecks from the Atlantic Fleet arrived, the marines numbering more than a thousand, assembled from the detachments serving in the ships of the fleet. Initially, Lejeune commanded the entire unit ashore. But as the size of the force increased to a brigade, command passed to Waller, with Lejeune assuming command of a regiment.

His marines conducted patrols and house-to-house searches to relieve marauding and rebellious Mexicans of their arms and otherwise bring the turmoil to a halt. By the end of April 1914, the Marine Corps counted 2,469 officers and men ashore. Two hundred navy officers and 3,760 sailors added to the sizable contingent. Colonel Joseph H. Pendleton and a regiment of marines embarked in the *South Dakota*, the *Jupiter*, and the *West Virginia* steamed off Mexico's other coast to intimidate the Huerta government further.

For the next seven months, the marines of the landing force swatted flies and mosquitoes, sweated, and fought tedium as the rebellious Mexican populace became pacified. Lejeune and his officers ordered defensive positions improved, conducted drills and exercises, and directed that strict attention be paid to field sanitation. Finally on 15 November 1914, the force departed Mexico and returned home. A grateful government showered the nation's highest military decoration, the Medal of Honor, on fifty-nine veterans of Veracruz. But most observers considered the awards somewhat specious, especially since the Marine Corps recipients were all officers—captain or above. Only thirteen Medals of Honor were given in World War I. Lejeune did not receive one, and his omission from the list of recipients did not apparently trouble him.[39]

Earlier, Biddle had asked Lejeune to serve as his assistant, but Lejeune begged off, citing personal reasons. This time, Barnett insisted, although Lejeune hoped privately to take up the new commandant's old post in Philadelphia. In Washington, Lejeune relieved his classmate Eli K. Cole. Their friendship had failed to survive in the years since graduation from the Naval Academy; whereas in 1904, Lejeune referred to Cole as "about the best friend I have in the service," by 1910 he had become "the man I am most afraid of among my juniors."[40]

In the next four years, Lejeune advanced from lieutenant colonel to major general. During this formative time, he hitched his political fortunes to Secretary of the Navy Josephus Daniels; in the process, Daniels groomed Lejeune to succeed to the commandancy. Coincidentally, the ambitious and frenetic Smedley D. Butler transferred his allegiance from Waller to Lejeune and grew increasingly convinced that only a veteran campaigner like Lejeune could save his Marine Corps from the leadership of the intellectuals from Annapolis. While less dogmatic than his erstwhile protégé, Lejeune nevertheless believed that the Marine Corps' raison d'être lay in expeditionary duty. In a letter to his sister written during the Elliott versus staff brouhaha of 1910, he scorned the machinations of "politicians" at headquarters to assert: "Fortunately, the real Marine Corps is elsewhere and consists of the 10,000 officers and men who are scattered around the world doing their duties."[41]

Notes

1. Senator Randall L. Gibson to JAL, 2 June 1890, reel 3, Lejeune MSS.
2. Edward C. Beach, "From Annapolis to Scapa Flow," unpublished memoir, privately held, pp. 54–57. Lejeune's version is in JAL, *The Reminiscences of a Marine* (1930; reprint, Quantico: Marine Corps Association, 1979), pp. 94–96. See also JAL to Rear Admiral James O. Richardson, Chief of the Bureau of Navigation, [1939], reel 7, Lejeune MSS.

3. Commandant of the Marine Corps to JAL, 28 July 1890, reel 13, Lejeune MSS; a copy is in entry 5, RG 127, NA.

4. "Status of Marine Corps," *ANJ* 24 (25 December 1886): 428.

5. Jack Shulimson, "The Transitional Commandancy: Colonel Commandant Charles G. McCawley and Uneven Reform," MCG 72 (October 1988): 70–77.

6. "Shrewd Annapolis Men," *NYT*, 8 September 1890; see also Joe Simon, "Lieutenant General John Archer Lejeune" (thesis, Louisiana State University, 1967), pp. 70–74.

7. JAL to Colonel Charles G. McCawley, 23 October 1890, entry 10, RG 127; see also JAL to AL, 3 and 21 September, 21 October 1890, reel 1, Lejeune MSS.

8. Cf. JAL, *Reminiscences of a Marine*, p. 101; and JAL to the Commandant, 10 May 1891, entry 10, RG 127, NA.

9. *Dictionary of American Naval Fighting Ships*, 6 vols. (Washington: GPO, 1959–) 1: 117; and log of the *Bennington*, RG 24, NA. The former indicates an enlisted compliment of 179 sailors and leathernecks, while the latter lists a total of 192 enlisted men on the day Lejeune reported aboard.

10. Commandant of the Marine Corps to JAL, 8 June 1891, entry 1, RG 127.

11. JAL to AL, 4 February 1892, reel 1, Lejeune MSS. Cf. JAL, *Reminiscences of a Marine*, p. 110.

12. The marriage received brief mention in both the *Portsmouth Star* and *Norfolk Virginian* on 23 October 1895. The wedding and reception were kept small because of the death of Ellie's brother in an accident a few months before.

13. JAL to AL, 14 June 1895, reel 1, Lejeune MSS. For a disturbing view of Lejeune's promotion possibilities, see "Promotion in the Marine Corps," *ANJ* 29 (24 October 1891): 148.

14. JAL, *Reminiscences of a Marine*, p. 115.

15. JAL to AL, 23 October 1897, and JAL to his mother, 25 December 1897, reel 1, Lejeune MSS.

16. JAL to AL, 2 January 1901, reel 1, Lejeune MSS.

17. Log of the *Massachusetts*, RG 24, NA.

18. JAL to the Commandant, [1935], reel 6, Lejeune MSS.

19. Ibid; see also JAL, *Reminiscences of a Marine*, pp. 150–51; and Adjutant and Inspector to Paymaster, 20 July 1903, entry 5, RG 127, NA.

20. JAL, *Reminiscences of a Marine*, pp. 151–54.

21. JAL to AL, 14 December 1903, reel 1, Lejeune MSS.

22. "Restraint on Naval Men," *NYT*, 20 December 1903; and *Annual Report of the Secretary of the Navy, 1903* (Washington: GPO, 1903), pp. 1209–62; see also, JAL to AL, letters from 23 October to 23 December 1903, reel 1, Lejeune MSS; and Lester Langley, *The Banana Wars: An Inner History of American Empire, 1900–1934* (Lexington, Ky.: University of Kentucky Press, 1983), pp. 20–50.

23. Commander-in-Chief, Caribbean Squadron, to JAL, 24 September 1904, reel 3, Lejeune MSS.

24. JAL to AL, 30 November 1903; see also, *Annual Report of the Secretary of the Navy, 1904*, p. 23.

25. JAL to the Commandant, 6 September 1906, reel 3, Lejeune MSS.

26. Commandant to JAL, 7 May 1906, reel 13, Lejeune MSS.

27. JAL to AL, 26 February 1906 and 2 January 1907, reel 1, Lejeune MSS.

28. JAL to AL, 5 June 1907, reel 1, Lejeune MSS.

29. Cf. JAL to AL, 19 March 1909; and JAL, *Reminiscences of a Marine*, p. 174.

30. JAL, *Reminiscences of a Marine*, p. 186.

31. Lejeune's first two papers are in Record Group 94 at the National Archives; his final paper, part of a class project on the military potential of Japan, is at the Army War College, Carlisle Barracks, Pennsylvania.

32. Harry P. Ball, *Of Responsible Command* (Carlisle Barracks, Penn.: Alumni Association of the Army War College, 1983), pp. 140–49; and Allan R. Millett and Peter Maslowski, *For the Common Defense* (New York and London: Macmillan, 1984), pp. 309–11.

33. Wayne A. Wiegand, "The Lauchheimer Affair," *Military Affairs* 40 (April 1976): 54–59; for contemporary accounts of the controversy, see the *NYT*; 16, 18, and 20 July 1910, and 4 December 1910. Lejeune's private views on the affair may be found in his letters to Augustine, 12 and 19 March 1910, reel 2, Lejeune MSS.

34. JAL to AL, 28 July 1910, reel 2, Lejeune MSS; and JAL, *Reminiscences of a Marine*, pp. 191–92.

35. Rear Admiral Eugene H. C. Leutze to JAL, 25 April 1911; JAL to the Commandant of the Marine Corps, 26 April 1911; and Biddle to Lejeune, 2 May 1911; reel 3, Lejeune MSS.

36. Jules R. Benjamin, *The United States and Cuba: Hegemony and Dependent Deployment, 1880–1934* (Pittsburgh, Penn.: University of Pittsburgh Press), p. 21; Whitney T. Perkins, *Constraint of Empire: The United States and Caribbean Interventions* (Westport, Conn.: Greenwood, 1981), pp. 5, 80; and Lester D. Langley, *The United States and the Caribbean in the Twentieth Century* (Athens, Ga.: University of Georgia Press, 1982), p. 66.

37. Graham Cosmas and Jack Shulimson, "The Culebra Maneuver and the Formation of the U.S. Marine Corps' Advance Base Force," in Robert William Love, Jr., ed. *Changing Interpretations and New Sources in Naval History* (New York and London: Garland, 1980), pp. 293–308.

38. Cf. Candidates for Commandant of the Marine Corps, 1913 file, container 531, Daniels MSS, Library of Congress; and Daniels, *The Wilson Years: Years of Peace, 1910–1917* (Chapel Hill, N.C.: University of North Carolina Press, 1944), pp. 322–323.

39. Jack Sweetman, *The Landing at VeraCruz* (Annapolis: Naval Institute Press, 1968), passim.

40. Cf. JAL to AL, 11 January 1904, reel 1, Lejeune MSS; and JAL to AL, 2 May 1910, reel 2, Lejeune MSS.

41. JAL to AL, 28 July 1910, reel 1, Lejeune MSS.

3

WORLD WAR ONE:
WASHINGTON
ST. MIHIEL, BLANC MONT

────────────── 1914–1918 ──────────────

> The flag was flung to the breeze as a signal to the sons of
> America that once again they were summoned to battle
> for God and for the right. Never before had a nation
> entered a state of war with a cleaner soul or a purer spirit.
> It was a mighty crusade.
>
> *John A. Lejeune,* The Reminiscences of a Marine

Lejeune reported for his new assignment as assistant to Major
General Commandant George Barnett. He had been promoted
to colonel, effective 25 February 1914. Increasingly, his long days
became dedicated to overseas deployments and personnel matters.
In July 1915, Secretary Daniels ordered the commandant to organize a force for immediate deployment to the troubled Caribbean
nation of Haiti. A landing force from the *Montana* had already
been sent ashore. Lejeune supervised the loading of the aged
Prairie with more leathernecks. The following week, additional
marines and a brigade staff under Colonel Littleton W. T. Waller
followed. Less than a year later, Lejeune prepared another contingent of leathernecks for duty in Latin America. This time, a
brigade commanded by Colonel Joseph H. Pendleton landed in
the Dominican Republic.

During Lejeune's tenure at Headquarters Marine Corps, no
issue came to dominate his work more than the personnel increases
to meet these deployments. From an overly committed small
force numbering approximately 10,000 officers and men in 1914,
the Marine Corps grew to more than 70,000 by the end of World

War I. For casual observers of the corps' administrative scene, the quantum increases appeared tied to the commitment on the western front; however, long before "over there" became a household phrase in the United States, Barnett and the staff of Headquarters Marine Corps had argued successfully for significant increases in numbers.[1]

In October 1915, Barnett and Lejeune told Daniels of their concerns about personnel problems. Increasingly, the Marine Corps found itself experiencing difficulty in meeting requirements both to support the fleet and to provide expeditionary forces for overseas service. On the heels of a demand by the navy for an increase of 7,500 men, Barnett and Lejeune argued for an increase of 1,500—based on a figure of twenty percent of navy strength. On 12 May 1916, the House Naval Affairs Committee reported its bill for naval appropriations for the following fiscal year to the House of Representatives. Much to the astonishment of Headquarters Marine Corps, it called for an increase of 3,079 enlisted men for the Marine Corps, approximately 700 more than requested. On 22 July 1916, the Senate passed an appropriations bill specifying an enlisted strength for the Marine Corps of 14,940—approximately 5,000 more leathernecks than called for in the estimates presented earlier, which surprised Barnett and his political supporters.

To the delight of Barnett and Lejeune, the Senate measure authorized the creation of eight brigadier generals. When the bill became law on 29 August 1916, Headquarters Marine Corps received immediate authorization to recruit an additional 5,000 men and to promote eight colonels to flag rank—five from among the line colonels and three from the staff. Lejeune became a brigadier general on 29 November of that year. Thus far, the increases in numbers and ranks had been tied to increasing expeditionary requirements—notably in Haiti and the Dominican Republic. Traditional overseas commitments in support of the fleet remained. The legislation of 1916 only foreshadowed the expansion of the Marine Corps as America drifted closer to war with Germany.[2]

Since the turn of this century, the Marine Corps had recruited under the colorful slogan "first to fight." With America's declaration of war against Germany in April 1917, the commandant took immediate steps to involve leathernecks in the conflict; obviously, failure to participate would result in a hollow ring to the corps' dramatic enlistment banner. In testimony before the House Naval Affairs Committee that month, Chief of Naval Operations Admiral William S. Benson argued that the corps should be limited to approximately 20,000 men and used solely for naval purposes. Barnett and Lejeune countered vigorously by claiming that in a land war, the Marine Corps should make its forces available to the army, provided commitments to the navy could be met.[3]

Even before additional marines had been authorized, the commandant approached the secretary of the navy with a request to accompany him to see the secretary of war. The commandant wanted to volunteer a brigade of marines for immediate service in France with the AEF. Bemused by Barnett's persistence, Daniels agreed and sought an audience with Newton D. Baker, President Wilson's secretary of war. Although Baker probably did not trouble himself over the finer points of military and naval organization, it became clear at the outset of the meeting that he had asked his staff for background information on the possible use of marines in the AEF.[4]

Baker insisted on the need for commonality among the troops sent to France and quizzed the commandant about such matters as uniforms, weapons, organization, and even insignia. Barnett countered by agreeing to whatever administrative changes the secretary requested, including a reorganization of the brigade to conform to army organization. Because the typical army regiment had almost twice as many troops as a Marine Corps regiment, the commandant agreed to combine the Sixth Marine Regiment with the Fifth so as to have an army-style regiment ready for immediate deployment.

Lejeune considered himself to have the best qualifications to lead the leatherneck force. As a brigadier general, graduate of the Army War College, and veteran of considerable expeditionary service, Lejeune believed Barnett would select him to command it. His enthusiasm reached as far away as Haiti, where his letter to Butler suggested that the frenetic campaigner might command a regiment in the brigade. When the brigade became only a regiment, the commandant selected Colonel Charles A. Doyen—his Naval Academy classmate—to command it. Lejeune took the news stoically, but Butler fumed disgusted from his lonely outpost in Haiti: "News has just come that . . . Doyen is taking a regiment of Marines abroad right way, that is what you get by staying on duty around Washington . . . [I have] far more hard work to my credit and get left out."[5]

At the eleventh hour, however, it appeared as if army officials sought to keep the marines out of the first troop deployment to France. After the meeting with Baker, neither Barnett nor Daniels received further information regarding the forthcoming embarkation. Barnett knew from his own sources that the sailing date would soon arrive but could not be certain just when. On the eve of the scheduled departure, Baker informed the commandant that no spaces in the troop transports could be found for the Fifth Marine Regiment; a smug Barnett responded by informing Baker not to trouble himself over the matter because he had arranged berths for the marines in the navy vessels escorting the troopships of the AEF.[6]

On 14 June 1917, 70 officers and 2,689 enlisted marines sailed for France. Upon their arrival, the headquarters of the AEF ordered the U.S. First Division into intensive training. Because the division already had four infantry regiments, the Fifth Marines received orders to guard duty behind the lines. When word of this decision reached Headquarters Marine Corps, Barnett complained bitterly to Daniels and any congressman that offered his ear. Quickly, word of the commandant's distress reached Pershing, who responded with a patient letter informing Barnett that when an additional regiment and a machine gun battalion of marines arrived, the AEF would form all of the marines into the Fourth Brigade and assign it to a division. Meanwhile, Pershing paid a visit to the units of the AEF and returned to his headquarters, visibly irritated because the leathernecks appeared more soldierly and polished than his beloved regulars.[7]

When the Fifth Marines crossed the Atlantic with the initial contingent of U.S. troops assigned to the AEF, Lejeune continued to press the commandant to allow him to be detached in anticipation of overseas duty in France. Barnett appreciated the yeoman work that Lejeune performed at Headquarters Marine Corps and was loathe to lose him. At one point, the commandant admonished Lejeune by suggesting that his repeated requests were motivated by belief that service in France was necessary in order to remain a viable candidate for the commandancy. Barnett softened his rebuke by suggesting that Lejeune was his logical successor for the corps' highest post. Nevertheless, Lejeune persisted in his request.[8]

In August 1917, President Wilson authorized the organization of the Sixth Marine Regiment for service in the AEF. In September and October, the force—along with a machine-gun battalion—sailed for France. Pershing ordered the formation of the Fourth Brigade (Marine) on 23 October 1917 and three days later assigned it to the Second Division, AEF. Subsequently, Doyen—promoted to brigadier general coincident with the formation of the Fourth Brigade (Marine)—became seriously ill and returned home in May 1918. General John J. Pershing, the commander of the AEF, informed Barnett that he had turned over command of the marine brigade to an army officer. Worse, he informed the commandant rather curtly that no replacement for Doyen need be sent; if one was, he would be assigned duties on the staff or in the rear with the Services of Supply (SOS). Undaunted, Lejeune continued to press for orders to France. When

Colonel Charles G. Long agreed to replace him as assistant to the commandant, Barnett consented to the transfer and Lejeune departed for Quantico in anticipation of an assignment to the AEF. He became the commanding general of the Marine Corps' most important post on 27 September 1917.

Throughout the fall and winter of 1917, Lejeune supervised the training of marines in the woods of northern Virginia. The call came in the late spring. On 17 May 1918, the officers and ladies at Quantico prepared a gala farewell. Before the evening meal for the troops, Lejeune addressed them in an assembly in the gymnasium. That evening, the ladies gathered for dinner separately, while the officers dined at the officers' club. Later, the two groups came together for a reception and a dance. The next morning, Lejeune passed command of the base to Butler—still fretting over his own lack of orders to France.

A few days later, the Lejeunes gathered in Yorktown for the christening of their first grandchild. Ellie, barely nineteen at the time, married Navy Lieutenant James B. Glennon the year before. In a sad farewell being repeated throughout wartime America, Lejeune said good-bye to his family on the train platform in Washington. Leaving home had not grown easier over the years and the farewell affected him deeply: "I would draw a veil over this scene. It is too sacred to portray. Suffice it to say that they bade me adieu with smiles on their lips and agony in their souls."[9]

Lejeune departed Headquarters Marine Corps carrying a special mission for the commandant. While one brigade of marines already served in France, Barnett had ordered another—the Fifth Brigade—outfitted and trained. Headquarters Marine Corps hoped that with the addition of support and service support elements Pershing would accept the units together as a Marine Corps division in the AEF. Barnett made it clear that Lejeune's assignment to the AEF had been made with the understanding that he argue the Marine Corps' case. Arriving in France on 13 June 1918, Lejeune first broached the matter with Pershing's chief of staff. Major General James W. McAndrew promised to arrange a meeting with the commander in chief.

At the promised conference, the unyielding Pershing repeated Secretary Baker's words about the need for commonality of units and equipment, leaving no doubt that he could do without the impediments of a Marine Corps division. At Belleau Wood the previous July, a news report identifying the involvement and heroic exploits of the Fourth Brigade (Marine) appeared in American newspapers. Although Pershing had forbidden the identification of specific units in journalistic coverage of AEF units, the author of the account had himself marched with the leathernecks at Belleau Wood and was severely wounded. When friends in the AEF press censorship detachment learned that the reporter, Floyd Gibbons of the *Chicago Tribune*, had fallen in the battle, they opted to honor his memory by releasing his final story unedited and uncensored. The windfall of journalistic coverage, although pleasing to the marines, irritated Pershing and the senior army officers on the AEF.[10]

While the staff of the AEF most likely suggested the importance of commonality, Pershing refused the offer of a Marine Corps division for other reasons. He had grown increasingly annoyed over meddling by the Department of the Navy and Headquarters Marine Corps in AEF affairs. Barnett's repeated queries over employment of the marines, between the arrival of the Fifth Marines in France and the formation of the Fourth Brigade (Marine), grew tiresome. The hyperbolic journalism about leatherneck prowess on the battlefield exacerbated the problem. After meeting with Lejeune and turning down his request, Pershing cabled the secretary of war in hopes of ending the matter once and for all: "[Lejeune] brings up the subject of the formation of a Marine division for service here . . . I am still of the opinion that the formation of such a unit is not desirable from a military standpoint. Our land forces must be homogeneous in every respect. . . . While the Marines are splendid troops, their use as a separate division is inadvisable."[11]

In a personal note to Barnett, Lejeune urged him to form the division anyway and offer it to Admiral William S. Sims, Commander of U.S. Naval Forces, Europe. Lejeune knew that Sims desired such a force, perhaps to employ in an amphibious role in the Baltic or Adriatic. Barnett chose to ignore Lejeune's suggestions, however, and proceeded to organize and train another brigade for service in France. When the Fifth Brigade arrived in the AEF, it took up rear-echelon duties. Butler, promoted to colonel and assigned to command one of its infantry regiments at the insistence of Secretary Daniels, concluded that interservice rivalry lay at the root of the army's refusal to accept a leatherneck division in France.[12]

Lejeune received orders to report to the Thirty-Fifth Division for a short period of orientation and observation. He fully expected to command an infantry brigade. On 5 July 1918, AEF headquarters posted him to the Sixty-Fourth Brigade, Thirty-Second Division. Composed of national guardsmen from Wisconsin, the brigade was then assigned to a French division astride the Swiss border. Major Earl H. "Pete" Ellis tagged along as his prospective adjutant. Before either he or Ellis heard a shot fired in anger, however, they found themselves back among fellow marines.[13]

Lejeune commanded the brigade of Wisconsin woodsmen for only three weeks. Before he had the opportunity to lead them into battle, orders arrived unexpectedly transferring Lejeune to the Fourth Brigade (Marine), Second Division, AEF. The brigade's commander, James G. Harbord—an army officer and close friend of Pershing—had just been promoted to major general. The commander in chief of the AEF took the opportunity to unseat the commanding general of the Second Division, Omar Bundy, and replace him with Harbord. For some time, the demanding Pershing had contained growing reservations with regard to Bundy's performance. On 9 June 1918, Pershing noted his concern in a pungent diary entry: "General Bundy disappoints me. He lacks the grasp. I shall replace him at the first opportunity." Then in a

memorandum to his chief of staff, he took the first step in replac-
ing a division commander: "I am inclined to think, from all
accounts, that the Second Division is not functioning well as a
division. They have done excellent fighting but it has been by
individual units and not under the direction of the division commander or his chief of staff."[14]

After giving the trusted and proven Harbord command of the
Second Division, Pershing needed a commander for the Fourth
Brigade (Marine). Perhaps to the commander in chief and his
staff, it made good sense to have a Marine Corps officer command marines. The availability of an officer of Lejeune's decided
character and professional reputation made the decision an easy
one. The assignment thrilled Lejeune. He shared his pride with a
message to his fellow marines: "I have this day assumed command
of the Fourth Brigade, U.S. Marines. To command this brigade is
the highest honor that could come to any man. Its renown is
imperishable, and the skill, endurance, and valor of the officers
and men have immortalized its name and that of the Marine
Corps."[15]

On 20 July 1918, the Second Division withdrew from the front
because of heavy combat losses and fatigue. While the division
recovered in rest camps in the vicinity of Nanteuil-le-Haudouin,
midway between Soissons and Paris, Harbord reported to Pershing at his headquarters on 23 July. After a perfunctory greeting
and a few platitudes about the Second Division's performance,
Pershing revealed to his old friend the dissatisfaction he felt over
the operation of the SOS under Major General Francis J. Kernan.

By midsummer of 1918, the combat service support area behind
the American units had become so muddled that the chief of staff
of the army and the secretary of war considered dispatching
Major General George W. Goethals—the legendary builder of
the Panama Canal—to France to assume command of the SOS.
Wilson's advisors believed Pershing's duties too much for one
man and grew increasingly concerned. With the assignment of

Goethals to command the SOS and Tasker Bliss to act as President Wilson's personal emissary to the French government, Pershing could concentrate on training and organizing an American army.

Additionally, Wilson and his advisors did not view Pershing as a skilled diplomat. President Wilson considered Bliss or possibly his confidant and advisor, Edward M. House, as better suited to deal with the French government. For the moment, however, Pershing considered only the implications resulting from a division of command within the AEF. In his memoirs, Harbord recalled Pershing's response condemning the proposal to split his command: "Divided control here in France would mean nothing but disaster."

The commander in chief revealed both his solution to the dilemma and the reason for summoning Harbord. Pershing wanted him to relinquish command of the Second Division and take over the Services of Supply. Earlier, the commander in chief discussed the problem with his staff. Everyone agreed that Harbord's reputation as a competent officer, both in staff work and in command of troops in combat, would put some drive into the SOS and restore its sagging morale. Pershing's flattery apparently turned Harbord's head. As much as he claimed to love leading the Second Division, its commander agreed to the change in duties. It was a bittersweet moment for Harbord. An ambitious officer, he hoped to command a corps before the war ended, with promotion to lieutenant general. But his loyalty and friendship to Pershing outweighed any personal goals.[16]

Although only a brigadier general, Lejeune enjoyed an enviable reputation among the senior officers of the AEF because of his superlative performance at the Army War College. Many of his former classmates and instructors now sat in the highest councils of the AEF. Pershing may have believed that by assigning a Marine Corps general to command a division, the notion of a leatherneck division in the AEF could be laid to rest. For Lejeune, the possibility that his new assignment might serve as a sop to

Barnett's aggrandizement never entered his mind. In any event, Harbord recommended Lejeune as his successor in the strongest terms.

Brigadier General John Archer Lejeune, U.S. Marine Corps, had reached the pinnacle of his military career. Of all the evidence underscoring Lejeune's pride in his accomplishments as a division commander in the AEF during the war, none is more illustrative than his memoirs, in which 197 pages cover his six months of wartime service in France, while only 25 pages are devoted to his nine-year tenure as commandant of the Marine Corps. Although the veteran First Division was the oldest and most thoroughly trained in the AEF, it had a reputation for being methodical and tenacious in its fighting. By contrast, the staff of the AEF characterized the Second Division as a fast-moving organization with dash and élan. The rivalry between the Second Division's two infantry brigades—one army and one Marine Corps—became intense at times as each attempted to outperform the other.[17]

The only problem remaining with regard to Lejeune assuming command of the Second Division lay in his rank; brigadier generals commanded brigades and major generals led divisions. Although before the war the only general officer in the Marine Corps was the major general commandant, the incumbent was entitled to the rank only while in office. Personnel increases because of the conflict resulted in an additional major general. Before he left for France, Barnett told him in strictest confidence that he could expect a second star because of strong support from Congressman Butler, Secretary Daniels, and the commandant himself.

With all barriers to his command laid aside, Lejeune assumed command of the Second Division on 28 July 1918. Three days later, he became a major general. Ahead lay paths of glory strewn with obstacles testing his leadership as never before. While friends in and out of uniform wrote to congratulate Lejeune on his command and promotion, only Secretary Daniels's letter seemed to foreshadow the intense political infighting to follow over the issue of the next commandant of the Marine Corps: "How gratifying it is to me to know that your appointment was approved universally . . . have every confidence in your leadership of the Marine Corps." As late as 5 August, however, Lejeune's hold on the division seemed tenuous for some reason. In a warm personal letter to Daniels, he informed his friend and political supporter, "I am at present in *temporary* command of a division."[18]

Four days before Lejeune's promotion, Pershing ordered the creation of the First American Army, AEF, and directed it to be operational by 10 August 1918. Pershing's force consisted of fourteen divisions organized into three corps, numbering over 550,000 American and 110,000 French troops. Nevertheless, the arguments among the Allies over the employment of U.S forces continued. In a stormy confrontation, Pershing and the supreme coordinator of the Allied armies, French Field Marshal Ferdinand Foch, came quickly to loggerheads.

Foch wanted the American divisions placed in the French lines, perhaps to stiffen the resolve of war-weary troops. By the time America entered the war, a stalemate had existed for almost four years and horrendous casualties had been suffered on all sides; worse, some units in the French army mutinied in 1917. The poor performance of the Allied high command—dominated by weary, trench warfare-minded French and British officers— made Pershing wary of giving the Allies carte blanche to use his forces to stiffen the wavering resolve of their units in the front lines. But on 24 July 1918, everyone agreed on a mission for the American troops: the reduction of the St. Mihiel salient, which threatened the railway lines essential for future operations.

Fortunately for Lejeune in the demanding days to follow, he inherited an experienced staff and commanders to support him. Initially, Colonel Preston Brown served as Lejeune's chief of staff. After graduating from Yale in 1892, he studied law for a year and then enlisted in the army to obtain his commission. The brilliant Brown made no attempt to conceal his contempt for officers whom he considered to be intellectually inferior. An officer with a monumental ego, Brown rubbed most juniors' sensibilities raw and often rankled his seniors as well. Apparently, he and Lejeune never crossed swords. The new commander of the Second Division made good use of Brown's skills as an extremely competent staff officer. Like Lejeune, Brown graduated from the Army War College.

Lejeune's other senior officers included Army Brigadier General Albert J. Bowley, commanding the artillery brigade; an Army War College classmate, Brigadier General Hanson E. Ely, commanding the Third Infantry Brigade; and a fellow leatherneck, Brigadier General Wendell C. Neville, commanding the Fourth Brigade (Marine). All of them were combat proven. In the difficult days ahead, Lejeune relied on their experience and professionalism; he never expressed disappointment in their performances.

Unconvinced by Foch's logic, Pershing continued to insist upon employment of U.S. forces as part of an American army under his personal command. The commander in chief of the AEF knew that he had the strong support of President Wilson and Secretary Baker. Furthermore, Pershing felt little confidence in the fighting abilities of his allies: "The infantry of both the French and British were poor skirmishers as a result of extended service in the trenches. Our mission required an aggressive offensive based on self-reliant infantry." He also grew weary of the critical and often patronizing comments heard by his staff from their counterparts in the British and French high commands: "The fact is that our officers and men are far and away superior to the tired Europeans. High officers of the Allies have often dropped derogatory remarks about our poorly trained staff and high commanders." Pershing then underscored his determination to put the matter to rest: "[I have told both the Allies] in rather forceful language, that we have been patronized as long as we would stand for it, and I wish to hear no more of that sort of nonsense."[19]

In the strategy to seize the St. Mihiel salient, the American army would aim at the head of the Hindenburg line from Dun-sur-Meuse to Grandpré, thus flanking the Aisne river positions and forcing a German withdrawal toward Mézières. With the French Fourth Army on the left of the Americans, the Allies hoped to prevent an orderly withdrawal of enemy forces into Germany by creating a bottleneck between the Ardennes and Holland. When a hesitant French high command turned over control of the area before the St. Mihiel salient, senior officers formally attired in dark blue frock coats and the traditional red trousers presented Pershing with two huge volumes containing the offensive and defensive plans for the salient. An amused Pershing accepted the books with the ceremony expected, even though he and his staff had prepared similar plans earlier: six pages for the offense and eight pages for the defense! At the time, Pershing's confidence grew considerably upon learning that between the Second Battle of the Marne and the upcoming attack to take the St. Mihiel salient, the Germans had lost over half a million men.

On 1 August 1918, Lejeune supervised the movement of his division to Pont-à-Mousson in the valley of the Moselle, an enormous logistical operation requiring several military railway trains. The division was then scattered in small cantonments over one hundred square miles around the French training area Camp Bois la Haie l'Evêque. There, the soldiers and Marines fired individual weapons, practiced grenade throwing, and received additional training in the employment of crew-served weapons. The engineers and communicators participated in special training provided by the engineer and signal units of a French division. Infantry battalions took to the field in terrain exercises followed by division-level maneuvers. As Lejeune noted in retrospect: "I deemed it my highest duty to be the welding of all units into a harmonious whole, and the kindling and fostering of a division spirit, or esprit, which would animate the hearts of all its officers and men."[20] Apparently, he succeeded. The division surgeon—who was, incidently, President Theodore Roosevelt's

son-in-law—remembered that "[Lejeune] maintained among officers and men the same high standard of morale and cemented the
ties of comradeship and respect between the two infantry brigades."[21]

The tables of organization and equipment for the Second Division listed a personnel strength of 979 officers and 27,080 enlisted
men. The equipment organic to the division included 1,078
horse-drawn vehicles, 678 trucks and cars, 74 artillery pieces,
260 machine guns, and 48 one-pounders and trench mortars.
The Third Brigade consisted of the Ninth and Twenty-third Infantry Regiments and the Fifth Machine Gun Battalion. The Fourth
Brigade (Marine) was composed of the Fifth and Sixth Marine
Regiments and the Sixth Machine Gun Battalion. The Second
Artillery Brigade counted three regiments—the Twelfth, the
Fifteenth, and the Seventeenth—and the Second Trench Mortar
Battery. Each of the four infantry regiments consisted of 108
officers and 3,718 soldiers or marines organized into two battal-
ions of four companies each; a typical company counted 258
men. The American divisions numbered almost twice as many
men as their counterparts among both the allies and the enemy.

By 9 August 1918, the division had moved to the Marbache
area near Pont-à-Mousson to be brought up to full strength and
to train for the forthcoming offensive. Because of the heavy
combat in mid-July at Soissons, its strength had dropped to
approximately twenty-two thousand men, more than six thousand doughboys and leathernecks short. Most of the shortages
appeared in the two infantry brigades, and the headquarters of
the AEF strove to fill the depleted ranks. When a replacement
battalion of a thousand marines had been used up, personnel
officers considered assigning soldiers instead of marines to the
depleted ranks of the Fourth Brigade (Marine).

Moving quickly to prevent the loss of unit integrity, Lejeune
asked Harbord to scour the rear echelon units for Marines assigned
to other duties. The chief of the SOS came through for his old

comrades. Marines assigned duties in the lines of communications received orders to the Second Division. Quickly, a stream of marine replacements appeared to fill out the thin ranks. By fall, Headquarters Marine Corps had corrected the imperfections in the replacement system. Significant shortages of leathernecks in France never appeared again. Pershing and his staff had been correct on the problem of replacements for a Marine Corps brigade, as Lejeune noted ruefully a decade later in his memoirs: "Headquarters could scarcely provide infantry replacements for the Fourth Brigade—impossible for an entire division."[22]

Lejeune realized very quickly that the replacements—soldiers and marines alike—needed intensive training before they could be employed effectively. He and his staff established schedules requiring the new men to fire their individual weapons, as well as the larger crew-served weapons such as machine guns and mortars. More than two-thirds of the new men had enlisted or been drafted for wartime service only and lacked the long years of experience of their comrades in the regular army and Marine Corps. Then, all too quickly, the days of orientation and training ended as they received orders for an attack to take the St. Mihiel salient.

Lejeune could not have found the terrain for a battle more familiar. During his classes at the Army War College, he and his fellow students studied another battle over the same terrain during the Franco-Prussian War. The salient, French territory held by the Germans since the first year of the war, interrupted the north-south railway and the highways that followed the Meuse River. From this redoubt, the Germans could fire artillery close enough to interdict road traffic on the Paris-Nancy highway. The terrain contained commanding heights and sheltered communications and almost two hundred square miles of French soil, with a town of ten thousand people who had not seen the tricolor flown for almost four years (see Map 1).

The salient threatened the flanks of the French army and made offensive action in Lorraine and the Meuse-Argonne impractical. Not only was it important to retake the contested ground for

WORLD WAR ONE

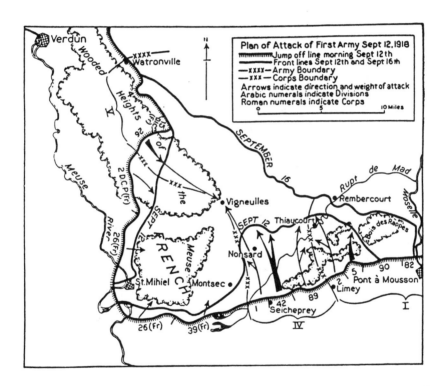

Map 1. American operations in the St. Mihiel Region, 13–16 September 1918. From *Second Division: Summary of Operations in the World War* (Washington: GPO, 1944), p. 69.

immediate strategic reasons, but also the battle would be the initial engagement of the American army and a key test to determine if a large U.S. force could operate effectively on the western front. Lejeune's message to his command on the eve of the battle left no doubt that the reputation of the entire AEF depended upon the outcome of the battle to take the St. Mihiel salient: "The approaching battle will constitute a great epoch in our country's history . . . the prestige and honor of our country are at stake."[23]

For nine cold and wet days, the soldiers and marines of the Second Division, AEF, lay shivering in the woods in front of the salient before relieving elements of the Eighty-ninth and Ninetieth Divisions on 10 September 1918. On the rainy night of 11–12 September, they marched into the front lines to join twelve other divisions—more than three hundred thousand men—for the attack on the salient. Six days previously, Lejeune had moved his headquarters to Franceville, closer to the assaulting units. As the soldiers and Marines filed into position for the assault, Pershing honored them with a brief visit and seemed pleased with what he saw.

As the Second Division moved into the lines in the Limey sector alongside the Fifth Division, the Eighty-ninth and Ninetieth Divisions stepped aside to allow the attacking units to fit between them. Lejeune's force relieved elements of both divisions and took its place for the offensive. Commanded by Major General Hunter Liggett, I Corps consisted of four divisions in line for the attack: Eighty-Second, Ninetieth, Fifth, and Second. Liggett retained the Seventy-eighth Division in reserve. To the left of I Corps, IV Corps stood poised to attack simultaneously by making a turning movement. To take the salient, the Allies had amassed three American corps, I (Liggett), IV (Dickman), and V (Cameron), and the II French Colonial Corps.

On the eve of the battle, a confident but anxious Lejeune observed the frantic preparations amid a monstrous traffic jam. Wheeled vehicles and horse-drawn carriages of all descriptions clogged the dusty roads leading into the lines. Shortly after 1:00 A.M. on 12 September 1918, a massive artillery preparation fired by twenty-nine hundred guns signaled the start of the battle. Four hours later, French and American soldiers, marines, and French colonials went over the top behind a rolling barrage. The Second Division attacked as the left division of I Corps. Its commander, Major General Hunter Liggett sat in his headquarters playing solitaire, waiting for reports from the attacking units. Lejeune watched nervously from a hilltop in front of the salient. In his memoirs, Lejeune reflected on the horrors of war as he recalled those anxious moments: "In war, if a man is to keep his sanity, he must come to regard death as being just as normal as life and hold himself always in readiness, mentally and spiritually, to answer the call of the grim reaper whenever fate decrees that his hour has struck."[24]

Lejeune positioned his division in column with the Third Brigade leading the assault. Its two infantry regiments attacked abreast, the Ninth on the right and the Twenty-third on the left. Each regiment placed its battalions in columns with a company of machine guns, a section of mortars and one-pounders, and engineers attached. Although resistance came from German machine-gun positions initially, Lejeune's doughboys outflanked them quickly.

By eleven the next morning, the army brigade in Lejeune's division—reinforced by an infantry battalion and a machine-gun company from the Sixth Marines—reduced Bois d'Euvezin and Bois du Beau Vallon. The assaulting forces seized Thiaucourt and the high ground north of the salient, capturing seventy German officers and thirty-two hundred enlisted men, ninety-two artillery pieces on railway cars, a hospital, an empty railway train containing fifty-two cars, a lumberyard, and a supply depot. The infantry regiments reported that their patrols had moved forward as far as Jaulny and Xammes. Lejeune then moved a forward command post to Loge Mangin, two kilometers south of Thiaucourt, to better control the rapidly unfolding situation. At 4:30 P.M. on

14 September 1918, he ordered the Fourth Brigade (Marine) to relieve the Third Brigade in the assault. Fearing a loss of contact with the retreating enemy, Lejeune ordered large reconnaissance patrols sent forward.[25]

On 15 September 1918, the Marine Corps brigade fought its way to Rembercourt up against the Hindenburg Line. The division occupied outposts against the northern edge of the woods north of Rembercourt-sur-Mad and Charny. Now, the Allies controlled the only Germany supply route into the salient. During part of the attack, Lejeune and one of his infantry brigade commanders took to horseback in order to get around the maze of vehicles clogging the roads. Casualties appeared low for the U.S. First Army in its initial engagement, largely because the German high command had already ordered the salient evacuated. Men and equipment appeared on the roads leading to Germany before the assault began. Lejeune's casualties totalled 1,437 men, including 30 officers. He glowed with pride for his gallant doughboys and leathernecks: "Nothing seemed to depress or daunt them. They played hard, they worked hard, and they fought hard. They were magnificent."[26]

The intense artillery barrage preceding the assault prevented German reinforcements from moving into the area once the attack began; thus, the Americans and French outnumbered the enemy by a considerable number. When the Seventy-eighth Division took over the lines of the Second and Fifth Divisions on the night of 15–16 September, Lejeune's command moved to the Ansauville-Royaumix area. During the informal change of command, German gas drifted into the division command post. The passing of control took place with Lejeune and the other officers wearing gas masks. Even as the Seventy-eighth Division relieved the Second Division, German forces counterattacked but were repulsed south of Toul.

The Second Division received orders to move by rail to an area south of Châlons-sur-Marne. At about the same time, Preston Brown received his promotion to brigadier general and a new assignment as chief of staff, IV Corps. The assistant chief of staff, G3, Colonel J. C. Rhea, became the division's new chief of staff. The Second Division claimed the capture of more than 3,300 German prisoners out of a total of 4,985 taken by the entire I Corps. General Liggett heaped praise on his subordinate: "Once more your corps commander has the proud knowledge of witnessing the Second Division maintain its splendid standards and proudly live up to his expectations."[27]

Liggett should have been pleased. His corps advanced ten kilometers along a seventeen-kilometer front, a significant penetration against the enemy in the conditions of World War I. Any further advance would have been impractical because of his corps' advance up to the guns of the Metz forts. I Corps captured prisoners from four German divisions. Even the enemy expressed admiration. A captured German major being marched to the rear paid a begrudging compliment to his captors as he passed a column of American infantry: "Those men are all young and fresh and vigorous," he observed. "We can't do it, but I wish I had had a 1914 battalion behind me. You wouldn't have had such a pleasant afternoon."[28]

After the success of Pershing's army, everyone wanted the fresh American divisions. The successful attack to retake the salient proved that an American army under American command and staff could be depended upon. Finally, the commander in chief released two divisions—the Second and the Fifth—to the French army for the forthcoming battle for Blanc Mont. From 16–24 September 1918, the Second Division acted as the reserve for the IV Corps in the Toul area in Champagne, to the west of the Meuse-Argonne/Lorraine area. The brief respite gave the bone-weary men an opportunity to rest. From 24–30 September, Lejeune and his troops moved by rail from Toul to an area south of Châlons-sur-Marne to take up a position behind the Fourth French Army.

From 30 September until 2 October, the division remained in reserve, cleaning trenches south of Somme-Py and mending equipment while preparing for the next battle. Lejeune established his headquarters just south of Navarin Ferme. For the upcoming offensive to take the Meuse-Argonne, the Germans had no intention of falling back; Lejeune and the Second Division could expect to face elements of nine different German divisions in the assault to take Blanc Mont. Lejeune's doughboys and leathernecks shivered in the early autumn chill and wet; winter clothing had not yet arrived.

The Americans classified the campaign to seize Blanc Mont as part of the Meuse-Argonne offensive. In reality, it was part of a general Allied offensive all along the western front. With the goal to clear all German forces out of France and Belgium, and to prevent their withdrawal into Germany, the Allies positioned their field armies to move east: the British towards Cambrai, the French to Aisne, and the Americans toward Sedan and Méziéres. The reduction of the St. Mihiel salient had been a necessary preliminary to the offensive. By the end of September, however, the French drive had stalled near Somme-Py in the Champagne area.

Between the Argonne and Somme-Py, the Fourth French Army had advanced almost eight kilometers, but its XXI Corps' attack stalled five kilometers north of Somme-Py. There, the French troops had been held up by the German trenches and concrete fortifications that made the desolate, chalky terrain of Blanc Mont such a formidable military objective. As the advance slowed and then ground to a halt, the Allied high command appealed to Pershing. Reluctantly, he released the Second Division in hopes of putting some starch into the war-weary assaulting force (see Map 2).

During the night of 1–2 October 1918, the Second Division relieved the French Sixty-first Division and a battalion of the French Twenty-first Division in XXI Corps. The Fourth Brigade (Marine) replaced the tired French division and Lejeune kept the Third Brigade in reserve south of the Butte de Sourain–Navarin Ferme ridge. His artillery brigade reinforced the fires of the Sixty-first French Division. Three French divisions, one Chasseur, a

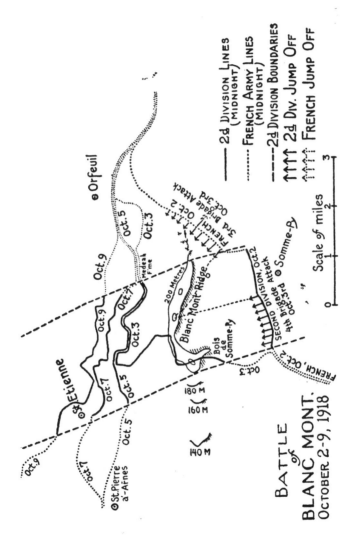

Map 2. Second Division operations with the Fourth French Army, 2–10 October 1918. From *Second Division: Summary of Operations in the World War* (Washington: GPO, 1944), p. 194.

colonial, and finally a line infantry division with Verdun on its
battle staff had already been shattered in futile attempts to seize
the Essen Hook and Trench.[29]

On 2 October, Lejeune established his headquarters on the
Sourain–Somme Py road a kilometer north of Souvain. On the
eve of the battle, XXI Corps appeared as: Twenty-first (French)
Division on the left; Second Division, AEF, in the center; and
Sixty-seventh (French) Division on the right. Lejeune reported
to his new commander, General Henri Gouraud. He met the
bearded, one-armed veteran of Gallipoli at a high-level staff conference at Fourth Army Headquarters before the offensive. Lejeune
brought his chief of staff and both infantry brigade commanders.
Besides his own staff, Gouraud introduced Lejeune's corps commander, Lieutenant General André Naulin.

At first, Gouraud proposed using Lejeune's troops as replacements to fill the depleted ranks of his French divisions. Alarmed
at the idea, Lejeune promised to take Blanc Mont if the Second
Division remained intact. Gouraud then underscored the importance of seizing the terrain: "This portion is the key to all the
German defenses in this sector, including the whole Rheims
Massif. If this ridge can be taken, the Germans will be obliged to
retreat along the whole front thirty kilometers to the River Aisne.
Do you think your division could effect its capture?"[30] Lejeune
replied emphatically that it could. Gouraud then put off a final
decision pending approval by Petain.

On 2 October, the commander of the French Fourth Army met
again with his subordinate commanders and their staffs. Gouraud
announced approval of Lejeune's request to keep the Second
Division intact. Then, Gouraud and his staff unveiled a plan
calling for an oblique advance from a neighboring sector, an
imaginative but flawed scheme in Lejeune's opinion. Apparently,
the idea originated from Naulin, who proposed that one brigade
attack half the distance to Blanc Mont while the other brigade
conduct an oblique attack to seize the objective. Lejeune argued
that the supporting artillery fires assigned to the Fourth Brigade

would endanger the troops of his Third Brigade, thus preventing the planned rolling barrage in front of the assaulting troops. Lejeune proposed instead that the Fourth Brigade conduct a frontal attack on the left of the objective simultaneous with an oblique attack by the Third Brigade.[31]

His plan approved, Lejeune hurried back to division headquarters. A harried staff worked through the night to prepare the operations orders and map overlays. Motorcycle dispatch riders delivered the instructions to waiting commanders; in some cases, the dispatches did not arrive until 3:00 A.M.. The operations order reached the division's subordinate commanders just in time to prepare their units to begin the assault at 5:30 A.M. on 3 October 1918. The operations order did not reach the Fourth Brigade (Marine) until 4:40 A.M.; the commander of the leading battalion of the Sixth Marines did not receive his copy until he had already reached the first objective.

John Thomason, the Marine Corps author and artist who fought with the Fourth Brigade (Marine) during the war, recalled the awesome artillery barrage: "The heavens seemed roofed over with long, keening noises—sounds like the sharp ripping of silk, magnified, running in swift arcs from horizon to horizon. There were the quickfiring 75s, the clear-cut bark of the discharge merging into a crashing roar . . . almost, one expected to look up and see them, like swift, deadly birds, some small, some enormous, all terrible."[32]

On 3 October 1918, XXI Corps aimed its attack towards Blanc Mont. The Fourth Brigade (Marine) attacked on the left and the Third Brigade on the right in a column of regiments. The Third Brigade advanced two kilometers north of the Médéah Ferme–Blanc Mont road, and the Fourth Brigade pushed up to the crest of Blanc Mont. A battalion of French tanks supported each infantry brigade. Lejeune's artillery brigade began the bombardment at 5:30, supported by the guns of the French Sixty-first Division. A creeping barrage followed to within three hundred meters of the first objective. The marines moved forward through the Essen Trench at H hour in ample time to position themselves for the assault, but the guides promised by the Fourth French Army assigned to assist the Third Brigade's move into position failed to arrive.

Stumbling forward in the black, starless night, Lejeune's soldiers arrived at their point of departure just minutes before H hour. The Third Brigade failed to establish a linkup with the Fourth Brigade as the advance began, creating a two-kilometer gap that did not close until the assault was well under way. By 8:30 A.M. on 4 October, the Second Division occupied its first objective. As darkness fell, elements of the Second Division reported an advance six kilometers to a point one kilometer south of Saint-Étienne-à-Arnes. Facing the fresh and energetic American troops, the Germans fell back.

The leathernecks and doughboys continued to move forward the following day, while French troops cleared the western slopes of Blanc Mont. However, the Germans still held the Essen Hook, a series of trenches and dugouts forming part of a defensive line taken by the Germans in the First Battle of the Marne in 1914. On 4 October, Lejeune's corps commander ordered him forward. Lejeune told both infantry brigade commanders to advance to a line one kilometer southwest of Scay Farm, to the Blanc Mont–Saint-Étienne Road south of Saint-Étienne.

Establishing a line of resistance there, Lejeune's infantry slowed their advance because the French divisions on their flanks failed to maintain the pace. Worse, the French Twenty-second Division on the left advanced to the east instead of to the north. At 4:00 P.M. on 4 October, Lejeune informed his corps commander that he might not be able to take his objective because of the exposed flanks. But by 5:00 P.M. on 4 October 1918, the Sixth Marines and the French Seventeenth Infantry Regiment had captured the machine-gun strong point on Blanc Mont, taking 204 prisoners and seventy-five machine guns and trench mortars.

Lejeune positioned his army infantry brigade on the right of the line and the marine brigade on the left for the advance over the crest of Blanc Mont. As the attacking units pushed into the German lines, Lejeune moved his own headquarters near Somme-Py closer to the front. On the night of 6–7 October, the Seventy-first Brigade of the Thirty-sixth Division relieved the Second Division in the lines. Four days later, the remainder of the Thirty-sixth Division relieved the Second Division. Command of the sector passed from Lejeune officially at 10:00 A.M. on 10 October 1918. Unit commanders marched the weary doughboys and leathernecks to an assembly area fifteen kilometers south of Saint-Étienne. On 14 October, the division moved to billets in the Suippes-Souain area.[33]

Lejeune praised the French troops that fought with him at Blanc Mont. Gouraud responded with a recommendation to the French high command to cite the Second Division in the French army's Order of the Day. The Second Division had broken the main German line of resistance, causing the enemy to retreat east of Rheims. The grateful French also presented two thousand croix de guerre to the officers and men of the Second Division. Lejeune received an appointment as a commander of the Legion of Honour.

The Second Division had been opposed by the Two Hundredth and Two Hundred-thirteenth German Divisions, both considered fresh and fit units, along with six other less energetic divisions. Mostly, Lejeune and his troops had faced German units demoralized and on the verge of crumbling. On the eve of the offensive, the commanding general of the Third Guards Division reported that "the troops have now arrived at the extreme limit of their endurance," while the commander of the Two Hundredth Division informed his superiors that "the troops have grown apathetic and indifferent to such an alarming extent that I can no longer guarantee that during a surprise attack, they will continue to hold their positions."[34]

Intelligence reports indicated signs of an enemy withdrawal all along the front. Patrols lost contact with the opposing forces and German long-range artillery began to fire—indications of a major retrograde movement in progress. Lejeune shared his pride in a message to the division. Gouraud praised Lejeune in a personal letter to Petain shortly after the offensive:

> The Second Division brilliantly commanded by General Lejeune played a glorious part in the operations of the Fourth French Army in the [campaign] in October 1918. On the third of October, the division drove forward and seized in a single assault the strongly entrenched German positions [which] resulted in the evacuation of the enemy [from] the positions on both sides of the River Suippe and his withdrawal from the Massif de Notre Dame des Champs.[35]

Between 2 and 10 October, Lejeune's force captured 48 German officers and 1,915 enlisted men. The Second Division suffered 209 casualties among its officers, and 4,771 enlisted men received wounds or died. For the next two weeks, the Second Division stayed in the Suippes area sprawled across the meadows and farms in reserve for the Fourth French Army.[36]

On 12 October, Lejeune visited the headquarters of the AEF to discuss his dismal personnel situation. He learned that the commander in chief had his mind on personnel problems of a different nature. Two days before, Pershing conducted a wholesale shuffling of general officers, visibly upset because some of his senior commanders failed to display the energy, loyalty, and aggressiveness he expected. Pershing relieved six general officers, and three new corps commanders appeared in Liggett's First Army. Lejeune's personnel problems seemed minor by comparison.

The Second Division badly needed army replacements for its infantry brigade. Some of its combat support and service elements had been detached to French units. Headquarters planned to replace the lost units with different but similar organizations. Lejeune pleaded with Liggett to give him back his own units for the sake of unit integrity. In a bit of bureaucratic legerdemain, Lejeune's personnel officer managed to divert twenty-five hundred army replacements destined for the Third Division to plug the holes in the ranks of the Second Division. Lejeune's appeal to Liggett resulted in the return of his original artillery and engineer units. Meanwhile, the Second Division assembled fifteen kilometers south of Saint-Étienne, recovering from the rigors of intensive combat to take Blanc Mont. At the time, Lejeune reflected on the superb record of his command, feeling especially proud of his fellow marines. The casualty figures troubled him. He expressed this concern in a letter to this successor as assistant to the commandant: "The Marine Corps has just cause to feel proud of its brigade . . . there isn't much left of the original crowd. [The hospitals] are full of wounded."[37]

Notes

1. Jack Shulimson, "First to Fight: Marine Corps Expansion, 1914–1918," *Prologue* 8 (Spring 1978): 5–16.
2. Assistant Secretary of the Navy Franklin D. Roosevelt, Chairman, Marine Corps Personnel Board, to the Secretary of the Navy, 3 February 1913, General Correspondence file 9236, RG 127, NA; and House Naval Affairs Committee, Hearings on Estimates by the Secretary of the Navy, 64th Cong., 1st sess., 29 February 1916.
3. House Naval Affairs Committee, Hearings on Estimates Submitted by the Secretary of the Navy, 65th Cong., 1st sess., 24 April 1917.
4. George Barnett, "Soldier and Sailor Too," unpublished memoir, chapter 25, Barnett MSS, MCHC.
5. Smedley D. Butler to Congressman Thomas S. Butler, 16 May 1917, Butler MSS, NewTown Square, Pennsylvania; Lejeune, not Barnett, apparently made the key personnel decisions for the Fifth Marines. See Frederick W. Wise with Megs O. Frost, *A Marine Tells It To You* (New York: Sears, 1929), p. 157.
6. Barnett, "Soldier and Sailor Too," chapter 25.
7. John J. Pershing to George Barnett, 10 November 1917, Barnett MSS.
8. JAL to Commandant of the Marine Corps, [1935], reel 6, Lejeune MSS, Library of Congress.
9. John A. Lejeune, *The Reminiscences of a Marine* (1930; reprint, Quantico: Marine Corps Association, 1979), p. 249.
10. Cf. Joseph T. Dickman, *The Great Crusade* (New York and London: Appleton, 1927), pp. 52–53 and 267–72; and Robert E. Lee Bullard, *Personalities and Reminiscences of the World War* (Garden City, New York: Doubleday, 1925), pp. 208–9 with Colonel Robert H. Dunlap to Major General Commandant George Barnett, 28 February 1919, entry 10, RG 127, NA; and Barnett, "Soldier and Sailor Too," ch. 28.
11. Pershing to Secretary of War, 18 June 1918, AEF 1331-S, entry 269, RG 120, NA.
12. For interesting views on interservice rivalry between the army and Marine Corps during World War I, see: Colonel Robert H. Dunlap to the Commandant, 28 February 1919, George Barnett's biographical file, MCHC; "AEF request for naval guns," memorandum for the record, n.d., 1918 file, container 2, Barnett MSS,

MCHC; and Brigadier General H. B. Fiske to the Chief of Staff, AEF, "Memorandum on Military Policy of the United Staff," 23 December 1918, container 16, RG 200, NA.

13. James G. Harbord to JAL, 12 July 1918, reel 3, Lejeune MSS.

14. Pershing to McAndrew, 9 July 1918, Commander-in-Chief file, Office of the Chief of Staff, RG 120, NA. Between 28 and 30 June 1918, Brigadier General André Brewster, the inspector general, AEF, inspected the Second Division. Brewster reported to Pershing that he believed Bundy lacked the faculty of command.

15. Quoted in Edwin N. McClellan, The United States Marines in the World War, rev. ed. (Washington: Headquarters Marine Corps, 1968), p. 47.

16. James G. Harbord, Leaves from a War Diary (New York: Dodd, Mead, 1925), p. 339. See also Harbord to Pershing, 25 October 1918, box 87, Pershing MSS; Harbord's Diary, 4 September 1918, Harbord MSS; Pershing's diary, 26 and 27 July 1918, box 6, Pershing MSS; all in the Manuscripts Division, Library of Congress; and Peyton March, The Nation at War, (Garden City, New York: Doubleday, 1920), pp. 193–97.

17. H. W. Edwards, "Harbord and Lejeune: A Command Precedent," Marine Corps Gazette 37 (July 1953): 12–15; and Rolf Hillman, "The Indianheads: Second to None," U.S. Naval Institute Proceedings 113 (November 1987): 40–48. For a less complimentary view of leatherneck-doughboy rivalry in the Second Division, AEF, see Brigadier General André Brewster's report of 12 July 1918, file 712-1, entry 588, RG 120, NA. When Clemenceau visited the Second Division to congratulate them on the epic battle for Belleau Wood, Bundy invited only the officers of the Third Brigade to meet the French prime minister.

18. Cf. Josephus Daniels to John A. Lejeune, 12 September 1918, Lejeune 1913–1919 file, container 88, reel 56, Daniels MSS; and Lejeune to Daniels, 5 August 1918, container 88, reel 55, Daniels MSS, Manuscripts Division, Library of Congress (emphasis in the original).

19. John J. Pershing, My Experiences in the World War, 2 vols. (New York: Stokes, 1931), 2:189–190 and 2:237.

20. JAL, Reminiscences of a Marine, p. 307.

21. Richard Derby, Wade in Sanitary (New York: Putnam's Sons, 1919), pp. 98–99.

22. JAL, Reminiscences of a Marine, p. 260.

23. Ibid., p. 314.

24. Ibid., p. 321.

25. Hunter Liggett, Commanding an American Army: Recollections of the World War (Boston: Houghton-Mifflin, 1925), pp. 63–65; Commanding General, Second Division, to Commanding General, I Corps, Report of Operations, 12–16 September 1918, Records of the Second Division (Regular), 9 Vols. (Washington and Fort Sam Houston, Texas: Second Division Association, 1930–1932) 6: Summary of the St. Mihiel Offensive; and Journal of Operations, Second Division, entry 271, RG 120, NA.

26. JAL, Reminiscences of a Marine, p. 316.

27. Liggett to Lejeune, 12 September 1918, reel 3, Lejeune MSS. See also Hunter Liggett, Ten Years Ago in France, (New York: Dodd, Mead, 1925), pp. 67–68.

28. Liggett, Ten Years Ago in France, p. 155.

29. John Thomason, "Marines at Blanc Mont," Scribner's, September 1925, pp. 227–31.

30. Edwin N. McClellan, "The Battle of Blanc Mont Ridge," Marine Corps Gazette 7 (March 1922): 4.

31. JAL to James G. Harbord, 29 June 1934, reel 6, Lejeune MSS.

32. John Thomason, *Fix Bayonets and Other Stories* (New York: Scribner's 1925; reprint, Quantico: Marine Corps Association, 1978), p. 115.
33. Ernst Otto, "The Battle at Blanc Mont," *U.S. Naval Institute Proceedings* 56 (June 1930): 9–10; Lejeune, "Resume of the Operations of the Second Division in Champagne, From October 2 to 9, 1918," *Marine Corps Gazette* 27 (September 1942): 17; Derby, *Wade in Sanitary*, pp. 137–38; and Thomason, "Marines at Blanc Mont," pp. 227–42.
34. Otto, "The Battle at Blanc Mont," p. 9.
35. Gouraud to Petain, n.d., Lejeune's officer qualification record, HQMC.
36. Summary of operations, Blanc Mont (Champagne), reel 11, Lejeune MSS; and "Operations of the 2nd United States Division with the IV French Army in Champagne," file 1034, entry 268, RG 120, NA.
37. Lejeune to Charles G. Long, 19 October 1918, reel 3, Lejeune MSS.

4

MEUSE-ARGONNE AND OCCUPATION DUTY IN GERMANY

—————————— 1918–1919 ——————————

> The endurance, the skill, the courage, and the fiery energy
> of the officers and men of the Second Division are unsur-
> passed in the annals of war.
>
> *Commanding General, Second Division, AEF*

On 25 October 1918, operational control of the Second Division passed to the United States First Army, then to V Corps.
Three days later, the corps staff informed its subordinate units
that the Germans had begun a general retreat along an eighty-
kilometer front. Allied units intended to launch a full-scale
offensive to break the stalemate on the western front. By the end
of the month, the U.S. First Army and the French Fourth Army
had accomplished the first part of the mission. The Americans
seized Bois de Forêt on the heights of Cunel and Romagne, and
Côte de Châtillon. Both armies joined at Grandpré as the
enemy was driven further from the Argonne. Now the Allies
were in a position to turn the German positions north of the
Aisne, and cut the Carignan-Sedan-Mézières railroad with a
goal to drive the enemy beyond the Meuse.[1]

In a subsequent staff conference, Lejeune's new corps commander, Major General Charles P. Summerall, left no doubt as to
the seriousness of the coming offensive with his thinly veiled
threats to relieve officers who failed to perform adequately. The
domineering Summerall had come to Pershing's attention because
he had the temerity to stand up to him, a quality admired by the
commander in chief. An opinionated, outspoken officer who
recognized no peer with his knowledge of supporting arms,

Summerall never hesitated to speak out when he thought he was right. In his initial encounter with Pershing and the staff of the AEF, Summerall surprised the conferees by arguing with Colonel Fox Connor, and then Pershing himself, over the amount and employment of artillery. Subsequently, Pershing cabled the war department requesting that Summerall remain in the AEF.

Summerall was cut in the mold of Pershing, with an abrasive and threatening style of leadership that Lejeune found offensive. Lejeune was to experience a troubled relationship with Summerall in the final drive to end World War I on the western front. While commanding the First Division, Summerall received a field report from an infantry battalion commander indicating that he had stopped. Irate, he responded immediately: "You may have *paused* for reorganization. If you ever send me another message with the word *stopped* in it, you will be sent to the rear for reclassification."[2]

At the time of the Second Division's arrival, the Forty-second Division held the front of V Corps. The Second Division would pass through it in preparation for the coming offensive. Combat objectives for the Second Division included Landres-et-St. Georges, St. Georges, Bois des Hazois, and Bois l'Epasse. As Summerall and his staff unfolded their battle plan, Lejeune pointed out that one of his flanks would be unprotected and requested modification of the proposed tactics. Unimpressed by his subordinate's logic, Summerall refused to change the operation order. On the eve of the offensive, Summerall joined Lejeune in a visit to each of the division's infantry battalions. Before departing, he again reminded Lejeune that he intended to relieve officers who failed to measure up.

The threat of summary relief hung heavy over Summerall's subordinates. At his first briefing with the staff and senior commanders of V Corps, he seemed to relish recounting the numerous cases of officers relieved of duty and sent to the rear for new assignments. Lejeune took exception to Summerall's style of leadership. On at least one occasion, he displayed the audacity to stand up to him: "General [Summerall], the Second Division's officers will carry out orders because of *esprit*, the pride and love for their division, and their devotion to the cause for which they are fighting."[3]

Earlier, Lejeune and the other division commanders received letters of guidance from Pershing that underscored the lack of confidence the commander in chief had in many of his subordinates. While not as threatening as the rhetoric used by Summerall, the tone of the official correspondence left no doubt as to what Pershing expected. Commanders should supervise personally and not allow their staffs to operate independently. Many young officers considered themselves in the same social class as their troops and often hesitated to give orders; senior officers must provide direction. When courage fails in the heat of battle, appropriate action must be taken: "When men run away in front of the enemy, officers should take summary action to stop it, even to the point of shooting men down who are caught in such disgraceful conduct . . . my sole purpose in writing the above is, by friendly suggestion, and perhaps, some criticism, to help you if possible to meet the great responsibility that rests upon you."[4]

Between 22 and 25 October 1918, the Second Division marched to the First Army area. During the night of 30–31 October, it relieved the Forty-second Division near Landres-et-St. Georges. The division's area of responsibility included La Tuilerie Ferme west to a point one kilometer south of St. Georges. On 1 November, the entire corps advanced towards its objectives. Pershing positioned Summerall's V Corps in the center of the American army to strike the main blow against the Germans and drive north to seize the heights of Barricourt. Composed of the Eighty-ninth and Second Divisions, V Corps was flanked by I Corps on the left (Eightieth, Seventy-ninth, and Seventy-eighth Divisions) and III Corps on the right (Fifth and Ninetieth Divisions). Seven veteran German divisions opposed them (see Map 3).

The last battle on the western front began for Lejeune at 3:30 A.M. on 1 November 1918. A massive artillery barrage lasted two

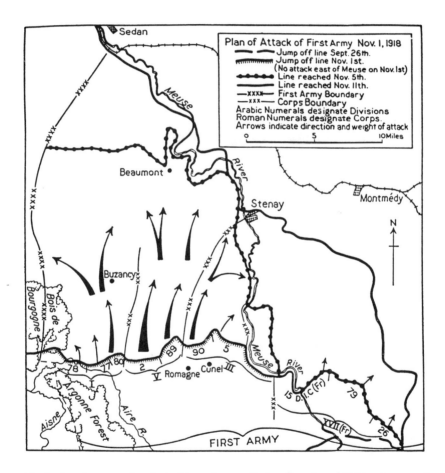

Map 3. American operations in the Meuse-Argonne Region. From *Second Division: Summary of Operations in the World War* (Washington: GPO, 1944), p. 127.

hours; H hour began at 5:30 A.M.. Lejeune planned a two-pronged attack. Initially, the Twenty-third Infantry would attack on the right towards Bois des Hazois, Bois l'Epasse, and Landres-et-St. Georges, then retire to join the Ninth Infantry as it supported the Fourth Brigade in an attack by a column of battalions on the left of the division's front. Just before the infantry assault, Lejeune shortened his lines five hundred yards and backed up the barrage. By doing so, he wiped out the German machine gun emplacements in no-man's land: "Bowley [brigadier general commanding the artillery brigade] and I both strongly believed that the artillery should be utilized to the extent of its capacity in order that victory might be achieved with the smallest loss of life among our assault troops."[5]

At the end of the first day of the offensive, all of the division's objectives had been taken as planned—St. Georges, Landre et St. Georges, and Bayonville et Chérnery—for an advance of nine kilometers. The entire First Army moved an equal distance while taking more than seventeen hundred German prisoners. Although the Eighty-ninth Division caught up with Lejeune and took its position on the right of the Second Division, failure of adjacent I Corps units on Lejeune's left to take their objectives made his flank vulnerable. Much to Summerall's dismay, the advance had to be halted to allow the other Allied units to catch up.[6]

As the victorious allies pushed the battered enemy forces back towards Germany, Lejeune pressed his troops with stirring messages: "The endurance, the skill, the courage, and the fiery energy of the officers and men of the Second Division are unsurpassed in the annals of war . . . when the history of America's part in winning this war is written, the renown of the Second Division will stand out pre-eminent."[7]

In a daring tactical movement during the night of 2–3 November, soldiers of the Ninth Infantry followed by the Twenty-third Infantry and one battalion of the Fifth Marines marched for six and a

quarter hours in total darkness and driving rain to surprise sleeping German units four miles behind the front without suffering a
single casualty. The resolute doughboys and leathernecks failed
by five minutes to capture a German division commander and his
staff. During the same night, the rest of the Second Division
advanced to the northwest edge of Bois de la Fotie. By noon on 3
November, the Ninth Infantry occupied the ridge running from
Le Champy Haut to Vaux-en-Dieulet. The Twenty-third Infantry
moved to a position three kilometers north of Fossé.

The advance continued unabated even though rations ran short.
Lejeune's soldiers and marines foraged for leftover German rations
and French foodstuffs and even devoured the remnants of a cab-
bage patch left behind by the retreating enemy. The determined
Lejeune ordered another night advance similar to the earlier one
and it too brought spectacular results. The Third Brigade advanced
five kilometers to the vicinity of Beaumont. German resistance
diminished rapidly following the initial Allied successes in the
Meuse-Argonne offensive. A German prisoner of war captured by
Lejeune's division underscored the obvious: "The penetration of
our line by American troops west of the Meuse caused us to
withdraw the front between the Aisne and Champineulle."[8]

Before noon on 4 November, units of the division attacked
towards Beaumont and began to look for intact bridges to cross
the Meuse. By midnight, the Third Brigade had reached La
Sartelle Ferme to seize bridges across the river and to protect the
right flank of the First Division moving to Mouzon. The Allied
high command continued to exhort its units to press the attack.
Success followed success on the battlefield, and Lejeune urged his
troops to drive even harder. By 5 November, the German lines
had begun to crumble. As the enemy high command attempted
to resist the Allied onslaught while negotiating for a better position at the peace table, Pershing insisted that the American army
group maintain its pressure on the enemy. After midnight,
Lejeune's 3rd Brigade moved to the vicinity of La Sartelle Ferme
in preparation to seize bridges across the Meuse.

On 6 November, Summerall told Lejeune to be prepared to attack Sedan. In the rapidly unfolding events on the western front, however, the attack to the north never came about. Instead, both the Second and Eighty-ninth Divisions received orders to cross the Meuse and seize the heights above the river. Colonel William A. Mitchell, commanding Lejeune's engineer regiment, conducted a reconnaissance of the Meuse. As he formulated his plan to bridge the river, Mitchell learned that the combat bridges promised by V Corps would not be ready in time. Fortunately, the division found two bridges intact. By the morning of 7 November, the division occupied Villemontry and Le Faubourg. A day later, the Second Division received orders to effect a crossing of the Meuse at Mouzon and Létanne in conjunction with the Eighty-ninth Division. But the Meuse on the right of the Americans could not be forded and was bounded by hills, which furnished observation and positions for artillery to fire into the approaches. To the left of the American army, the Argonne forest with its heavy growth and steep ravines blocked access to the enemy.[9]

On 9 November 1918, Summerall and his staff unfolded their battle plan and Lejeune found it riddled with faults. To begin with, he wanted the area across the river cleared of machine guns before attempting a crossing; instead, Summerall ordered the Second and Eighty-ninth Divisions to cross the river simultaneously on the night of 10–11 November. It would be the final night of the war and the commanding general, Second Division, spent it without sleep: "The night of the last battle of the war was the most trying night I have experienced," he recalled.[10]

Doughboys and leathernecks cleaned their weapons and checked their equipment in preparation for what they hoped to be the final battle of the war. Their commander reflected on the deaths to come even though the conflict seemed about to end. The tired, wet, and cold marines and soldiers of the Second Division had little difficulty taking their last objective of the war from the disheartened Germans. The influx of fresh American troops had proven too much for the war-weary enemy. By the end of October

1918, some German soldiers had mutinied. Turkey surrendered on 30 October and Austria-Hungary four days later; Bulgaria had been out of the war for over a month.

Lejeune ordered another crossing of the Meuse on the night of 9–10 November by the Fourth Brigade (Marine) after an earlier attempt that day failed. The Sixth Marines took up a position on the riverbank under cover of darkness, but enemy fire forced the supporting engineer detachment to abandon work on the bridges. The next evening, the Fifth Marines fared better downstream, where the engineers threw two bridges across the Meuse. Thirty minutes before midnight on 10–11 November 1918, the Second Battalion, Fifth Marines, crossed the river; by daybreak, the Eighty-ninth Division had crossed the barrier alongside the Second Division.[11]

Pershing ordered his staff to signal all U.S. units to cease fire at 11:00 A.M. The Second Division halted in the vicinity of Sénégal Ferme, two kilometers southeast of Mouzon. Along the western front, combatants of all nationalities sat down in numb disbelief. For the commanding general, Second Division, triumph in France in this noble crusade had been part of an ideal nurtured since his boyhood days in Reconstruction-era Louisiana, as a military cadet at Louisiana State University, a naval cadet at the U.S. Naval Academy, a midshipman with the fleet, and an officer in the Marine Corps since 1890.[12]

While Lejeune reflected on the sweetness of victory, the soldiers and marines of his command mostly counted their blessings for having survived. Many of the doughboys and leathernecks who crossed the Atlantic more than a year before fell in the struggle to break the long stalemate that had ground down the Western Allies. Of the approximately thirty-one thousand marines who served in France during the war, more than half suffered wounds or were killed. A decade later, Lejeune could still recall the emotional impact of the cease-fire in vivid detail:

> A few minutes before eleven o'clock, there were bursts of fire from the two antagonists and then—suddenly there was complete

silence. It was the most impressive celebration of the armistice that could have possibly taken place. There was a solemn and an earnest joy in the hearts of every man at the front . . . we were happy because fighting, death, and destruction had ceased. I offered up a prayer of thanksgiving to Almighty God.[13]

As the announcement of the cease-fire spread from trench to dugout, soldiers and marines spilled out into the shell-pocked meadows to light warming fires. Many of the troops would be warm and dry for the first time in weeks. Long-forgotten harmonicas appeared from the bottoms of haversacks. The patriotic songs that had become the emotional staple of the wartime era could be heard across the barren fields of battle. In a thoughtful gesture, Lejeune wrote to the next of kin of his officers who had lost their lives in the war. As numb as his soldiers and marines, Lejeune found solace in his belief that war was an ennobling experience: "While war is terribly destructive, monstrously cruel, and horrible beyond expression, it nevertheless causes the divine spark in men to glow, to kindle, and to burst into living flame, and enables them to attain heights of devotion to duty, sheer heroism, and sublime unselfishness that in all probability they would never have reached in the prosecution of peaceful pursuits."[14]

The final drive for the Meuse-Argonne to end the war had cost the Allies more than 120,000 casualties, but together they had captured forty-seven German divisions. While his command attempted to recover from the horror and fatigue of the endless days of combat, Lejeune sought the assurance of his corps commander that his weary troops would be withdrawn for a much-needed rest in warm, dry billets. He even appealed to his good friend Hunter Liggett to use whatever influence he had. Instead, Pershing and his staff had other plans for Lejeune's division.

Rather than withdrawing the Second Division from the lines and providing a train trip to the port of embarkation at Brest, Pershing selected them for occupation duty in Germany with the Third Army. Supplies, horses, and mules poured in from adjacent divisions to bolster the Second Division. From 11–16 November

1918, Lejeune and his troops remained in the mud of the Beaumont area, then began the long march through Belgium and
Luxembourg in preparation to cross the Rhine into Germany.
But just as the weary columns formed for the journey, Lejeune
had occasion to demonstrate his determined character to his new
corps commander, Major General John L. Hines.

When the Second Division received orders transferring it from
V Corps to III Corps in the Army of Occupation, Lejeune and
his staff prepared in earnest for the long march ahead. Third
Corps ordered the Second Division to begin its march from Stenay
on the east bank of the Meuse, believing that all of the bridges
closer to the divisions' encampment had fallen. It ordered Lejeune's
command to march forty kilometers to the nearest intact span
and return another forty kilometers on the opposite side of the
Meuse in order to begin the trek there. Meanwhile, forward
elements of the Second Division reported an intact bridge considerably closer to the division's position. Lejeune notified III Corps
headquarters and assumed that the march of the Second Division
would begin at the closer point.

An exhausted Lejeune woke in the middle of the night to
overhear the duty officer in a telephone conversation with III
Corps headquarters. Taking the field telephone, Lejeune learned
that General Hines still wanted his division to cross the Meuse at
a point forty kilometers to the north. When he questioned the
order and asked to use the closer span, the staff officer at III
Corps headquarters responded rather testily that the general had
ordered it; moreover, he had gone to bed! Outraged, Lejeune
insisted that the matter be brought to the attention of his superior immediately or he would motor over and wake him up to
discuss the issue. As Lejeune recalled the incident more than
twenty years later, it seemed better to rouse one sleeping general
than to march twenty-five thousand sick and exhausted men all
night for no reason. Sensing Lejeune's determination, the exasperated staff officer woke up Hines to relay the request. He called
back quickly with the authority to use the closer bridge. Although

Lejeune won this bout, the incident probably added to the misgivings many of his superiors shared with regard to the stubborn Louisianan.[15]

After the complete American army had formed in the fall of 1918 for the final drive to end the war, Pershing directed his corps commanders to prepare candid appraisals of the major generals. Instead of the customary inflated reports of fitness on general officers, the reports that Pershing wanted would be more useful in evaluating the professional character of his senior commanders. Lejeune received two such evaluations, the first from Hunter Liggett, which did nothing to mar his image as the consummate professional soldier: "Qualified for staff or line duties; a very good disciplinarian; very good knowledge of supply; is aggressive; has excellent qualifications for leadership; and has shown himself to be an excellent division commander in the field."

Summerall's frank report, while attributing some good professional qualities to Lejeune, suggested criticism of his performance: "[Lejeune's] attitude towards higher authority is lacking in that absolute subordination and eager acceptance of difficult tasks imposed on his command is lacking." Moreover, the report added that all too often Lejeune decided when his mission had been completed, sometimes in the face of adversity; nevertheless, "[When Lejeune] commits himself to an undertaking, he pursues his objective with admirable vigor, resourcefulness, and self-sacrifice. A strong will as well as resolution on the part of superiors will obtain the finest results from this officer."[16]

Doubtless, Lejeune would have been miffed and hurt had he the opportunity to read the second candid appraisal of his professional character. From the outset, he had resisted Summerall's style of leadership and questioned the tactical direction coming from V Corps headquarters. As a result of this temerity, Summerall now took the opportunity to criticize Lejeune and damn him with faint praise. Although Lejeune never served under Major General Robert E. Lee Bullard, his performance came to Bullard's attention as well. Like Summerall, Bullard apparently did not consider Lejeune to be a superlative combat commander. In a collection of essays written after the war, Bullard praised Preston Brown and the Second Division without mentioning Lejeune: "Through three changes of commanders [Bundy, Harbord, Lejeune] and three battles [Belleau Wood, Soissons, St. Mihiel], Brown had continually stood forth as the striking, dominant personality of the division."[17]

Throughout his military career, Lejeune had chosen to lead by gaining the loyalty and devotion of his men. The threatening style used by Pershing and imitated by many of his subordinates—especially, Summerall—won no praise from Lejeune. In a summary of his wartime experiences written more than two decades later, he underscored his feelings by referring to Liggett and Gourand as "leaders of men." Significantly, he failed to mention either Pershing or Summerall. In Lejeune's opinion, such officers were "drivers of men," and they failed to gain the unquestioned loyalty of their subordinates.[18]

In mid-November 1918, Lejeune and his weary troops began the long march through Belgium and Luxembourg preparatory to crossing the Rhine into Germany. No matter how proud Lejeune was of his troops, he had to admit that they displayed the effects of the last offensive. Soldiers and marines marched in the freezing rain as if in a stupor. When the long columns halted for a brief rest, most callapsed in place to be roused after too few minutes by equally weary officers and sergeants. Influenza struck the western front with a vengeance and Lejeune's division felt the fury of the dreaded disease. New uniforms arrived for the soldiers and marines, along with poorly fitting English shoes. Lejeune appealed continually to higher headquarters for relief in the form of warm billets and trucks to transport his command, but to no avail. Eventually, Pershing paid attention to the tired doughboys and leathernecks, but not in the fashion that Lejeune had hoped.

Sometime that month, Pershing passed by the marching columns in his staff car. Noting the ragged condition of Lejeune's command, he expressed his displeasure after arriving at Third Army headquarters. Almost immediately, Lejeune received an official letter from an old friend and classmate from the Army War College. Brigadier General Malin Craig, then serving as chief of staff, III Corps, reported the commander in chief's concerns over the unkempt appearance of the Second Division.

Pershing had apparently stormed into the III Corps command post livid over what he had seen, calling Lejeune's command an "eyesore." As Craig took notes, the commander in chief ticked off a litany of complaints. As the staff car carrying him passed the tired columns, Pershing noted the slovenly appearance of the soldiers among the division's two army infantry regiments. The year before, he had been mortified to see that the marines of the Fifth Regiment appeared more polished than his beloved regular soldiers during an inspection of the First Division. Now his soldiers walked and shuffled along rather than marched, and they appeared unshaven and dirty. As an old cavalryman, Pershing was outraged by the condition of Lejeune's horses and mules. Many of the animals required grooming, and the harnesses needed oiling and polishing. Malin Craig passed on a warning from Pershing: "If the officers can't lead, they will be replaced by others waiting in the rear."[19]

Furious at this slur on his command, Lejeune responded immediately to Craig's letter, suggesting that if AEF headquarters wanted the division's appearance improved, it might have honored his request for a period of rest and re-outfitting before ordering it to march into Germany. As Lejeune smarted under the insult, he and his division continued their long, slow march through Belgium and Luxembourg. Men and animals suffered in silence, no longer the spirited unit they once had been. Wet clothing wore out quickly and most of the men needed new shoes and equipment. Horses and mules appeared near exhaustion, and a lack of decent forage and a persistent form of mange worsened their condition. Finally, on 10 December 1918, the Rhine appeared in sight.

After the cease-fire, command became sometimes even more

difficult than in the thick of combat. Pershing's chief of staff sent letters of caution to each division commander, citing several concerns of the exacting commander in chief. While officers commissioned for wartime service usually performed to the satisfaction of Pershing and his staff, many of these patriots in uniform lacked the experience necessary to maintain discipline, unable to keep the largely conscript and "service-for-wartime-only" American force from unraveling. Immediately after the cease-fire, Pershing shared his concerns over the military efficiency of the AEF. Demobilization and occupation duties demanded more from the soldiers and marines than combat. In a sternly worded memorandum to his senior commanders, Pershing's chief of staff underscored the demands that lay ahead: "There remains now a harder task which will test your soldierly qualities to the utmost. Success in this and little note will be taken and few praises will be sung; fail, and the light of your glorious achievements of the past will sadly be dimmed."[20]

Lejeune responded immediately to McAndrew's letter, promising to maintain the military posture of his division according to Pershing's high standards. McAndrew's letter cited several additional problems that had surfaced recently, apparently due to a lack of harmony between regular army officers and those commissioned just for wartime service. In his reply, Lejeune stated that he already noted some grumbling among the officers in his command and listed two reasons for the unhappiness: too many recommendations for Distinguished Service Crosses being disapproved by higher headquarters and unit citations for the major battles failing to include the Second Division. Especially disconcerting to Lejeune and his officers was the omission of the Champagne (Blanc Mont) and the Château-Thierry (Belleau Wood) offensives from the list of separate and distinct campaigns.[21]

In addition, Lejeune knew the comradeship between his doughboys and leathernecks to be tissue thin. Many of the army officers in the Second Division bridled over the excessive publicity given to the exploits of the Marine Corps brigade at the expense of its

sister army infantry brigade or the division as a whole. One of
Lejeune's army regimental commanders, Paul D. Malone, shared
this animosity with Harbord after being promoted to brigadier
general and leaving Lejeune's command: "The enclosed sheet
announcing that 10,000 Marines are being allowed for service in
France and fixing the rate of pay for them inspires my letter
herewith. Once more the Marines see an opportunity . . . with
characteristic disregard to everybody and everything, we are likely
to send to the Rhine . . . a bunch of adventurers, illiterates, and
drunkards."[22]

The extensive publicity given to the exploits of the Marine
Corps brigade in Lejeune's division rankled most of the Army
infantrymen, who believed that they had fought just as bravely.
The members of the Third Brigade rarely received mention in
combat dispatches, while soldiers in other units in the division
earned even less publicity. Most doughboys came to conclude—
just as did Pershing and most of his senior officers—that the
token force of leathernecks in the AEF earned far more acclaim
than was warranted.[23]

The ruffled feelings between soldiers and marines continued,
even outside the boundaries of the Second Division's area. A
Marine Corps captain reported disgustedly to Lejeune an unpleasant incident that occurred as he marched his company past a
group of lounging soldiers from an adjacent division. When the
doughboys spied the leathernecks approaching, they burst into
song with doggerel not likely to win friendships among those who
wore forest green:

> The Marines have won the croix de guerre, parlez-vous?
> The Marines have won the croix de guerre, parlez-vous?
> The Marines have won the croix de guerre,
> But the sons of bitches were never there,
> Hinky dinky, parlez-vous.[24]

Apparently, the offensive song had even appeared in the newspaper of the Third Army, much to Lejeune's dismay. He wrote

immediately to the commanding general, who promised to have the insulting behavior cease. However, not all army officers found fault with their Marine Corps contemporaries. The year before, Pershing recommended that applications be accepted from qualified Marine Corps officers for transfer to the regular army.[25]

Until 15 July 1919, the Second Division occupied an area around the bridgehead at Coblenz on the Rhine from Ehrenbreitstein castle to the northern boundary of the American sector and the Valley of the Wied. Lejeune established his headquarters in Heddesdorf, a suburb of Neuwied. The town strained under the load of occupation when Headquarters, III Corps, established itself alongside Headquarters, Second Division. For the troops, the inadequate bathing and delousing facilities contributed to their discomfort.

The Second Division formed part of the Third American Army centered east of Luxembourg, while the Tenth French Army occupied an area to the right of the Americans near Metz. The Allied high command positioned the Fifth French Army opposite Bastogne. As his officers worked to maintain discipline and prepare their troops for the eventual trip home, Lejeune continued to seethe over the casual insult dropped by Pershing. Although Lejeune's first chief of staff, Preston Brown, had been the subject of severe professional criticism from Pershing himself, he had apparently corrected his shortcomings to the satisfaction of the commander in chief. In the months since leaving Lejeune's command, Preston Brown received two promotions and now held the powerful position of chief of staff at the forward headquarters of the AEF. Not willing to forget Pershing's snide insult, Lejeune penned a personal note to his former subordinate.

In it, Lejeune asked Brown to invite Pershing to send a general officer to conduct a thorough inspection of the division. A week later Major General André Brewster, the inspector general of the AEF, arrived in Coblenz to spend more than a week with Lejeune's command. Brewster visited every unit, speaking to both officers and enlisted men, and reported to Pershing that the division appeared to be in superb condition. A copy of Brewster's letter reached Lejeune, assuaging his professional pride and ego.[26]

After the cease-fire, the politically important streamed across the Atlantic to pay homage to America's victorious fighting men. Those with an interest in the Marine Corps came to Germany to visit Lejeune and the Second Division, AEF. The arrival of some visitors served later to fuel nasty rumors that a cabal had been formed to oust the commandant of the Marine Corps, Major General George Barnett.

· The chief of naval operations, Admiral William S. Benson, came early in 1919 with the assistant secretary of the navy, Franklin D. Roosevelt. Benson and Lejeune had become warm friends during the latter's tour as assistant to the commandant and enjoyed each other's company, more so than Benson's cronies in navy blue, who found him abrasive and aloof. But the most important visitor for Lejeune's future came in the person of the wily politician and Democratic party loyalist, Secretary of the Navy Josephus Daniels.[27]

After Lejeune came to the attention of the secretary of the navy in 1913 when Daniels interviewed prospective candidates for the commandancy, the two men became close friends. Their personal correspondence is filled with warm personal notes of mutual admiration: "[Our] deep friendship formed in the days when we [were] in the Navy is permanent and lasting on both sides. You know that nowhere outside of your own kin have you friends who hold you in more affectionate esteem."[28]

Apparently as a favor for the shrewd secretary, Lejeune arranged a minor personnel transfer before Daniels's junket to Germany. At least one person suggested political currying as the reason for the action. A few months before the arrival of his distinguished visitors, Lejeune ordered the transfer of the secretary's son, Second Lieutenant Josephus Daniels, Jr., then serving in the Fifth Brigade as aide-de-camp to Smedley D. Butler. No stranger to the political scene, Butler knew the importance of assuaging the correct important people. Soon after his arrival in France, he informed his father of plans for the secretary's son: "When I get my promotion [to brigadier general], I shall make Josephus Daniels, Jr., an aide [de camp] on my staff as he is a fine, devoted friend and we are all very fond of him."[29]

However, both the younger Daniels and Butler experienced disappointment in the days to follow as their careers took unexpected paths. In February 1919, Lejeune arranged the transfer of young Daniels to his command for duties on his personal staff. Disgusted and reluctant to leave the Fifth Brigade now that Butler had been promoted to brigadier general, Josephus Daniels, Jr., lost no time in complaining to his powerful father: "When the time comes to pick the next MGC [major general commandant], you will see why this major general [Lejeune] is doing me this way without asking myself or General Butler."[30]

Earlier in September 1918, Butler learned to his dismay that Pershing had no intention of employing an additional Marine Corps brigade except as a rear-area unit. The colorful and ambitious commanding general of the Fifth Brigade then received an assignment far from the sound of guns. Before America entered the war, Butler used his political connections to gain an assignment in Haiti in 1915, where he remained satisfied until America's entry into the war. Then, when his repeated requests for orders to France failed to move Headquarters Marine Corps, Butler pulled his important political strings again. This time, Daniels ordered Barnett to transfer Butler from Haiti to a Marine Corps unit earmarked for France. Merely being in the AEF, however, did not guarantee combat duty, as Butler soon learned to his despair.[31]

When U.S. forces began to arrive in increasing numbers in France, Pershing ordered the establishment of a replacement and processing camp near the port of Brest. Camp Pontanezen soon became a ramshackle city of leaking tents amid a sea of mud; worse, the influenza epidemic of that year struck the desolate installation without mercy. On the day that Butler assumed command, more than a hundred men died. Butler's assignment to straighten out the mess may well have been the product of interservice rivalry, as most observers considered it an impossible task. With Butler's failure, the myth of leatherneck infallibility would end. Butler did not fail, however, as Assistant Secretary of the Navy Roosevelt noted in a letter of praise to Secretary Daniels: "Butler deserves all possible credit but no officer can do the impossible."[32]

Arriving with the fury and energy of a dozen men, Lejeune's old comrade in arms raised the quality of food in the mess halls, ordered military bands to entertain the troops to raise morale, and secured adequate medical treatment for the ailing transients in the camp. Because of his fetish for locating duckboards to raise the walkways above the sea of mud, Butler became known throughout the AEF by the sobriquet "General Duckboard." However, when Butler applied for a commission in the Marine Corps in 1898, he wanted to march to the sound of guns. His quest for the noble thrill of feeling a bullet's whiz past a cheek had not diminished. In gloom and despair, Butler wrote to his father, convinced that his military days had ended: "I feel at the present time and have felt for the past five months that my days of soldiering are over. For over twenty years, I worked hard to fit myself to take part in this war which has just closed, and now when the supreme test came my country did not want me."[33]

As Butler brooded despondently near the western seacoast of France, Lejeune and his division remained in Germany to ensure that the defeated government accepted the terms of the surrender. Secretary and Mrs. Daniels received a gracious welcome from Lejeune when they visited Germany. He hosted his friends each evening at dinner during their week-long visit. As usual, the egalitarian Daniels wanted to visit the enlisted men. Lejeune arranged as much visiting as the secretary desired and allowed him to distribute medals. After the tumultuous removal of Barnett from the commandancy, critics charged that a political intrigue had been formulated during Daniels's visit to Germany in 1919. Lejeune denied it vehemently. But his friendship and attachment to Daniels grew increasingly stronger: "One seldom meets these kind [Secretary and Mrs. Daniels] among those who occupy high positions," he commented in a letter to his sister.[34]

After the entourage left, the command returned to its routine of garrison duties, equipment maintenance, and tourism. Anxious to return home, most of the soldiers and marines became bored. Lejeune learned that he had to toughen up, just as McAndrew's stern letter of guidance some months before had suggested. In a memorandum to his officers, Lejeune decried a lessening in discipline. As an example, he cited the leniency shown an officer after conviction by a court-martial.

Lejeune had his portrait painted by celebrated artist Joseph Cummings Chase, who traveled to Europe following the cease-fire to paint the leadership of the AEF. The original of Lejeune's portrait is kept by the Smithsonian Institution, and a good likeness graces of the foyer of Lejeune Hall at the U.S. Naval Academy.[35]

Before the Second Division left for home, Pershing found time to pay them one last visit. Lejeune marched his division by the commander in chief with a stirring parade, one that apparently pleased Pershing. When the troops had again massed on the parade ground, the official party presented more than one hundred Distinguished Service Crosses, earned for gallantry during the Meuse-Argonne offensive. Pershing pinned the Distinguished Service Medal on Lejeune and gave him an invitation for one last official act before leaving France.[36]

The government of France planned a gala victory celebration and parade for Bastille Day, 1919. All senior American officers who could ride a horse received an invitation to participate. More than one thousand blind, lame, and mutilated French veterans led the long line of marchers. Foche and Joffre followed, leading a military contingent of more than a thousand picked troops representing each nation among the victorious Allies. Pershing led the American participants. An officer carrying his four-star flag rode next, followed by Harbord and Pershing's three aides-de-camp. Major General Henry T. Allen, the commander of the U.S. occupation forces in Germany, followed directly in front of his predecessor, Major General John L. Hines. Four ranks of American generals followed—including Lejeune—totaling thirty of them in ranks eight abreast. The band of the AEF came next. Finally, a composite regiment of U.S. soldiers—all handpicked and each more than six feet in height—marched in this stirring end to the war, carrying the unit colors of all the American regiments. More than twenty thousand French and French colonial troops marched as well. The parade provided an emotional finish to Lejeune's finest hour.[37]

Under first Harbord and later Lejeune's command, the Second Division earned a record unequaled by a division in the AEF. The division captured 288 German officers and 11,738 enlisted prisoners, 74 heavy and 269 light artillery pieces, 58 trench mortars, 8 antitank guns, and 1,350 machine guns. Moreover, the division advanced farther—sixty kilometers—against the enemy than any other division. But in the process, the Second Division counted 5,150 leathernecks and doughboys killed in action (KIAs) and another 18,066 wounded (WIAs). Of the other divisions in the AEF, only the First Division (4,196 KIAs and 11,324 WIAs) and Third Division (3,401 KIAs and 12,000 WIAs) even approached the Second Division in the number of friendly casualties.[38]

Members of Lejeune's command earned a total of 7 Medals of Honor, 675 Distinguished Service Crosses, 10 Distinguished Service Medals, 6 Belgian Crosses, 17 Legions of Honor, 42 Medals Militaire, and 2,740 croix de guerre. For his wartime service, Lejeune wore the Distinguished Service Medal, the Cross of a Commander of the Legion of Honour, the croix de guerre with palm, and the World War I Victory Medal. Service with the AEF was the apogee of Lejeune's military career and provided the most meaningful memories of his long years of service to his country.[39]

As the division passed through Camp Pontanezen for processing and embarkation, Lejeune stayed with his old friend Butler. Disappointed that he had failed to see action in the war, Butler played the gracious host without revealing any rancor or bitterness. Instead, Butler vented his sorrow and frustration in letters home. In his jaded view, failure to see combat in France had been part of a political vendetta instituted by Barnett and the staff at Headquarters Marine Corps. Earlier, the subject of his assignment in France had been discussed by Harbord and Lejeune; both senior officers agreed that Butler should remain at Camp Pontanezen. After his return home, Butler continued to fume. His frustrations would be important factors in the political machinations rocking the commandancy in 1920.[40]

Lejeune and most of his command embarked on the aged *Henderson* for the trip home, while the remainder of the division found passage in other transports. During Daniels's visit, Lejeune had planted an idea with the shrewd secretary that took seed quickly. As their transports steamed across the Atlantic, Lejeune received a cablegram from the secretary of war inviting the Second Division to parade through the streets of New York City upon their arrival. The acceptance of the invitation depended upon the willingness of the rank and file of the division to postpone their departure for home. The spirited unit endorsed the idea enthusiastically. Eventually, more than twenty-five thousand soldiers and Marines formed on 110th Street to march past Central Park amidst the thunderous ovation of the civilian population. Lejeune rode on horseback ahead of the marching columns to join the mayor and Assistant Secretary of the Navy Roosevelt to review the troops. Only one parade remained to end Lejeune's participation in the noble crusade; however, he had not been invited.

With orders to once again command the Marine Corps post at Quantico, Lejeune enjoyed a well-deserved leave with his family, visiting relatives and friends, and then a vacation in Atlantic City. Reading his morning newspaper one day, he learned that President Wilson would review the Fourth Brigade (Marine) in a parade past the White House. Stunned, Lejeune wondered why he had not been invited to march with the marines or sit in the reviewing stand with the official party. After all, he had once commanded the brigade. Later, it had been part of his division.

Donning his uniform and buckling up his Sam Browne belt, Lejeune called on the commandant of the Marine Corps to inquire about his omission from the parade or reviewing party. Barnett replied rather testily that no provision had been made for Lejeune to appear in the parade with the troops; however, perhaps a place could be found in the reviewing stand if he insisted on attending. Arriving obviously unwanted, Lejeune found his assigned seat prevented much of the view. His constant jumping up and down and craning of the neck attracted the attention of the assistant secretary of the navy. The gracious Roosevelt invited Lejeune to the front of the stand, introduced him to President Wilson, and left him to stand just behind the front near the commander in chief to watch the leathernecks march past.

Lejeune's presence at the event and his conspicuous absence from the original guest list contributed to the discomfort of Barnett. The commandant of the Marine Corps intended the event to underscore his yeoman service in preparing marines for combat duty in France. He did not wish to share the limelight with anyone else. The affair foreshadowed the bitter infighting to follow for the corps' highest post, a series of events that marred and almost prevented Lejeune's expected accession to the commandancy.[41]

Notes

1. Edward M. Coffman, *The War to End All Wars: The American Military Experience in World War I* (New York: Oxford University Press, 1968), pp. 296–356.
2. Quoted in Donald F. Smythe, *Pershing: General of the Armies* (Bloomington: University of Indiana Press, 1986), p. 157. See also Harbord, "Personalities and Personal Relationships in the American Expeditionary Forces," Army War College Talk, 24 April 1933. For a flattering opinion of Summerall, see Johnson Hagood, *The Services of Supply: A Memoir of the Great War* (Boston: Houghton Mifflin, 1927), p. 5.
3. JAL, *The Reminiscences of a Marine* (1930; reprint, Quantico: Marine Corps Association, 1979), p. 380.
4. Pershing to Lejeune, 24 October 1918, copy in container 116, Pershing MSS, Manuscripts Division, Library of Congress.
5. JAL, *Reminiscences of a Marine*, p. 383.

6. *Second Division: Summary of Operations in the World War* (Washington: GPO, 1944), pp. 69–95.
7. Second Division order, 5 November 1918, container 88, reel 55, Daniels MSS, Manuscripts Division, Library of Congress.
8. Liggett to Lejeune, 13 November 1918, reel 3, Lejeune MSS, Library of Congress. See also Summary of Operations, Meuse-Argonne, 1–11 November 1918, reel 11, Lejeune MSS; and war diary, 1–11 November 1918, *Records of the Second Division (Regular)* 9 vols. (Washington and Fort Sam Houston, Texas: Second Division Association, 1930–1932): 6.
9. Coffman, *The War to End All Wars*, pp. 299–356.
10. JAL, *Reminiscences of a Marine*, p. 400.
11. D.L.S. Brewster, "An Analysis of the Crossing of the Meuse River by the Second Division AEF on 10–11 November 1918," *Marine Corps Gazette* 25 (March 1941): 22–23; 50–51.
12. JAL, *Reminiscences of a Marine*, p. 233.
13. JAL, *Reminiscences of a Marine*, pp. 402–3. See also, Summary of Operations, Meuse-Argonne Offensive, 1–11 November 1918, reel 11, Lejeune MSS.
14. JAL, *Reminiscences of a Marine*, p. 321.
15. Lejeune to the Commandant of the Marine Corps, 22 October 1940, Lejeune's officer qualification record, Headquarters Marine Corps.
16. The two reports on Lejeune are in container 1953, AEF central file 201.6.e.e, RG 120, NA. Pershing's memorandum directing the special fitness reports is Pershing to Chief of Staff, 9 July 1918, office of the chief of staff files, entry 15, RG 120. Cf. Summerall's fitness report on Lejeune with Summerall to the Adjutant General, AEF, 24 December 1918, RG 120. Hind's fitness report on Lejeune, apparently critical as well, is not extant.
17. Cf. Robert E. Lee Bullard, *Fighting Generals*, p. 190; with James G. Harbord to Lejeune, 14 November 1918, reel 3, Lejeune MSS.
18. Lejeune to the Commandant of the Marine Corps, 22 October 1940, Lejeune's officer qualification record, Headquarters Marine Corps.
19. Malin Craig to the Commanding General, III Corps, 22 November 1918, reel 3, Lejeune MSS. See also Lejeune to Craig, 25 November 1918, reel 3, Lejeune MSS; and Richard Derby, *Wade in Sanitary* (New York: Putnam's Sons, 1919), pp. 189–92.
20. AEF general order 203, 12 November 1918, Pershing correspondence file, 1917–1919, Harbord MSS, Manuscripts Division, Library of Congress.
21. JAL to Major General James McAndrew, 5 March 1919, office of the chief of staff files, entry 15, RG 120, NA.
22. Malone to Harbord, 13 June 1919, file 21676-A-592, RG 120, NA.
23. Brigadier General André Brewster to General John J. Pershing, 12 July 1918, entry 587, RG 120; Pershing's diary, 18–21 August 1917, Pershing MSS; and Lieutenant General Robert E. Lee Bullard, *Personalities and Reminiscences of the War* (New York: Doubleday, 1925), pp. 208–9.
24. Captain Frederick G. Wheeler to Lejeune, 29 March 1919, reel 3, Lejeune MSS.
25. Pershing to the Secretary of War, 5 June 1918, cable 1249, reel 59, Josephus Daniels MSS, Manuscripts Division, Library of Congress.
26. Lejeune to Pershing, 31 December 1918, container 116, Pershing MSS, Library of Congress.
27. JAL to AL, 23 March 1919, 16 April 1919, 1 May 1919, 18 May 1919, 5 June 1919, and 15 June 1919, all on reel 2, Lejeune MSS.
28. Daniels to Lejeune, 5 March 1941, reel 5, Lejeune MSS.

29. Butler to his parents, 30 October 1918, Butler MSS, NewTown Square, Pennsylvania.
30. Josephus Daniels, Jr., to Josephus Daniels, 23 February 1919, family correspondence, container 23, reel 12, Daniels MSS.
31. Josephus Daniels, Jr. to his mother, 28 October 1918, reel 12, Daniels MSS; and Dessez interview by the author, 11 July 1979.
32. Roosevelt to Daniels, 13 January 1919, container 94, reel 59, Daniels MSS.
33. Butler to his father, 20 March 1919, Butler MSS, NewTown Square.
34. JAL to AL, 5 June 1919; see also, JAL to AL, 1 March and 16 April 1919, all on reel 2, Lejeune MSS.
35. Joseph Cummings Chase, *Soldiers All: Portraits and Sketches of the Men of the AEF* (New York: Doran, 1920), p. 311.
36. JAL to AL, 15 March 1919, reel 2, Lejeune MSS.
37. Smythe, *Pershing: General of the Armies*, pp. 256–57.
38. *A Guide to the American Battlefields of Europe* (Washington: GPO, 1927), p. 268; and *Second Division: Summary of Operations in the World War* (Washington: GPO, 1944), pp. 267–68.
39. Edwin N. McClellan, "A Brief History of the Fourth Brigade," *Marine Corps Gazette* 4 (December 1919): 368; and Lejeune to Barnett, 1 February 1919, container 64, Daniels MSS. Lejeune's citations are in his officer qualification record at HQMC.
40. JAL to James G. Harbord, 31 December 1918 and 15 March 1919, Harbord MSS, Manuscripts Division, Library of Congress; also, Cf. Merrill L. Bartlett, "Old Gimlet Eye," *U.S. Naval Institute Proceedings* 112 (November 1986): 65–72 and Hans Schmidt, *Maverick Marine* (Lexington: University Press of Kentucky, 1987), pp. 96–109.
41. Lejeune to the Commandant of the Marine Corps, [1935], reel 6, Lejeune MSS.

5

THE QUEST FOR THE COMMANDANCY
1919–1920

Secretary Daniels came in. He had really nothing on his
mind, except to say how-do-you do. He is a queer character,
a combination of ignorance, kindheartedness, and shifty
opportunism.

Theodore Roosevelt, Jr., Diary entry

Hurt and puzzled by his exclusion from the original list of
officials reviewing the parade of the Fourth Brigade (Marine),
AEF, Lejeune returned to his family for the remainder of his
leave. The incident caused him to wonder if his professional and
personal relationship with Barnett remained intact. But the commandant never mentioned the incident and spoke to Lejeune
only with regard to his next assignment during a subsequent
meeting. On 27 October 1919, Lejeune took up anew his former
position as commanding general at Quantico.

He found the installation in a shambles because of frantic
preparations for wartime service. Besides seeing to repair of the
physical plant, Lejeune had plans for his marines based on personal criticisms over the way the war had been fought. Lejeune
returned from the western front convinced that military personnel needed more education. At the enlisted level, he believed
the men to be bored and overtrained to the point of disinterest in
their military profession. The antimilitary attitude following World
War One exacerbated the problem. Many marines wondered how
their military training would help them succeed in the difficult
postwar employment situation. With Butler's assistance, Lejeune

introduced a novel solution to the problem of educating and training marines.

Lejeune suggested that his marines would perform better if officers reduced the hours of purely military training. More than two hours of military training in the classroom or on the drill field each day made the average enlisted man muscle-bound and stale. In Lejeune's program, Quantico-based Marines trained, drilled, and performed routine maintenance from reveille until the noon meal. In the afternoon, they had the opportunity to study one of three vocational subjects: automotive mechanics, music, or clerical skills. Lejeune's plan attracted immediate support, both from within and outside the corps.[1]

Enlisted marines warmed to a training scheme that seemed to have long-range utility. Moralistic reformers encouraged any plan that appeared to improve the lot of the lower ranks. The egalitarian secretary of the navy, Josephus Daniels, supported Lejeune's program enthusiastically. After each visit to Quantico, he returned to Washington trumpeting Lejeune's accomplishments. In a euphoric personal note, Lejeune claimed as a goal the establishment of Quantico as the Fort Leavenworth of the Marine Corps, apparently planning to include the education of his officers in his reforms. While the bond between Daniels and Lejeune grew stronger, the personal and professional relationship between the secretary of the navy and the twelfth commandant of the Marine Corps deteriorated rapidly. Although the canny Daniels grew increasingly wary and combative in his professional relationship with Barnett, he continued to prepare and sign fitness reports on him that ranged in the "excellent to outstanding" category. No matter what inflated reports Daniels might write on Barnett, however, he concluded that the twelfth commandant had to go; Lejeune would replace him.[2]

On 20 September 1919, Lejeune received a telephone message requesting that he report to Daniels's office. After an exchange of pleasantries, the secretary abruptly changed his manner of speaking. Daniels became very grave, expressing concern over the state of the corps. The secretary related the circumstances surrounding the reappointment to second terms in office both for Barnett as commandant and the navy's bureau chiefs in 1918. Had it not been for the war, the officers' terms would have ended; reappointment was not possible under the policy of single four-year terms or the "single-oak" scheme advocated by Daniels. Because of the war, Daniels set aside his rigid administrative mandate and reappointed everyone. Later, he claimed that the bureau chiefs and commandant all understood that they would leave office once the war had ended. Now that it had, the secretary of the navy dusted off his old edict.[3]

Charging Lejeune with strictest confidence, Daniels revealed that he intended to ask for Barnett's resignation as commandant as soon as he had seen President Wilson and obtained his approval; moreover, Daniels intended to nominate Lejeune as the new commandant of the Marine Corps. Stunned, Lejeune walked outside to his car to join Butler for the return to Quantico. To his surprise and dismay, he learned that his earnest subordinate already knew of the plan through his congressman father. The plan— related to Lejeune "in strictest confidence"—began to take on the characteristics of an unsavory cabal. The elder Butler encouraged Daniels, recommending Lejeune as the next commandant in the strongest possible terms. Daniels, in turn, hoped for Smedley D. Butler to succeed Lejeune at the helm of the corps—presumably after a single four-year term of office. Lejeune had expected to become the next commandant of the Marine Corps, but not until Barnett's second term ended in 1922. A year after that, Barnett reached mandatory retirement age.[4]

The commandant of the Marine Corps that Josephus Daniels hoped to oust deserved better treatment from the government that he served so faithfully. After graduating with the Naval Academy class of 1881, Barnett's career followed a pattern typical of Marine Corps officers in the nineteenth century: sea duty in command of a detachment of marines in one of the navy's ships, alternating with tours in a barracks at a navy yard. From the date

of Barnett's commission in 1883 and Lejeune's in 1890 through
the period of the Spanish-American War, both officers performed
similar duties, with Barnett probably accumulating the better
service record; however, their life-styles differed considerably.[5]

Like many of his contemporaries, Barnett made a conscious
decision to forego marriage as a junior officer because of the lengthy
family separations occasioned by tours of duty at sea. A handsome young man with polished manners, Barnett earned a deserved
reputation as a "dandy" or "lady's man" by the time he achieved
his majority. Because of increasing commitments for leathernecks
in expeditionary missions following the Spanish-American War,
field-grade officers began serving overseas. Barnett continued to
put off marriage because of the likely family separations. All of
his logic went askew, however, when he met Lelia Montague
Gordon in 1907.[6]

Still in mourning for the death of her first husband, a wealthy
and prominent Virginia politician, Mrs. Basil Gordon was coaxed
by friends out of her fashionable home in DuPont Circle to
attend a dinner dance at the Washington Navy Yard. There she
met Barnett, the commanding officer of the Marine Barracks.
Smitten, the confirmed bachelor launched a campaign to gain
her hand. Although pressing his case with the determination
characteristic of a leatherneck, Mrs. Gordon refused to respond
to his proposal of marriage. Meanwhile, the beautiful and wealthy
widow gathered an impressive number of suitors from among the
capital's eligible bachelors, including several titled European
diplomats.

Undaunted, Barnett made inroads with daily deliveries of flow-
ers and by charming Mrs. Gordon's three small children. Barnett
finally obtained the acceptance he sought following notification
from the commandant that he would soon receive orders overseas.
In conference with Major General George F. Elliott, Barnett
learned that his choices lay between commanding the Marine
Corps Legation Guard in Beijing or assignment as the Marine
Corps officer to accompany the "great white fleet" around the

world. Confronting Mrs. Gordon, Barnett pressed for an answer
to his proposal: marry him now or he would sail with the fleet.
The crafty Elliott told Barnett that any woman would jump at the
opportunity to see China. Perhaps the commandant knew his
women, because the following month the couple exchanged vows
in a Baltimore church. A thoughtful Elliott sent part of the Marine
Corps band.[7]

The three years that the Barnetts enjoyed in China contrast
sharply to the period that the Lejeunes endured in the Philippines,
shopping for themselves in native markets and surviving in a
harsh tropical climate. The Barnetts lived very well, as did most
foreign diplomats and military officers in imperial China. Surrounded by a platoon of Chinese servants, Mrs. Barnett quickly
gained the reputation of being the most sparkling and gracious
hostess in the foreign legation. A woman with ambition and
drive, in the next decade she would propel her husband into and
out of the commandancy; in the process, Lelia Montague Barnett
would cause Lejeune no end of worry.[8]

At this juncture in their respective careers, Lejeune and Barnett appeared to be on separate paths. While Barnett had just as
much sea duty and overseas time, his uniforms bore few powder
burns or tropical sweat stains. Barnett's life-style, first as a young
blood and then upon marrying into inherited wealth, contrasted
sharply with the conservative and strongly Episcopalian Lejeune
sitting upright at the dinner table leading his family in prayer. As
Naval Academy graduates, both officers appreciated the importance of keeping the corps tied with the mission of the navy and
in support of the fleet—something that Butler never could or
would accept. Lejeune and Barnett used the old school tie to
their own advantage during their respective careers and for the
good of the Marine Corps. For the most part, however, their
paths and careers rarely crossed until they came into contention
for the commandancy.

Although Lejeune submitted his name for consideration in
1910, he presented a weak case for the corps' highest post. Given

the number of qualified colonels, only extraordinary circumstances could cause Secretary of the Navy George von Lengerke
Meyer to select a lieutenant colonel rather than a colonel from
among the line officers. Major General William P. Biddle—the
successful candidate—fared well under the Taft administration,
gaining a reputation as an unobtrusive albeit lethargic administrator. With the troublesome Elliott in retirement, Meyer paid
scant attention to the affairs of the Marine Corps for the remainder of his tenure as secretary of the navy.[9]

When the Democrats took the White House in 1912, it took
Biddle—known by the unkind sobriquet "Sitting Bull" because of
a propensity to spend most of the day resting his ample girth in a
padded officer chair—less than a year to see the advantages of
retirement. As in the Taft years, the choice of President Woodrow Wilson for a new commandant of the Marine Corps was
influenced by partisan politics. This time, a craftier than usual
politician in the person of Secretary of the Navy Josephus Daniels arbitrated the decision. Daniels had come to his office
convinced that the administration of the naval services demanded
firm, steady civilian leadership. A North Carolina newspaper
editor and party loyalist, Daniels satisfied Wilson's requirement
for an articulate spokesman for the New South, Prohibition,
progressive reforms, and religious fundamentalism. The new secretary of the navy brought with him a propensity to meddle in
internal administrative affairs and a Machiavellian streak as a
political schemer.[10]

Senator John Weeks lobbied hard for Barnett, his Naval Academy roommate. Barnett had a good record, but the secretary
thought him lacking in drive and energy. Waller's case reappeared,
this time with renewed vigor; thirty-one Democrats in the Senate
signed a petition to President Wilson urging the appointment of
the veteran campaigner. While no one disputed Waller's reputation as a tough and capable Marine Corps officer, Daniels sought
an educated officer free of political controversy. Another veteran
campaigner, Lincoln Karmany, lost out as well. Daniels's diary

entry for 13 November 1913 leaves no doubt as to why: "Karmody [*sic*]—divorced."[11]

Thus, Secretary Daniels considered only two of the candidates for commandant of the Marine Corps in 1913 to be acceptable: Barnett, over whom Daniels harbored reservations; and Lejeune, a contender too junior in rank. While the leading aspirants for the corps' highest post enjoyed powerful political support, Lejeune had few cards to call or present. Senator Estophinal of Louisiana lent his shoulder to the problem, as did old friends from the class of 1888. None of Lejeune's supporters had significant political clout, however. The name of Lejeune's Naval Academy classmate Eli K. Cole even appeared briefly among the list of candidates, but Daniels disqualified him as well because of rank.

In his memoirs Daniels claimed to have considered Lejeune the best-qualified candidate, but he felt compelled to bow to service custom and select the more senior Barnett. Observers of Department of the Navy politics believed that no one except the corps' colonels were being considered seriously for the commandancy. The secretary raised no false hopes for Lejeune during his interview in the late fall of 1913. He left the office of the secretary of the navy convinced that the new commandant would be Waller or Barnett. For Lejeune's old friend Smedley D. Butler, the selection left only one choice.[12]

At this point in his colorful career, Butler enjoyed a reputation for courage and decisiveness under fire, hard work, a willingness to accept arduous duty in inhospitable climes, and an outspoken temperament prone to hyperbole. Dreadfully anti-navy and anti-Naval Academy, his pungent observations both amused and horrified listeners who considered the feisty Quaker a bit eccentric. His letters home were meant to influence Congressman Butler, no matter to whom they were addressed. The following excerpts from Butler's correspondence, written during his tour in Haiti, are revealing:

Really, these Navy people are not fit to be put ashore . . . now this sort of warfare will pass and gain you much credit and high marks in a million dollar war college . . . I am simply the very subservient chief of a nigger police force. Some day, my grandchildren will be subjected to the remark "where was your grandfather during the big war?" And they will have to hide their heads in shame and either lie or say "he was a policeman in the service of a foreign black republic."[13]

By the time of deliberations to select a successor to Biddle, Butler had hitched his coattails to Waller. The frenetic campaigner had become convinced that the future of the Marine Corps lay in expeditionary duties in support of America's brief period of neocolonialism. In his view, only a seasoned combat veteran should lead an elite body of fighting men such as the U.S. Marine Corps. Twenty-five years later, Butler could still exclaim: "Waller was the greatest soldier I have ever known . . . Waller might have liked to talk about himself, but he had plenty to talk about."[14]

Butler's letters to his wife concerning the selection of Barnett reveal just how strongly he felt: "I am afraid Colonel Waller has absolutely no chance . . . This is an awful mess." Less than a week later, he sputtered: "If Colonel Waller could only win them over—thing[s] would be exactly as [they] should be."[15] Although Butler intended for his wife to show his letters around the family, his histrionics apparently had scant influence on Congressman Butler at this point. The elder Butler seems to have had little or no say in the choice of Barnett, leaving his more powerful colleagues to decide the issue. Thus, if not exactly the epitome of a "soldier of the sea," George Barnett, a fellow Navy Academy graduate seven years senior to Lejeune, became the twelfth commandant in February 1914.

For hardy campaigners like Butler, the selection of a Naval Academy graduate with a minimum of foreign duty or sea service in his record meant the eclipse of their hopes for the future leadership of the Marine Corps. Butler's outburst, typically emotional, probably embodied the conclusion of many leatherneck officers who had attached their professional stars to a Marine

Corps embodying the colonial infantry role: "All my hard work has been thrown away and I am broken. The only hope [was] Colonel Waller's appointment."[16]

A capable administrator, Barnett proved a skillful player of Capitol Hill politics. With the aid of his indefatigable wife, one of Washington society's most prominent members, the new commandant gave the corps' highest post a luster it lacked for many years. Knowing full well how the staff versus line controversy had tainted the Marine Corps during the tenure of Major General Commandant Elliott, Barnett chose to let his three principal staff officers—Colonel Charles H. Lauchheimer, the adjutant and inspector; Colonel Charles L. McCawley, the quartermaster and son of a former commandant; and Colonel George Richards, the paymaster—continue in office with little interference from the commandant.

Each of the three staff officers created his own fief with a small staff of assistants and clerks. The new commandant found it prudent to leave their organizations intact. The staff officers enjoyed appointments by congressional fiat, and the incumbents had cultivated a wide circle of important political friends and supporters. Only Lejeune as the assistant to the commandant of the Marine Corps effected any small change, and that in the assignment of two bright young majors, Earl H. "Pete" Ellis and Ralph Keyser, to the office of the commandant to perform staff duties. Lejeune supervised the functions of Headquarters Marine Corps as de facto chief of staff. Mostly, Barnett spent his days testifying on Capitol Hill or in conferences with the secretary of the navy. He sought to gain personnel increases for a Marine Corps assigned additional responsibilities at a more rapid pace than at any time in its history. But in the process of arguing for more marines, Barnett began to alienate Daniels.

In his last annual report before retiring, Biddle had underscored the inability of the corps to meet a growing number of commitments with such a small force. On 30 June 1913, the Marine Corps reported a strength of 331 officers and 9,625 enlisted men; a year later, the numbers had increased only slightly to 336 officers and 10,386 enlisted men. Besides the brigade of leather-necks in the Philippines and the Legation Guard in China, traditional detachments serving in the navy's ships still demanded a large share of personnel assets. During Barnett's first term as commandant, unsettled political developments in the Domini-can Republic and Haiti resulted in deployment of two additional brigades to the Caribbean. After April 1917, a commitment to the American Expeditionary Forces in France devoured personnel assets at a furious pace. In the negotiations over requests for increases, Daniels supported Barnett, but always with a skeptical eye. Often, Barnett used the proposed legislation to argue for an increase in the number of general officers. In 1918, he and his political supporters raised the ante to dizzying heights. [17]

When the Senate Naval Affairs Committee considered appro-priations for fiscal year 1919, Barnett's friends among the Republicans in the upper house attached a proviso calling for the promotion of the commandant of the Marine Corps to the rank of lieutenant general and the elevation of the three principal staff officers to major general. Barnett claimed later to have had noth-ing to do with the genesis of the proposal. He denied vehemently that his supporters planned to prevent passage of the naval appro-priations bill if legislation calling for the promotions did not pass. Despite Barnett's disclaimer, he used all the political influence available to gain passage of legislation affecting the rank of the commandant of the Marine Corps. As Lejeune prepared to board his troopship for France, he received a telegram from Barnett asking for political support to ensure passage of the bill. [18]

The naval appropriations bill passed back and forth between the House and the Senate without either side giving on the issue of promotions. Senior Navy officers expressed outrage over a plan that elevated the commandant of the Marine Corps to the level of the chief of naval operations and his principal staff officers to that of the bureau chiefs. "As you may judge, there is great opposition to this in the line and staff of the Navy for it gives great prominence to small accomplishments," snarled one admiral.[19]

Smedley Butler cast his opinion into the fray as well in a letter home, asking his father to oppose passage of the legislation. Although the frenetic Butler harbored a deep disgust for Barnett, believing that it was the commandant himself who prevented his assignment to the Fourth Brigade (Marine), AEF, he had always denigrated the staff officers of the Marine Corps. On 27 June 1918, Congressman Butler rose in the House of Representatives to denounce the legislation. Armed with the knowledge that Secretary Daniels opposed the promotions as well, the fiery Quaker condemned the increases in rank. Pointing in the visitors gallery, he implied that they were "rocking-chair warriors" and added: "When the rewards are handed out for service in the war, they will go to the men that have earned them, and not to those who may perchance be favored by certain beautiful social surroundings in the capital of the United States."[20]

Those in attendance did not fail to appreciate the reference to Mrs. Barnett. Smelling blood, another congressman jumped up to suggest that Barnett be court-martialed for going over Daniels's head to seek a promotion. Earlier, Congressman Butler shared his outrage in a personal letter to Assistant Secretary of the Navy Franklin D. Roosevelt, speaking of "the selfishness of these men who are endeavoring to take care of themselves only."[21]

Both the elder Butler and Daniels received indications from Barnett's Republican supporters that failure to pass the general officer promotion portion of the naval appropriations bill would result in defeat of the entire legislative package. Afterward, Daniels rebuked Barnett for his bureaucratic ploy; the commandant denied any direct involvement. But Barnett's personal papers and his eleventh-hour telegram to Lejeune contradict his disclaimer. And despite Daniels's claim to be outraged over Barnett's machinations, his fitness reports on the commandant failed to reflect anything untoward: "An able and capable officer, a wise advisor, and competent executive. As Major General Commandant of the Marine Corps during the period of the war, he has shown initiative and ability of a high order."[22]

Nevertheless, the wily secretary had crossed swords with his senior Marine Corps officer over another matter that added to the poison of their professional relationship. Daniels always maintained that he secured Barnett's promise to step down when requested. Moreover, he insisted that his elevation of Lejeune to the commandancy had been his alone. Years later, Daniels wrote to Lejeune comforting him over fears that Mrs. Barnett intended to publish a magazine article suggesting that a cabal composed of Daniels, Lejeune, and the Butlers brought about her husband's professional ruin. Daniels remained firm in his denial: "You [Lejeune] never requested the appointment, nobody ever offered it to you, and no influence was ever brought to bear upon me to appoint you. . . . Barnett promised to resign when requested . . . 'I am an officer and a gentleman and I would not remain in office a minute when either you or the President wanted to make a change.' "[23]

When Barnett's four-year appointment drew to a close in February 1918, Daniels summoned the commandant to his office and offered to reappoint him for another term despite the "single-oak" policy limiting naval officers to one tour of duty in Washington. Given the exigencies of the war, Daniels's decision to retain Barnett made good sense. At the meeting, however, the secretary of the navy requested an undated letter of resignation and indicated that he would submit it to President Wilson once the war was over.

Barnett bridled at the request and reminded the shrewd ex-newsman that all military and naval officers served at the pleasure of the president. When he no longer needed or wanted such services, the president had only to so indicate. Sensing a stubborn streak in a subordinate usually willing and subservient, Daniels backed down quickly. At a subsequent meeting, he told the commandant to forget the matter; however, in his published memoirs, Daniels claimed to have secured Barnett's promise to step down after the war.

Because no other officials witnessed either meeting, the self-serving statements of both Daniels and Barnett must be taken in their proper context. In any event, Barnett's maladroit attempt to gain a promotion through a rider to an annual naval appropriation bill and his refusal to sign an undated letter of resignation fueled Daniels's suspicions further about his commandant of the Marine Corps. Sadly, the efficient commandant appeared to be more and more just another self-serving bureaucrat in uniform. Barnett seemed to typify the type of naval officer that Daniels hoped to remove from the Department of the Navy when he received his portfolio in 1913. Worse, Barnett's socially prominent wife appeared to contribute to the poison of the relationship.[24]

By 1920, Lelia Montague Barnett had a reputation equaled by few among the capital's social elite. She was known to set one of the best tables in Washington, and few of its prominent residents declined her hospitality or the opportunity to witness Mrs. Barnett's witty repartee at the expense of pretentious politicians. All too often, the pompous Daniels appeared as the butt of her humor. Early in his tenure in office, the moralistic secretary promulgated several edicts that he thought might elevate the moral tone of the naval services. Naval officers of that generation never forgave Daniels for corking the bottles in the officers' messes aboard ships. When Daniels decreed that alcoholic beverages would no longer be served at official dinners at navy or Marine Corps stations, he garnered the swift attention of Lelia Montague Barnett.

Unwilling to imagine a formal dinner without aperitifs and wines, she obtained Daniels's permission to use alcoholic beverages in cooking. Then, she prepared a meal that the secretary of the navy would not likely forget. Daniels and the Barnetts' other guests sat down to a several-course dinner at the historic home of the commandants of the Marine Corps, "Eighth and Eye." Each dish of the memorable meal had been laced heavily with alcohol:

grapefruit doused with two cocktails, soup consisting most of sherry, terrapin in Madeira sauce, a roast beef, champagne frappe, and brandied peaches for dessert. Pressing a second peach on the senator sitting on her left, Mrs. Barnett received a grave reply: "Madame, I really can't eat another drop."[25]

Although the stuffy Daniels laughed along with the other guests at the joke played on him, the humor had a hollow ring to it. Clearly, Mrs. Barnett contributed to her husband's demise by irritating the secretary of the navy. Daniels and his wife scorned inherited wealth and socialites such as the commandant's spouse. More than one society columnist suggested that Mrs. Barnett snubbed both Mrs. Daniels and the second Mrs. Wilson. Uncomfortable social exchanges among the protagonists in the drama, such as Mrs. Barnett's baiting of Daniels, may have reinforced the decision to oust the twelfth commandant of the Marine Corps.

Journalists delighted in poking fun at the pompous Daniels and his propensity for involving himself in the intimate details of the navy and Marine Corps. On the heels of Daniels's selection of William S. Benson as the first chief of naval operations, rather than the more popular and better-qualified Bradley A. Fiske, a member of the Fourth Estate lashed out: "We could make shift to live under a debauchee or a tyrant, but to be ruled by a busybody is more than nature can stand."[26]

After the stormy events of 1918, Daniels grew increasingly suspicious of Barnett and began to scrutinize the routine correspondence leaving the office of the commandant. Although the two officials occupied offices in the same building, formal letters passed back and forth just as if they worked miles apart. Many of the letters between the two became puerile memoranda in which Daniels might inquire as to why Barnett ordered more field coats and blankets, only to have the commandant respond testily that Quantico experienced colder temperatures than Parris Island. Through one such exchange over supply matters, Daniels revoked the authority of Headquarters Marine Corps to make routine requisitions without sending the purchase requests to his office for approval. A want of faith extended to personnel matters, and Lejeune sometimes became involved.[27]

Daniels's lack of trust and confidence in Barnett even extended to the commandant's administration of minor personnel matters. Rear Admiral William B. Caperton's son, a Marine Corps second lieutenant, ended an unwise marriage in the divorce courts, and the incident came to the attention of the moralistic Daniels when the young man fell behind in his alimony payments. Learning of the matter, Barnett sent the recalcitrant a scorching letter of admonition, ordering him to send the required funds through the commandant's office to ensure compliance with the edict of the divorce. Meanwhile, Daniels summoned Lejeune from Quantico and asked him to inquire "discreetly" into the affair, suggesting that he could not trust Barnett in the matter because Caperton was Mrs. Barnett's nephew.[28]

Although Lejeune met with the Danielses socially several times after that meeting in the fall of 1919, the subject of Barnett's dismissal never came up again. The secretary continued to indicate an unwillingness to bother Woodrow Wilson because of the president's ill health. In May 1920, Lejeune received a summons to meet with Daniels at his office in Washington. At first, the secretary asked only for a recommendation of a brigadier general to receive the vacancy resulting from Major General Waller's decision to retire. That Daniels would seek out the opinion of Barnett's subordinate on such an important matter reveals just how little he thought of the commandant by then. Lejeune recommended Wendell C. Neville—hardly a surprise, given Neville's superlative performance in command of the Fourth Brigade (Marine), AEF. Then, Daniels revealed the real reason why he had summoned Lejeune.

Barnett's request for an inspection tour of Marine Corps installations on the West Coast received unusually speedy approval. The secretary of the navy wanted the commandant out of town while he undertook his ouster. Pompous as usual and brimming confidence in his official position, Daniels intended to clear his plan with the ailing President Wilson in a White House meeting before acting. Although Lejeune claimed later to be surprised at the information, a witness came forward later to provide evidence that Lejeune and Butler knew of Daniels's plan even before the secretary disclosed it. According to this account, the political machinations of the secretary of the navy resulted in heated discussions at Quantico earlier that spring.[29]

The informant—a former Marine Corps officer on duty at the post headquarters on successive Sundays—claimed to have overhead Lejeune and Butler discussing the forthcoming relief of Barnett. In the first exchange, Butler merely told Lejeune that Daniels had informed his father of the proposed date of Barnett's dismissal; everything seemed to be progressing as planned. In the second conversation, Lejeune appeared to object to the duplicity involved. Butler dismissed Lejeune's protestations and referred to Barnett as a "god-damned old fogy who had outworn his usefulness . . . who had alienated congressional [support for the Marine Corps] by trying to gain a promotion for himself."[30]

Butler added that Mrs. Daniels grew increasingly jealous of Mrs. Barnett's social position. Although Lejeune continued to express his reservations over the unprofessional conduct of the matter, Butler brought the conversation to a close by suggesting that if Lejeune did not want the commandancy, then someone else would be found. In any event, Barnett had to go! Events moved quickly after Daniels made his decision to act. On 10 June 1920, he recorded in his diary: "Barnett returned from the Pacific. It is a rather troublesome problem on my hands."[31]

On Tuesday, 17 June, he spoke to President Wilson, informing him that under the terms of Barnett's reappointment in 1918, the commandant of the Marine Corps agreed to step down. Barnett had made no such pledge and Daniels knew it. No evidence exists to support Daniels's contention that he met with Barnett during the period immediately preceding the conference with the president. The shrewd secretary thought that by clearing his

actions with the Oval office he had smooth sailing for his Byzan-
tine drama; however, an interested observer witnessed the meeting
between Daniels and Wilson.[32]

Daniels dictated a letter informing Barnett of his removal from
office, effective 30 June 1920. In it, Daniels asked that the commandant indicate a preference to retire as a major general or to
remain on active duty in his permanent rank of brigadier general.
The secretary left town for the week, claiming to have official
business. A messenger delivered the curt dismissal to Barnett, ill
at home with influenza. The arrival of the unexpected letter
roused him from a sickbed.

Arriving at 1:30 P.M. on Friday, 20 June 1920, the messenger
told Barnett that he had been instructed to wait until 4:30 for a
reply. Later, the commandant noted rather ruefully that a discharged servant usually receives thirty days' notice! After discussing
the affair with his wife, Barnett decided not to go quietly but
instead to fight the dismissal order. In response to Daniels's letter,
Barnett opted to stay on active duty; asked for promotion to
major general, because with Lejeune's elevation to the commandancy a vacancy in that rank became available; and requested
assignment to command the base at Quantico. The secretary
anticipated none of Barnett's responses, expecting him to march
proudly off into retirement as an honorable old soldier of the sea.

Even the scheming Daniels could not have predicted the maelstrom to follow. The evening of the disclosure of the dismissal,
the Barnetts held a council of war at their home. Rear Admiral
Cary Grayson, President Wilson's personal physician, joined his
friends to reveal what he had witnessed earlier in the week.
Pledged to secrecy, Barnett took the name of his informant to the
grave; however, Mrs. Barnett disclosed Grayson's participation in
the table of contents to her unpublished autobiography.[33]

Daniels hoped that the commandant would bow out gracefully
and accept Lejeune as his successor, but Barnett instead vowed to
seek redress. First, he wrote directly to President Wilson complaining of his treatment at Daniels's hands. But in compliance

with the punctilios of military and naval correspondence, Barnett's letter went via Daniels. When Wilson's secretary queried Daniels on the matter, the wily secretary of the navy—still out of town— cabled a request that no action be taken until his return to Washington. Clearly, Daniels hoped by then that the uproar would have subsided. When it did not, he added a strong recommendation of disapproval to Barnett's letter.[34]

The chief of naval operations, Admiral William S. Benson, advised Barnett to seek an audience with Daniels immediately and put the rancor to rest. Although appearing to be Barnett's counselor and friend, Benson applauded Lejeune's appointment. Barnett's constant pleas for expansion of the Marine Corps had irritated Benson as well as Daniels because the chief of naval operations believed strongly that leatherneck forces should be used exclusively in support of the fleet. Ignoring Benson's advice, Barnett turned to his powerful Republican friends in hope of blocking Lejeune's confirmation in the Senate. Finally, the ousted commandant endured a painful meeting in Daniels's office.[35]

By the time that Barnett met with the secretary to discuss his removal from office, Daniels knew that a powerful array of Senate Republicans had lined up to support the former commandant. Even a Democrat, Claude A. Swanson, joined Senators John Weeks and Henry Cabot Lodge in protesting Daniels's actions. Barnett asked Daniels several embarrassing questions in their final meeting: If the secretary thought so little of him, why had he continued to submit outstanding fitness reports on his performance of duty? Why had Daniels recommended him for the Distinguished Service Medal? Furthermore, in all of their recent meetings, Daniels had never expressed any displeasure with his performance. Clearly, Daniels had no real grievance against Barnett and the ousted commandant knew it. Despite his later protestations, Daniels considered Barnett a capable and efficient administrator. In an undated memorandum, buried in Daniels's files, he revealed his candid evaluation of Barnett: "He stands equal to the ablest men who have been at the head of this important branch of the service."[36]

While Barnett claimed to be shocked and surprised over his dismissal, ample correspondence among his personal papers indicates that rumors of the ouster reached his ears months before the arrival of Daniels's letter of dismissal. Clearly embarrassed, the secretary cut short the encounter with a curt dismissal. Daniels might have felt more comfortable knowing of the almost universal acceptance of Lejeune's appointment by those whose opinion counted most—those who wore forest green or navy blue.

Among senior Marine Corps officers, only Joseph H. Pendleton supported Barnett. The array of notable leathernecks who expressed approval of Lejeune's appointment included Waller, Cole, Butler, Ben H. Fuller, Harry Lee, Charles H. Lyman, and John Russell. Former commandants Biddle and Elliott chimed in with warm letters of support as did several navy flag officers, including William S. Benson and Cary Grayson—the same Grayson whom the Barnetts considered a close friend. Congressman Butler exuded warmth and admiration: "Take it from me that we are soon going to have a Marine Corps and it is now commanded by a real soldier," adding, "My, I am pleased with your appointment & mean to assist you in any way to make your administration a great success . . . the right thing has been done. Tell me always when I can serve you."[37]

In contrast, the letters of regret received by Barnett contained mostly condolences and offered little encouragement in the way of redress. Many of the officers who wrote to Barnett deploring his unfair treatment, such as Benson, Fuller, and Lyman, dashed off congratulations to Lejeune at the same time. Admiral Benson, whom Barnett considered a confidant in the brouhaha, opined to Lejeune that it "should have taken place a year ago, but better late than never."[38]

While Daniels appeared smug and sure of his decision to replace Barnett, he may have been motivated by the uncertain political future of the Democratic party in the upcoming presidential election. A war-weary America had experienced enough of Woodrow Wilson's great crusade. The refusal of the Senate to ratify the Treaty of Versailles underscored the feelings of many citizens. Despite public optimism, most Democrats felt that their party stood no chance to keep the White House. As a lifelong Democrat and close friend of Daniels, Lejeune could easily be squeezed out of the running for the commandancy because of partisan politics. Daniels chose to give Lejeune the post he deserved while it was in his power to do so. In public, however, the secretary of the navy continued to espouse his belief that Lejeune deserved the commandancy because of his superlative record of tropical campaigning and wartime service in France: "I always gave preference to men who won distinction at the cannon's mouth . . . I always regard General Lejeune as the ablest soldier in the United States. He is dedicated to the Marine Corps, which he has brought to the highest standard of efficiency and I would rather act upon his judgement about Marine [Corps] matters than upon my own or anyone else's."[39]

Democrats took control of the Senate in the elections of 1920. Ironically, Barnett's best friend—a Republican—offered a logical solution to put the controversy to rest. Barnett's Naval Academy roommate and soon to be secretary of war attempted to gather support on Capitol Hill for the ousted commandant. Increasingly, he found that support and sympathy were lacking. Most Americans felt obliged to reward veterans of the fighting in France, not Washington bureaucrats in uniform like Barnett. Moreover, Barnett and his Republican supporters dealt with an unbending official in the person of Daniels, angry because Barnett had not stepped down gracefully. Critics could detect no blemishes on Lejeune's record to brandish against his appointment. In thoughtful letters to Barnett and his wife, Weeks suggested a compromise; ironically, Lejeune proposed the same solution to Daniels.[40]

Six days after the secretary informed Barnett of his dismissal and released the news to the press, Lejeune wrote to Daniels with a possible solution. He told the secretary that he had

Lejeune receiving the Distinguished Service Medal from General John J. Pershing, Germany, 1919. Courtesy of the Marine Corps Historical Center.

Major General Charles P. Summerall, Brigadier General Smedley D. Butler, and Lejeune, Camp Pontanezen, France, 1919. Courtesy of the Marine Corps Historical Center.

Lejeune and Brigadier General Wendell C. Neville on the transport *Henderson*, returning from France in 1919. Courtesy of the Marine Corps Historical Center.

Major General Commandant John A. Lejeune, San Diego, 1923.
Courtesy of the Naval Historical Center.

Lejeune, Secretary of the Navy Edwin Denby, and Captain William A. Moffett at the Great Lakes Naval Training Center in the early 1920s. Courtesy of the Marine Corps Historical Center.

Lejeune with Brigadier General Smedley D. Butler at a baseball game, Quantico, 1922. Courtesy of the Marine Corps Historical Center.

Lejeune and the faculty, Virginia Military Institute, early 1930s. Courtesy of the Marine Corps Historical Center.

The funeral cortege of Lieutenant General John A. Lejeune assembles along Constitution Avenue prior to moving to Arlington National Cemetery, 20 November 1942. Courtesy of the Marine Corps Historical Center.

considered the best interests of the Marine Corps and wished to eliminate factionalism: "I am proposing for your consideration the appointment of B [Barnett] to the rank of major general-
. . . this appointment would be an extremely generous act on your part and would heal his wounds . . . I am also proposing for your consideration a plan for B's [Barnett's] assignment as an assistant [to the commandant] on the west coast."[41] Despite Neville's popularity and his distinguished record in World War I, most observers concluded that Daniels' nomination of the veteran campaigner for a second star—instead of Barnett—was spiteful and petulant.

Righteous in his wrath, Daniels submitted Neville's name for the vacant major general's appointment instead of Barnett's. He did approve the former commandant's assignment to a newly created post in San Francisco, however. Obviously, having the troublesome Barnett out of town at a distant post far from his Republican supporters appeared advantageous to both Daniels and Lejeune. As the secretary and his protégé marched through the controversy created by Barnett's abrupt removal from the commandancy, the most painful encounter of all remained for Lejeune.

At 11:40 A.M. on 30 June 1920, Lejeune reported to Barnett's office at Headquarters Marine Corps. Both of the incumbent's aides-de-camp remembered the embarrassing and uncomfortable scene. Clifton B. Cates recalled that Barnett merely asked Lejeune why he failed to inform him of the plot. Lejeune replied lamely that "his hands were tied." Charles I. Murray remembered a more acerbic exchange in which Barnett ordered Lejeune to stand at attention in front of his desk. The outgoing commandant delivered a stern tongue-lashing, charging his subordinate with disloyalty and unprofessional conduct and being a false friend. Once again, according to Murray, Lejeune repeated that "his hands were tied." At twelve o'clock, Barnett ordered an aide-de-camp to remove one star from his shoulders. The twelfth commandant marched out of the office, without so much as a handshake with Lejeune, and left the adjutant and inspector to administer the oath of office to Lejeune.[42]

While the Butlers—father and son—reveled in the removal of an officer they both had grown to dislike to the point of blind hatred, Smedley D. Butler had to be as close to the scene as possible. On the last day of Barnett's commandancy, the younger Butler and his aide-de-camp waited outside Headquarters Marine Corps in a staff car to have the pleasure of seeing a demoted and humiliated Barnett walk out of the building. To a close friend, Major Alexander A. Vandegrift, Butler chortled: "The Barnett faction has been making a big noise and yelling for vengeance, which vengeance I do not believe they will get."[43]

Mrs. Barnett never forgave those who had destroyed her husband's career and tarnished her social position in the process. Initially, she showered government officials with her version of the affair. Her polite notes detailing the events leading to Barnett's dismissal can be found among the personal papers of almost any public figure of the era. On the eve of his relief, she held a farewell party that left no doubt as to her feelings. When the guests arrived at "Eighth and Eye," movers had already taken all of their possessions to Wakefield Manor. The traditional artifacts belonging to the historic residence had been placed in closets. Only one thing remained on the bare walls—a framed photograph of Daniels affectionately inscribed to Barnett. None of the guests missed the point.[44]

In 1932, Lelia Montague Barnett produced the two letters from a former Marine Corps officer purporting to shed new evidence on the sorry events of 1920. Excited with her discovery, Mrs. Barnett corresponded immediately with Lejeune, threatening to have the revealing and offending material published: "You not only had knowledge of the plot to remove General Barnett but . . . you took part in it and finally gave in to General Butler. . . . The thing that was done helped kill my husband. . . . He loved you as a friend . . . [He] bore that pain [of his dismissal] to his death."[45] Alarmed, Lejeune notified Daniels immediately.

The former secretary of the navy took pains to calm his fears and reminded his former protégé that Lejeune's elevation to the commandancy had been his alone. Despite Mrs. Barnett's revelation of material purporting the existence of a cabal to remove her husband from office, the overriding evidence suggests that the Machiavellian Daniels orchestrated the ouster himself.

Two years later, one of Lejeune's former aides-de-camp, Captain John Craige, wrote an account of the Marine Corps in Haiti. The author suggested Barnett contrived to spend an entire career in the Marine Corps without hearing a shot fired in anger: "He was a rocking chair warrior par excellence." The book, *Cannibal Cousins* (New York, 1934), implied further that the brains and drive behind Barnett's commandancy had been Charles H. Lauchheimer, the longtime adjutant and inspector. Mrs. Barnett began legal action to stop publication of the book. Upon the advice of her attorney, however, she dropped the matter. But Mrs. Barnett believed that Lejeune knew of the book and its offending passage, yet failed to correct his former subordinate. Two decades later, her worst enemy wrote his memoirs. In the second volume of his autobiography, Daniels recalled the events surrounding the ouster of Barnett and suggested that it had merely been a feeble attempt to kill the single-oak policy. In his memoir, Daniels chose to denigrate Mrs. Barnett. The former secretary of the navy claimed he discussed the affair with an admiral—most likely, Benson—who suggested that if Barnett had been an Indian, his name would have been "the man-afraid-of-his-wife."[46]

Again Mrs. Barnett's attorney advised against further legal action because her husband had been a public figure and not immune from criticism. To Lejeune's embarrassment, Mrs. Barnett refused to let the matter slip into the dustbin. She told and retold her version of the affair to anyone who would listen, to the point of becoming a bore on the subject. For the rest of her life, Smedley D. Butler could only be "Smelly Butler." Mrs. Barnett's eldest daughter, admittedly not particulary fond of Barnett, offered little sympathy for her mother. In her opinion, Barnett was "putty in her mother's fingers—she made him and she broke him."[47]

Even their old friend John Weeks found the constant harangue boring and oppressive. The new secretary of war shared a critical commentary with Secretary of the Navy Edwin H. Denby: "I have had a call this morning from our ubiquitous friend, Mrs. Barnett, who is anxious that in some address to be made of the Marines, some mention be made of General Barnett's conduct of the Marine Corps during the period of the war. If I did not feel so friendly to you I would not put a thing of this sort up to you, but I do submit it for your consideration and shall be perfectly content with whatever action you take."[48]

John Archer Lejeune took office as the thirteenth commandant of the Marine Corps and served by executive fiat into the fall. Barnett accepted the new post in San Francisco, but without a second star. Mrs. Barnett would have none of his exile and remained in Washington. Barnett refused to leave with his head bowed and continued to embarrass both Lejeune and Daniels with such public statements as "I love the Corps so much I shall remain on the active list performing any duty assigned me to the best of my ability."[49]

Mrs. Barnett would simply not give up, entreating public figures to assist her in seeking redress. Her letter to Daniels's former assistant Franklin D. Roosevelt is typical: "He [Barnett] had to stand quietly and see his rightful honors given to a Daniels favorite [Lejeune], a man who had already received his just share of preferment . . . If you had seen his eyes as we took his stars from his shoulders."[50]

For more than a decade, her infrequent public outbursts on this dreary subject served to alarm and embarrass Lejeune. More ominously, the Republicans took the White House in the elections of 1920. The Senate set aside all previous appointments by a lame-duck administration to await the pleasure of a new president. The machinations of Secretary Daniels, supported by Congressman Butler and his ambitious son, appeared to have come to naught.[51]

Notes

1. Charles A. Fleming, Robin A. Austin, and Charles A. Braley III, *Quantico: Cross-roads of the Marine Corps* (Washington: GPO, 1978), pp. 38–42; JAL to AL, 3 April 1920, reel 2, Lejeune MSS, Library of Congress; JAL to Josephus Daniels, [?] December 1919, container 88, reel 55, Daniels MSS, Library of Congress; and Earl H. Jenkins, "The New Marine Corps," *Marine Corps Gazette* 5 (September 1920): 254.

2. George Barnett, fitness reports, 1914–1920, Barnett's officer qualification record, Headquarters Marine Corps.

3. Josephus Daniels to Woodrow Wilson, 5 April 1913, and Wilson to Daniels, 14 May 1913, USMC 1899–1913 folder, container 531, Daniels MSS; Headquarters Marine Corps to the Secretary of the Navy, 8 October 1913, USMC September-December 1913 file, container 531, Daniels MSS; and Lejeune to CMC, [1935], reel 6, Lejeune MSS.

4. Lejeune to the CMC, [1935], reel 6, Lejeune MSS. Daniels's plans are revealed in Daniels to Franklin D. Roosevelt, 20 December 1934, container 95, reel 59, Daniels MSS. The original of Daniels's letter to Roosevelt cannot be located in the Roosevelt MSS, Hyde Park, New York.

5. Cf. George Barnett, "Soldier and Sailor Too," unpublished memoir, Barnett MSS; and JAL, *Reminiscences of a Marine*, pp. 93–242; cf. fitness reports, George Barnett and John A. Lejeune, officer qualification records, Headquarters Marine Corps. See also Josephus Daniels to files, [1915], subject file—Bureau Chiefs (1913–1915), container 549, Daniels MSS.

6. George Barnett to the Naval Academy Class of 1881, 23 February 1900, Fourth Report, Class of '81, Naval Academy archives. Cf. fitness reports, Barnett (1883–1898) and Lejeune (1890–1898), officer qualification records, Headquarters Marine Corps.

7. Lelia Gordon Lucas (Mrs. Barnett's daughter), interview with author, Huntley, Virginia, 7 June 1979.

8. Lelia Montague Barnett, "Command Performances," unpublished memoir, n.d., n.p., Lelia Montague Barnett MSS, Wakefield Manor, Huntley, Virginia.

9. Wayne A. Wiegand, "Patrician in the Progressive Era: a Biography of George von Lengerke Myer," (Carbondale, Ill.: diss., Southern Illinois University, 1975), pp. 110–15.

10. Lejeune to Commandant of the Marine Corps, [1935], reel 6, Lejeune MSS; Paolo E. Coletta, "George von Lengerke Meyer," in Coletta, ed., *American Secretaries of the Navy*, 2 vols. (Annapolis, Md.: Naval Institute Press, 1980), 1: 495–518; and Merrill L. Bartlett, "Secretary of the Navy Josephus Daniels and the Marine Corps, 1913–1921," in William B. Cogar, ed., *New Interpretations in Naval History: Selected Papers from the Eighth Naval History Symposium* (Annapolis, Md.: Naval Institute Press, 1989), pp. 190–208.

11. Cronon, ed., *The Cabinet Diaries of Josephus Daniels 1913–1921* (Lincoln: University of Nebraska Press, 1963), p. 53. See also Senator Claude A. Swanson to President Woodrow Wilson, 2 December 1913, container 531, Daniels MSS.

12. Josephus Daniels, *The Wilson Years: Years of Peace, 1910–1917* (Chapel Hill, N.C.: University of North Carolina Press, 1944), pp. 322–23; Louis McGill to Joseph H. Pendleton, 27 December 1913, folder 10, Pendleton MSS; and Victor Blue to Pendleton, 30 January 1914, folder 11, Pendleton MSS, MCHC.

13. Smedley D. Butler to his mother, 16 August 1915; to his father, 1 and 5 October 1916; and to his parents, 6 October 1917, Butler MSS, New Town Square, Pennsylvania.

14. Smedley D. Butler as told to Lowell Thomas, *Old Gimlet Eye: The Adventures of Smedley D. Butler* (New York: Farrar & Rinehart, 1933; reprint, Quantico: Marine Corps Association, 1981), pp. 36–37.

15. Smedley D. Butler to his wife, 5 February 1914, Butler MSS.

16. Smedley D. Butler to his wife, 31 January 1914, Butler MSS.

17. *Annual Reports of the Secretary of the Navy,* 1913–1917; and Jack Shulimson, "First to Fight: Marine Corps Expansion, 1914–1918," *Prologue* 8 (Spring 1978): 5–16.

18. Lejeune to the Commandant of the Marine Corps, [1935], reel 6, Lejeune MSS.

19. Leigh Palmer to William S. Sims, 29 May 1918, Sims MSS, Manuscripts Division, Library of Congress.

20. *Congressional Record,* House, 65th Cong., 2d sess., 27 June 1918, p. 8374. See also Barnett to Daniels, 28 June 1918, Barnett 1914–1918 file, container 64, Daniels MSS; and Lejeune to the Commandant of the Marine Corps, [1935], reel 6, Lejeune MSS.

21. Thomas S. Butler to Franklin D. Roosevelt, 27 April 1918, container 80, Roosevelt MSS. See also Smedley D. Butler as told to Lowell Thomas, *Old Gimlet Eye,* p. 243.

22. Barnett's fitness report, 1 April–30 September 1918, signed by Daniels. Barnett's officer qualification record, Headquarters Marine Corps.

23. Daniels to Lejeune, 2 May 1932, container 88, reel 55, Daniels MSS. See also Daniels to Claude Swanson, 27 July 1933, container 102, reel 62; and Daniels to Franklin D. Roosevelt, 26 December 1934, container 95, reel 59, Daniels MSS.

24. Cf. Josephus Daniels, *The Wilson Years: Years of War and After, 1917–1923* (Chapel Hill, N.C.: University of North Carolina Press, 1947), p. 155; and Barnett, "Soldier and Sailor Too," chapter 29, Barnett MSS.

25. Lelia Montague Barnett, "Washington Dinner Disasters," n.d., Lelia Montague Barnett MSS.

26. George Harvey, "The Rt. Hon. N.C.B. (North Carolina Boy), Our First Lord of the Admiralty," *North American Review,* April 1915, p. 481.

27. Daniels to Barnett, 11 October 1919 and 11 October 1919, container 64, Daniels MSS.

28. Daniels to Lejeune, 29 May 1920, container 88, Daniels MSS; and Barnett to Second Lieutenant Arthur I. Caperton, 26 August 1919, Barnett June–December 1919 file, container 64, Daniels MSS.

29. Lejeune to Commandant of the Marine Corps [1935], reel 6, Lejeune MSS.

30. Raymond J. Bartholomew to Mrs. George Barnett, 11 and 27 January 1932, Barnett MSS. Butler's biographer, Hans Schmidt, in *Maverick Marine: General Smedley D. Butler and the Contradictions of American Military History* (Lexington: University Press of Kentucky), p. 119, dismisses this correspondence because it is typed and unsigned; however, the author read the handwritten versions from Bartholomew while interviewing Mrs. Barnett's surviving daughter, Lelia Gordon Lucas.

31. Daniels's diary, 10 June 1920, Daniels MSS.

32. Cf. George Barnett, "Soldier and Sailor Too," chapter 29, Barnett MSS, with Daniels's diary entries, 1–16 June 1920, Daniels MSS.

33. Cf. Lelia Montague Barnett, "Command Performances," n.d., table of contents page, Lelia Montague Barnett MSS, with George Barnett, "Soldier and Sailor Too," chapter 29. A handwritten copy of the letter of dismissal is in the Barnett 1920 file, container 64, Daniels MSS, and a typed copy appears in the Edwin H.

Denby MSS, Burton Collection, Detroit Public Library. The typed, signed order dismissing Barnett, dated 19 June 1920, is in his officers qualification record, Headquarters Marine Corps.

34. George Barnett to President Woodrow Wilson, 21 June 1920, copy in Barnett's officer qualification record, Headquarters Marine Corps; Josephus Daniels to Wilson, 29 June 1920, copy in Barnett 1920 folder, container 64, Daniels MSS.

35. Cf. William S. Benson to George Barnett, 27 August 1920, container 15, Barn-Barr file, Benson MSS, Manuscripts Division, Library of Congress; with Benson to JAL, 20 June 1920, reel 12, Lejeune MSS.

36. Josephus Daniels, undated memorandum, Bureau Chiefs 1913–1916 file, container 549, Daniels MSS.

37. Thomas S. Butler to Lejeune, 6 July 1920, reel 12, Lejeune MSS. All of Lejeune's letters of congratulations are on the same reel.

38. Benson to Lejeune, 20 June 1920, reel 12, Lejeune MSS.

39. Daniels to Claude A. Swanson, 27 July 1933, container 102, reel 62, Daniels MSS.

40. John Weeks to Barnett, 17 August 1920; and Weeks to Mrs. Barnett, 2 September 1920, 1920 file, Barnett MSS. Cf. Charles H. Lyman to Barnett, 21 June 1920, Barnett MSS; and Lyman to Lejeune, 21 June 1920, reel 12, Lejeune MSS.

41. Lejeune to Daniels, 26 June 1920, Lejeune 1920–1924 file, container 88, Daniels MSS.

42. Major General William A. Worton and General Clifton B. Cates, oral histories, MCHC.

43. Smedley D. Butler to Alexander A. Vandegrift, 6 August 1920, copy in the Butler MSS, MCHC. Butler's actions on the day of Lejeune's assumption of office and Barnett's last day as commandant are revealed in the oral history of Major General Ray A. Robinson (MCHC), Butler's aid-de-camp in 1920.

44. Interviews by the author: R. Frederick Roy, Washington, 11 July 1979; Lelia Gordon Lucas, Huntley, Virginia, 7 June 1979; and Vice Admiral Lloyd M. Mustin (Mrs. Barnett's nephew), Alexandria, Virginia, 5 June 1979. See also Mrs. Barnett to Franklin D. Roosevelt, 18 July 1920, container 80, Roosevelt MSS.

45. Lelia Montague Barnett to Lejeune, [1932], Barnett MSS.

46. Daniels, *The Wilson Years: Years of War and After*, p. 155.

47. Lelia Gordon Lucas, interview with the author.

48. John Weeks to Edwin Denby, 20 June 1921, June 1921 folder, 1910–1921 container, Denby MSS, Burton Collection, Detroit Public Library, Detroit, Michigan.

49. *Army-Navy Journal*, 30 June 1920, n.p., copy in Barnett's biographical file, MCHC.

50. Lelia Montague Barnett to Franklin D. Roosevelt, 16 July 1920, container 80, Roosevelt MSS; also interviews by the author: Vice Admiral Lloyd Mustin and Lelia Gordon Lucas.

51. For contrasting views of this unsavory and unprofessional brouhaha, cf. Hans Schmidt, *Maverick Marine*, pp. 110–28; and Merrill L. Bartlett, "Secretary of the Navy Josephus Daniels and the Marine Corps, 1913–1921," pp. 190–208.

6

THE COMMANDANCY

————————— 1920–1929 —————————

> Let each one of us resolve to show in himself a good
> example of virtue, honor, patriotism and subordination,
> and to do all in his power, not only to maintain, but
> to increase the prestige, the efficiency, and the esprit
> of the grand old Corps to which we belong.
>
> *Major General Commandant John A. Lejeune, 1922.*

Despite Lejeune's strong desire to be the thirteenth commandant, Secretary Daniels's abrupt ouster of Barnett disturbed him.
The duplicitous nature of the scheme ran against his personal
code of honor and integrity. Knowing that Congressman Butler
and his spiteful son had encouraged Daniels added to Lejeune's
misgivings. Throughout the remainder of the summer and into
the fall of 1920, Barnett's Republican supporters continued to
criticize the Wilson Administration for its unfair treatment of the
twelfth commandant. The election of Warren G. Harding, a
Republican, prompted the Senate to set aside their confirmation
of Lejeune to await the pleasure of the new president. Lejeune
began to believe that his brief tenure at the helm of the Marine
Corps might end abruptly. As late as December, the issue appeared
still in doubt and caused Lejeune to declare to his sister: "I'm not
going to sit still and let my nomination slide while they wait for
the next administration."[1]

As Lejeune fretted and worried, Congressman Butler—now the
ranking member of the House Naval Affairs Committee—sought
the advice of Secretary Daniels. The canny politician advised
that Butler and the entire committee call on Edwin H. Denby,

President Harding's designate to receive the portfolio of the Department of the Navy. Butler believed that such a bipartisan show of support might just suffice to convince Denby and Harding to retain Lejeune in office. In the ensuing meeting, Denby was cordial but noncommittal. The new secretary of the navy knew Lejeune by reputation, however. During World War One, Denby enlisted in the Marine Corps. Although overage and overweight, he completed recruit training and then accepted a commission. For the remainder of the war, Denby served at Parris Island teaching patriotism and citizenship to leatherneck recruits undergoing basic training.[2]

Still unsure of his future, Lejeune appeared on the steps of the Capitol on 4 March 1921 to attend the inauguration ceremony. Meanwhile, Denby had reached an easy conclusion: bringing Barnett back into office—as some Republicans demanded—might serve no purpose except to exacerbate the political controversy surrounding his ouster. Worse, a continuation of the brouhaha threatened to tarnish the image of the Marine Corps in the eyes of an electorate already weary of political bickering. As the crowds gathered, Lejeune felt a hand on his shoulder. Denby came right to the point: "General Lejeune, would you serve as Commandant of the Marine Corps during my administration?"[3]

When Lejeune replied in the affirmative, Denby asked for a recommendation of a brigadier general to fill the unoccupied major general's position made vacant by his elevation to the commandancy. Without hesitating, Lejeune nominated Barnett. By that afternoon, Denby had obtained the confirmation of the Senate and the signature of President Harding. Just as Lejeune and Senator Weeks had predicted months before, the simple act of restoring Barnett's second star defused further criticism of the twelfth commandant's removal from office.

Apparently, however, in their thirst to end the controversy, no one considered the consequences. As long as Barnett remained in uniform, the corps' quota of major generals remained filled. Although Denby had authorized the promotion to permanent brigadier general for Smedley D. Butler, Logan Feland, and Harry Lee, all three of the ambitious officers had to wait at least until Barnett retired—probably in 1923—for another star. Another brigadier general, Eli K. Cole—a Naval Academy classmate of Lejeune's—had already received his permanent promotion to brigadier general. Cole, an officer despised by Butler, would most likely be the next leatherneck to become a major general because of seniority. But for the moment, Denby's warm letter of congratulations to Barnett underscored the desires of most observers to end the controversy once and for all: "I know of nothing that would have given me more pleasure, other than having it one of my first official acts, [than] to have nominated you to be [a] major general."[4]

Immediately upon taking the reins of the corps on 30 June 1920, Lejeune began a major reorganization of Headquarters Marine Corps so as to alter its traditional functions. The act of 11 July 1798 authorized the appointment of additional officers to assist the commandant in his duties. Legislation on 3 March 1903 added to the number of assistants and increased the rank of some of them. The passage of significant personnel legislation during World War One resulted in the promotion of the commandant's principal assistants—adjutant and inspector, quartermaster, and paymaster—to brigadier general. Not surprisingly, by the time Lejeune became the thirteenth commandant, the incumbents on the staff had established their own fiefs.

Lejeune knew all too well the sorry and unprofessional squabble that occurred during the Elliott commandancy. During the Biddle and Barnett tenures, both senior leathernecks decided to remain aloof from the staff and otherwise avoid a repeat of the disagreement of 1910. Lejeune chose instead to reorganize the staff of Headquarters Marine Corps and, in the process, to eclipse the power of the principal staff officers. What the new commandant sought was a staff that responded to direction from his office to the demands and requirements of the Marine Corps at large.

While serving as the assistant to the commandant, 1914–1917, he had urged Barnett to form a planning section at headquarters. On 1 December 1920, Lejeune ordered the expansion of the planning section into the Division of Operations and Training (DOT). The new organization had responsibility for operations, training, military education, intelligence, and aviation. Significantly, the director of the new division, Lieutenant Colonel Robert H. "Hal" Dunlap, reported directly to the commandant. Three new sections appeared at Headquarters Marine Corps along with the DOT: personnel, education, and recruiting. Their section chiefs reported directly to the commandant as well. Lejeune's reorganization left the traditional members of the staff responsible only for routine "housekeeping" and "maintenance." Lejeune assigned a wartime comrade and fellow alumnus of the Naval Academy, Major General Wendell C. Neville, as his assistant.[5]

Even as his staff began to function in its new assignments, Lejeune encountered a major controversy that threatened to tarnish the reputation of the Marine Corps. Near the end of his tenure as commandant, a stunned Barnett had expressed outrage over an allegation of "indiscriminate killing of natives" by marines assigned to the Gendarmerie d'Haiti. According to the material in a transcript of a court-martial sent to the commandant for approval of sentence, two marines had summarily executed a pair of native insurgents. Shocked at what he read, Barnett ordered an official investigation. He then followed his correspondence with a "confidential and personal" letter to the Marine Corps commander in Haiti to express his concern. The second letter cautioned Colonel John H. Russell to take whatever action necessary to ensure that such atrocities did not recur. The matter might have ended then and there, except for mounting opposition to American involvement in Haiti—especially during a U.S. presidential election.

Criticism of U.S. intervention in Haiti increased in intensity in 1920, especially from political organizations representing blacks.

Advisors to presidential hopeful Harding hoped to embarrass the Wilson administration with a series of provocative materials. In the summer of 1920, a journalist returned from a fact-finding trip to the troubled island nation and reported in a weekly magazine that "I have heard officers wearing the United States uniform [presumably marines] in the interior of Haiti talk of 'bumping off gooks' as if it were a variety of sport like duck hunting." The reporter added that reports of torture and murder by leathernecks were commonplace. He concluded his scathing report by suggesting that the marines assigned to duties in Haiti were, for the most part, "ignorant and brutal."[6]

Sensing a major political controversy in the making, Daniels ordered former commandant Barnett to prepare a detailed report on the history of Marine Corps activities in Haiti. In compiling the information requested, Barnett added a copy of his "personal and confidential" correspondence to Russell. By the time he delivered the report to Daniels, however, the controversy appeared to have subsided and the material received only a cursory reading. But someone else read the entire report carefully and apparently revealed its contents to a journalist. Revelations of the letters between Barnett and Russell added to the mounting criticism over U.S. involvement in the region. Republican opponents of the Wilson administration seized on the information with glee; Harding delighted in telling eager crowds that "thousands of Haitians have been killed by American Marines."[7]

An outraged Daniels summoned Barnett to his office. At first, the canny secretary of the navy denied receiving the report. But Barnett had taken the precaution of asking Brigadier General Henry C. Haines to accompany him that day. Thus, Daniels could no longer deny acquiring it. Summoning Lejeune and Butler to his office, Daniels ordered them to Haiti to conduct an investigation. For most of September 1920, they visited American military installations and conferred with local commanders. Returning to Washington, Lejeune and Butler reported only a few cases of misconduct on the part of leathernecks assigned to

Haiti; in each instance, courts-martial followed and heavy prison sentences were awarded. When a smug Daniels announced the results of the Lejeune-Butler fact-finding trip, he suggested that Barnett had failed to act aggressively upon learning of the atrocities—an unfair allegation that exacerbated the confrontation that began with Barnett's ouster the previous September. Most observers remained unconvinced; the Lejeune-Butler report and Daniels endorsement of it did little to soften Republican criticism of U.S. involvement in Haiti.[8]

Even as the residual problems from Barnett's tenure in office—Lejeune's stormy appointment and the Haitian scandal—appeared to have subsided, the new commandant faced another controversial situation that had its origins during the administration of his predecessor. In April 1917, only 431 officers were forest green; by the end of World War I, the ranks had swollen to over 2,400. Although from 1883 until 1897, and then again from 1915 onward, Marine Corps accessions to its commissioned ranks had all been from the Naval Academy, new officers commissioned during the war years came from the ranks and recent university graduates. Faced with the inevitable reductions following the war, most of the temporary and reserve officers faced reduction in rank or outright discharge.

A board—named the Russell Board, after its chairman, Colonel John H. Russell—that convened during the closing weeks of Barnett's commandancy stunned the officer ranks by "plucking" or reducing in rank many officers with distinguished records of tropical campaigning or heroic combat in France. Disappointed observers charged that the Russell Board had concentrated too heavily on education and pedigrees. Reportedly, Russell advised the conferees to select officers for retention "whom they would invite into their quarters and whom their daughters might marry."[9]

Many promising officers found their hopes for a career as a Marine Corps officer shattered by a rather arbitrary and perhaps capricious administrative procedure. Lejeune moved quickly to correct the perceived inequities and restore morale to the ranks of his officers. A new board—chaired by Neville—met to examine each case anew. When it submitted its report in May 1921, the results suprised few observers. Two of the board members dominated the proceedings: Butler argued for the retention of officers from the ranks, suggesting that they formed the backbone of the corps; Harry Lee championed the cause of the veterans of the Fourth Brigade (Marine), AEF. The Russell board may have overcompensated in favor of gentlemanly and educational qualities, but the Neville board leaned in another direction to favor officers with combat decorations. Many of the temporary and reserve officers selected by the Neville board possessed limited education or were simply too old and lacked the potential for professional growth.

The failure of both boards underscored the inadequacies of the Marine Corps' officer promotion system, a problem perplexing Lejeune during his years in office. The thirteenth commandant sought to replace the corps' antiquated custom of promotion by seniority with an effective system of examination. He proposed a regimen of examining boards and presented his plan first to the House Naval Affairs Committee (HNAC). Lejeune's proposal won speedy approval because of the strong endorsement of Congressman Butler. He cautioned potential critics that he did not foresee any wholesale pruning of the officer ranks, but merely a thinning out of the aged and redundant:

> There is a class of officer of mediocre practical ability who, by reason of some limitation of character of accomplishment or by lack of efficiency in the performance of the more exacting duties, are usually continued in the performance of the minor duties, in which they are able to establish fair records. They do not, therefore, have on their official records any sufficient unfavorable data which would justify an examining board in recommending against promotion. [10]

Lejeune hoped to force out those officers who had failed selection for at least five years or who had become too old to lead troops on maneuvers or into combat. Legislation affecting Marine Corps officer promotions had remained essentially unchanged since 1892, allowing headquarters only the prerogative to purge the ranks of the professionally or physically unqualified. Lejeune believed that colonels over age fifty-six and lieutenant colonels reaching age fifty should be retired, while officers in the ranks of lieutenant through major should not be retained beyond their forty-fifth birthday.

Lejeune's proposed legislation passed quickly through the HNAC but failed to survive senatorial scrutiny. In sharp questioning, one senator after another wondered just how such a system could remain equitable. Lejeune attempted to mollify his skeptical audience by promising to retain any officer who had completed ten years of service until he would be eligible for retirement. The commandant reminded detractors that of all the armed services, only the Marine Corps remained tied to such an inefficient system. Nevertheless, his critics seemed convinced that the proposed system invited a callous misuse of administrative power. Despite Lejeune's eloquent pleas, the controversial legislation failed to receive approval in the Senate.[11]

Rejection by the Senate for such a relatively minor administrative change in the regulations governing the Marine Corps mirrored the general disenchantment and malaise pervading the body politic. As Lejeune struggled to maintain the efficiency and morale of the Marine Corps, he encountered retrenchment as severe as that faced by leathernecks following the Civil War. In July 1919, Congress cut the Marine Corps to 1,093 officers and 27,100 enlisted men. By the end of Lejeune's first year as commandant, that figure dropped to fewer than 21,000 men. Attempts at further reductions followed. Lejeune galvanized what political forces he had at his disposal and managed to forestall further cuts in 1922. Despite his frustrations and misgivings over the reductions, however, Lejeune managed to trumpet to the HNAC on 20 November 1922 that "the Corps had recovered from the post-bellum lassitude and laxness, and is in a highly efficient condition."[12]

Although Congress continued to demand further reductions in personnel and operating expenses, traditional leatherneck commitments with the fleet and overseas remained the same. The potential for overseas deployment of a naval force continued. On 20 August 1920, President Wilson ordered a marine guard to provide security at the American mission in Tungchow, China. In August 1921, a battalion of leathernecks deployed to the waters off Panama because of local disturbances near the Canal Zone. In January 1922, Marines from the *Galveston* landed at Corinto, Nicaragua, to reinforce the legation guard in Managua following an intensification of anti-American feelings. More of Lejeune's marines marched into China, this time when leathernecks from the *Albany* landed on 28 April 1922 to reinforce the legation guard in Peking. The following month, a composite battalion of marines and bluejackets from the ships of the Asiatic Fleet landed at Tientsin following renewed fighting between two Chinese warlords. Despite these continuations of traditional leatherneck service to the nation, Lejeune began to fear for the survivability of the Marine Corps.

Lejeune decided to focus the indefatigable Butler's energies on the public's perception of the Marine Corps and formulate a program to demonstrate leatherneck prowess and élan. Quantico became the showplace of the corps in a series of events designed to please the citizenry and Congress. Renewed emphasis on marksmanship appeared—a Marine Corps tradition dating from the age of sail—and leatherneck sharpshooters dominated the annual interservice matches during Lejeune's commandancy. More colorful and entertaining, Quantico's athletic teams—with the base band thundering in the background and the colorful Butler acting as head cheerleader—competed successfully against college teams in baseball and football.[13]

Between Butler and Lejeune, an even more spectacular display of leatherneck prowess emerged. Beginning in 1921, the Quantico-based East Coast Expeditionary Brigade reenacted a Civil War battle each fall. The first such display took place at the site of the Battle of the Wilderness. Lejeune hoped to demonstrate that tactics in modern warfare had changed considerably due to technology and weaponry. The Quantico marines used the weapons and equipment of the 1920s but carried out the scenario of 1864. Large crowds of spectators, including prominent politicians, attended the events and gave them a festive air. Following the success of 1921—even President Harding attended—the maneuvers continued: Gettysburg (1922), New Market (1923), and Antietam (1924).[14]

Through a seemingly insignificant deployment of leathernecks, the Marine Corps earned fresh laurels during the early years of Lejeune's commandancy. Alarmed over the growing number of robberies of railway mail cars, the postmaster general requested assistance in the form of federal troops. President Harding responded by directing Secretary of the Navy Denby to employ marines. On 8 November 1921, the initial contingent of leathernecks—fifty-three officers and twenty-two hundred enlisted men—began their new duties. Denby sent them off with stirring orders: "If attacked, shoot, and shoot to kill. The mail must be delivered or there must be a Marine dead at the post of duty."[15]

While the Quantico marines in their public relations efforts and their comrades riding shotgun on railway mail cars served to keep the public's acclaim and esteem for their leathernecks high, Lejeune knew that ultimately he answered to a niggardly Congress. Fiscal restraint dominated hearings of both the House and the Senate Naval Affairs Committees. Assistant Secretary of the Navy Theodore Roosevelt, Jr., recorded the frustrations of the Department of the Navy in a pithy diary entry: "The House Naval Affairs Committee, in my opinion, is perfectly willing to grant us a good Navy, but is unwilling to stand against the Appropriations Committee. In other words, they mean well weakly."[16]

In February 1921, Lejeune appeared before the Senate Naval Affairs Committee (SNAC) as Congress pondered a budget for fiscal year 1922. Chief of Naval Operations Admiral Robert E. Coontz concluded his testimony by supporting Lejeune's position that the strength of the Marine Corps be one-fifth the size of the navy. Lejeune argued his case with dismal facts and figures: If Congress slashed the size of the Marine Corps to twenty thousand men, it left only five hundred Marines to man the two expeditionary brigades. Lejeune reminded his audience that almost half of his leathernecks served overseas or at sea, performing expeditionary duties or traditional roles in support of the fleet. In contrast to Lejeune's difficulties with the SNAC, he experienced little difficulty with the HNAC—mostly due to the influence of Congressman Butler.[17]

To both officers and enlisted marines, Lejeune maintained an image of uncompromising professionalism. An inspiring and stimulating speaker, he spoke without notes. On 31 October 1921, Lejeune brought the annual convention of the American Legion to its feet in thunderous applause. Comparing the heroic deeds of the Marine Corps to those of the French Foreign Legion that charged against the forces of Austria and Russia in the Battle of Wagram, Lejeune quoted Marshal Ney: "Hear them shoot; see them charge! It's in their blood! It's in their blood!"[18]

On 12 January 1922, he addressed the officers at Quantico to explain his goals. Trumpeting his motto, "In time of peace, prepare for war," Lejeune admonished his audience to assist in his aims. In an emotional plea, he referred to the corps' priceless heritage and reminded his listeners that it had come to them from the heroic dead. In closing his address, the commandant offered advice on leadership, a favorite theme: "Discipline must be maintained; military punctilio observed; but there is also the obligation to deal justly, fairly, kindly, and honorably with those who are under our command; and to serve loyally and faithfully those who command us." Then, Lejeune pointed directly to his officers for emphasis: "This obligation is mutual."[19]

Faced with the inevitable reductions, Lejeune undertook several steps that he hoped would mollify Congress. In testimony before the SNAC in 1922, he promised to reduce expenses by 40 percent; in the following fiscal year, Lejeune planned to cut an additional 10 percent. He had already closed two-thirds of the recruiting stations and raised the minimum age for enlistment to twenty-one. Given further reductions, Lejeune planned to order a halt to all new enlistments. In testimony before the HNAC, Lejeune attempted to demonstrate that he had managed the fiscal affairs of the Marine Corps prudently: in Haiti, marines moved from tents into native huts; at Quantico, Butler and his Marines would build the new athletic stadium using scrap lumber and stone from a quarry on the base. Lejeune noted, somewhat laconically, that although Congress had authorized a Marine Corps Reserve, no funds had been approved to pay the leathernecks.[20]

Although leatherneck aviation elements did not deploy to France with either of the Marine Corps brigades, Lejeune remained committed to the participation of aviation in any modern amphibious or military force. On 30 October 1920, he approved an expanded and revised table of organization for his aviation assets: four wings of two to four squadrons each, with each squadron divided into two or more flights. In his testimony before the SNAC on 4 May 1922, Lejeune requested the purchase of land at Quantico for an aviation field so that leatherneck aviators could train with marines in the expeditionary force. With the approval of the fiscal year 1923 appropriations, Lejeune ordered the formation of the First Aviation Group at Quantico—three squadrons, comprising observer aircraft, fighter planes, and kite-balloons.[21]

Despite the long hours at his desk, Lejeune followed a strict regimen of temperance and exercise. Each morning at seven, his aides-de-camp, Captains John Craige and Lemuel C. Shepherd, Jr., met him at "Eighth and Eye" with horses. The three of them rode to Haines Point and then to Headquarters Marine Corps. Although the social whirl of Washington demanded much of his time, Lejeune never attempted to emulate his predecessor or his indefatigable wife—a professed doyenne of society. Social functions at the historical home of the commandants consisted mostly of the weekly "at home" common to the military and naval community. The contrast to the Barnetts disappointed at least one observer: "[The Lejeunes] never entertained, you know," complained Neville's daughter decades later.[22]

The administration of President Harding grew to a close because of the series of scandals surrounding the Oval Office. Following the public outcry over the lease of the navy's oil reserves, the secretary of the navy submitted his resignation. Lejeune enjoyed his relationship with Denby, especially since he devoted his attentions to the Washington Naval Arms Limitation Conferences. Trusting the commandant more than Daniels had Barnett, Denby left Lejeune relatively free to manage the affairs of the Marine Corps without civilian interference. When President Calvin Coolidge announced his choice for secretary of the navy, it pleased Lejeune; privately, the commandant and the secretary-designate addressed each other as "Gabe" and "Magic."[23]

Lejeune had every reason to express delight and satisfaction with President Coolidge's selection of a Naval Academy classmate, Curtis D. Wilbur, as secretary of the navy. Wilbur had resigned following graduation in 1888 and studied law. In 1918, he became a California state supreme court justice and a year later its chief justice. The conservative jurist appeared ideal for the new president, anxious to rid his administration of any taint remaining from the Harding years. Having an old friend and classmate in office made Lejeune's administration of the Marine Corps less onerous. Congressman Butler remained as chairman of the HNAC, which promised a continuation of smooth relations in the lower house. But the younger Butler waxed critical over Wilbur's appointment: "A fine quality of jelly fish isn't he—but just like all of this administration. This old slob [Wilbur] will retire soon enough and pass to the Supreme Court bench and maybe we will get a stronger man."[24]

Lejeune experienced few of the administrative difficulties and personality conflicts that plagued Barnett's tenure in office. Neither Denby nor Wilbur shared Daniels's distrust of bureaucrats in uniform. Both secretaries expressed confidence in Lejeune and left him to manage the affairs of the Marine Corps without civilian hindrance. Denby's assistant secretary of the navy, Theodore Roosevelt, Jr., spent his term in office representing the Department of the Navy at the Washington Naval Arms Limitation Conferences, and the press of these meetings prevented him from becoming involved in Marine Corps affairs. When Roosevelt left office in 1924, his successor—a cousin, Douglas Robinson—acquired duties throughout the department rather than as a watchdog over leatherneck activities. As Barnett's date for mandatory retirement on 1 September 1923 approached, Lejeune concluded that the seemingly meaningless post at the Department of the Pacific required a senior general officer. Knowing that Neville's wife—a semi-invalid—would welcome a warmer climate, he selected Neville to replace Barnett. Then, Brigadier General Logan Feland replaced Neville as assistant to the commandant.[25]

Meanwhile, an important administrative change took place with regard to Lejeune's most frenetic and ambitious subordinate. Corruption among municipal officials in Philadelphia became so rife during the turbulent 1920s that the mayor appealed directly to President Coolidge for assistance. The Oval Office sent the mayor's letter to the secretary of the navy, who passed the request for assistance to the HNAC. When Congressman Butler mentioned the matter to his restless son, already bored with the peacetime routine at Quantico, the request for federal help became a summons to supply a general officer—specifically, Smedley D. Butler. Thus, Lejeune continued to battle congressional retrenchment without Butler's energies at Quantico.[26]

For the remainder of his commandancy, Lejeune fought a continuous battle over appropriations and manpower. After initial postwar demobilization, leatherneck enlisted strength dropped to 16,085 in 1920. In 1926, it had risen slightly to 17,976 Marines. Drastic cuts for the rest of Lejeune's tenure in office made it difficult, if not impossible, to meet both traditional Marine Corps missions and increasing commitments overseas. Initially, it even appeared as if the cutbacks worked in Lejeune's favor: In late 1923, he ordered the minimum height standard raised to sixty-five inches. The following spring, Lejeune decreed that only native-born Americans or naturalized citizens could enlist. On 1 April 1924, he ordered the minimum enlistment increased from three to four years. Nevertheless, Lejeune learned to his dismay that during 1923 alone, 1,595 of his Marines deserted; only 269 had been captured, court-martialed, and sentenced to long terms in naval prison, and given dishonorable discharges.[27]

Lejeune continued to strive for fiscal prudence and responsibility. In 1925, he reported to Wilbur that he had spent fifteen million dollars less in the last fiscal year than had been expended during any of the previous five years. Despite the commandant's demonstrated frugality, Congress singled out the Marine Corps—alone among the armed services—for a reduction in strength for the following fiscal year. As a result, the West Coast Expeditionary Brigade, composed largely of the Sixth Marine Regiment, reverted to cadre status. Although Lejeune harbored grave concern over the state of the smaller of the naval services, he promised Wilbur that he could keep the Marine Corps intact under the proposed, miserly budget for fiscal year 1926.[28]

Lejeune's initial appointment for a four-year term of office ended in 1925. The notion of Josephus Daniels's policy of single four-year terms of office for senior naval officers surfaced briefly, but both Denby and Wilbur had discarded the single-oak edict as unrealistic and unworkable. Moreover, Lejeune's stewardship of the Marine Corps had been sound and had drawn no criticism from important political sources. Congressman Butler led Lejeune's reconfirmation swiftly through the HNAC, and then sent it on to Wilbur: "It's [HNAC] action [was] largely induced because of the conspicuous service he [Lejeune] rendered this country during the great war."[29]

Lejeune believed strongly that his alma mater provided the best junior officers for the Marine Corps—despite the protestations of Smedley D. Butler. When his vacancies could not be filled from

Annapolis, he turned to other sources. The Marine Corps had demonstrated an egalitarian streak by commissioning promising young NCOs; in 1925, ten corporals and sergeants became second lieutenants. During that same year, ten graduates of the Naval Academy entered the Marine Corps. To fill the remaining twenty-five openings, Lejeune's staff solicited nominations from colleges and universities that offered Army ROTC training. Eventually, twenty young men were accepted from among the eighty-one who applied.[30]

The previous summer, Lejeune learned that Butler—frustrated in his dealings with the municipal government in Philadelphia— contemplated a return to the colors. Lejeune waited almost two months before replying, then wrote to welcome him back into forest green. In the same correspondence, Lejeune informed Butler of several proposed changes in the assignment of general officers: Harry Lee to Parris Island, Eli Cole from Parris Island to Quantico, and Dion Williams to Headquarters Marine Corps. These transfers left the post at San Diego available for Butler upon his return. Clearly, Lejeune had selected the Marine Corps' least important post for the unpredictable Butler. Still, the commandant shared a rare personal sentiment in his letter: "I have missed you more than I can tell you since you have been in Philadelphia."[31]

During congressional testimony in 1925, Lejeune argued for an increase in the number of major generals. He noted that the army had one officer of such rank for every thirty-two hundred soldiers, and the navy counted one rear admiral for every three thousand sailors. Lejeune wanted only one major general for each thirty-five hundred Marines. The proposed legislation became common knowledge throughout Washington and Quantico, precipitating considerable speculation over who might benefit from the increases. In a stern letter to his general officers, the commandant admonished them to stop the idle gossip. Lejeune feared a congressional backlash that might block passage of the legislation. Despite Lejeune's caution, Butler wrote, impatiently inquiring about the promotions. In a footnote to his important political connections, Butler informed Lejeune that unless his chances for gaining one of the promotions appeared certain, he would not ask his congressman father to help in securing the legislation. Butler even attempted to patronize Lejeune to soften his disrespectful and unprofessional threat: "I have always maintained that you were the only man to keep this ship [the Marine Corps] on an even keel."[32]

In any event, the legislation failed to survive congressional scrutiny. Nonetheless, Lejeune ignored Butler's impudent remark. The commandant continued to plead for personnel increases in the face of an unyielding Congress. He reminded his audiences in the House and Senate Naval Affairs Committees that a continuing predilection to use his marines for any and every situation— including the guarding of the mails—might no longer be possible if the strength of the corps were further reduced. The proposed budget for fiscal year 1927 contained funding for only 16,800 marines, rather than the 18,000 men requested. The commandant reminded both the HNAC and SNAC of his personnel problems: In 1922, the Marine Corps had been reduced to 21,000 enlisted men; between 1923 and 1925, that figure had been slashed further to 19,500; now in 1926–27, Congress appeared to mandate a further reduction to 16,800 leathernecks. Nevertheless, Lejeune's commitments to the fleet and overseas had not diminished but actually increased. The situation appeared so serious that Lejeune feared for the mental health of his marines. He expressed this concern to the secretary of the navy in 1926: "To reduce the Corps would be highly detrimental to its morale and efficiency. All Marines know that the Corps is now too small and consequently overworked, and they would feel that any further reduction of its strength was an indication that those in authority did not regard very highly its value to the nation."[33]

The tedium and frustration of Lejeune's official duties made Sundays with his family all the more important and enjoyable. The Glennons visited often and a proud grandfather doted on his grandchildren. When Laura's school presented a musical program, the commandant attended to hear his daughter sing. In early 1925, Lejeune took Ellie to New York for a short vacation. While there, they shopped and enjoyed two Broadway shows, *The Student Prince* and *What Price Glory?* But such escapes from the grind of the commandancy came all too seldom. Lejeune seemed always to face yet another session of testimony before a congressional committee, and he found the commandancy increasingly tiresome and frustrating.[34]

In testimony before the SNAC on 10 January 1927, Lejeune continued his plea for a restored or increased budget. Again, his marines had been called out to protect the mails. The increased cost of separate rations for the men had to be taken out of the corps' operating budget. Lejeune reminded his listeners' that the Marine Corps' traditional missions aboard ship, and in support of the fleet at home and overseas, remained. Meanwhile, there was also the occasional demand for expeditionary forces. When one senator questioned why only marines seemed to be required for such expeditionary duties, Lejeune took the oportunity to remind the SNAC of a questionable point of international law. Most Western governments believed at the time that employment of naval forces overseas amounted to little more than a police action; the peoples of the underdeveloped nations did not object. Wilbur advised President Coolidge of the same debatable interpretation of international law: "[Intervention by U.S. Marines] . . . does not constitute an act of war. Normally, if the Army was used, it would be tantamount to a declaration of war." Wilbur opined that the president had the authority to order marines ashore, as part of a naval force, without concurrent congressional approval.[35]

Despite the belief that the Marine Corps constituted the spearhead of America's armed forces during the 1920s, Lejeune continued to fret over readiness in the face of reductions mandated by a retrenchment-minded government. Caught up in the spirit of international disarmament, some politicians believed that the smaller of America's naval services should be reduced as well. Wilbur shared Lejeune's concerns and took the opportunity to remind the president of the potential for deployment of marines in 1924: Domestic political unrest in Cuba might require a leatherneck force; a revolution had just occurred in Honduras; Mexico severed diplomatic relations with Great Britain, and the political future of America's closest southern neighbor seemed uncertain. Disorder in Nicaragua, political peace in Haiti only because of the presence of marines, and the real possibility of sending leathernecks back to the Dominican Republic all suggested significant reasons to maintain a ready force of Marines for potential expeditionary duties.[36]

In his annual report for 1925, Lejeune reminded readers that his corps—already stretched thin because of overseas commitments—had been cut to eighteen thousand men, a reduction of fifteen hundred marines. As a result, he ordered one infantry regiment disbanded and the size of some posts reduced. Meanwhile, leathernecks continued to serve at sea in the large warships of the fleet, just as their predecessors had in the age of sail. In 1926, thirty-three ships had detachments of marines in them and this commitment represented twenty-one percent of the Marine Corps' strength. Finally, Lejeune argued once again for the construction of permanent buildings at Quantico. Maintaining the temporary structures of the World War I era grew increasingly wasteful. Then, in the second half of his commandancy, Lejeune faced two new and demanding commitments.[37]

After a major U.S. intervention in Nicaragua during the first decade following the Spanish-American War, only a small legation guard of marines remained. The token force in Managua provided a controversial and inflammatory reminder of Yankee imperialism and contributed to the internal political turmoil. In October 1925, rebels angered by the American-backed government took to the streets and focused their grievances on the considerable U.S. economic presence. When rebels murdered an American businessman and began to plunder U.S. businesses in late 1927, President Coolidge ordered in a naval task force—mostly marines. Initially, the force came from the ships of the fleet; eventually, however, an entire expeditionary brigade of marines—two regiments of infantry, a battalion of artillery, an aviation squadron, and headquarters elements—deployed to Nicaragua. Lejeune selected Brigadier General Logan Feland, rather than Butler, to command the brigade.[38]

Meanwhile, another significant overseas commitment surfaced. When Generalissimo Chiang Kai-shek and the Chinese Nationalists, the Kuomintang, broke ranks with the communists in the united front to unify China in the late 1920s, foreign lives and properties once again appeared to be threatened. In July 1926, Kuomintang Army units marched north into the Yangtze Valley. Landing parties of bluejackets and leathernecks from the U.S. Asiatic Fleet came ashore in response to the plea of foreign missionaries and businessmen.

On 25 January 1927, President Coolidge approved the assembling of the Fourth Marine Regiment in San Diego. A week later, the force sailed for China. A brigade headquarters, two more battalions of leathernecks—later expanded to form the Sixth Marine Regiment—an artillery battalion, a tank platoon, and aviation elements followed. Because Butler commanded the West Coast Expeditionary Brigade, Lejeune selected him to lead the leatherneck force in China. In the following months, Butler and his marines established cantonments in Shanghai and Tientsin. Remaining aloof from the turbulence of local politics, the leathernecks mounted patrols and staged elaborate military reviews to remind a restless population of their presence. Quickly, the potential for violence against foreigners diminished. During the last half of 1928, the brigade headquarters and one of the two infantry regiments returned to San Diego. But to Lejeune's dismay, the Fourth Marine Regiment remained in Shanghai and appeared to be a permanent fixture; the deployment added to the commandant's concerns over his diminishing personnel assets.[39]

As Lejeune approached the end of his second term as commandant (5 March 1929), he felt serious misgivings about the
condition of his Marine Corps. Although almost everyone
expected Lejeune to serve another term, the weight of the office
began to tire him. Lejeune's personal appearance suggested that
he had begun to lose that special pride in his uniform; he appeared
rumpled and disheveled at times and began to gain weight. More
important, Lejeune grew increasingly weary over the unrealistic
decisions of Congress. Only the HNAC appeared supportive of
the Marine Corps, and then only because of the determination of
Congressman Butler.[40]

On 26 May 1928, one of Lejeune's staunchest political supporters died. The death of Congressman Butler reduced the
commandant's influence with the powerful HNAC markedly.
Lejeune had maintained a cordial relationship with the feisty
Quaker from Pennsylvania's Eighth Congressional District. Only
a month before his death, Butler attempted to honor Lejeune
with a special favor. On 27 April 1928, he advised the secretary
of the navy that he had sponsored House Resolution 13341
calling for the creation of the rank of lieutenant general for the
commandant of the Marine Corps. In less than a week, however,
Wilbur responded forcefully and negatively. The secretary of the
navy could see no reason why the commandant should hold a
rank equivalent to that of a fleet commander—and those flag
officers relinquished their third star upon leaving such assignments.
Finally, Wilbur noted that H.R. 13341 conflicted with Title 37,
U.S. Code of 10 June 1922—meaning, simply that if the legislation passed into law, no means existed to fund the increase in
salary and allowances. The HNAC agreed with Wilbur and allowed
the bill to die in committee.[41]

The previous September, presidential hopeful Herbert C. Hoover announced his candidacy. He indicated no willingness to
retain Curtis Wilbur as secretary of the navy if elected, even
though Wilbur supported Hoover's candidacy. Thus, Lejeune faced
not only another term by a new administration with Hoover's

election, but also a continuation of the niggardly policies of the SNAC. This time, the HNAC without Congressman Butler would be less inclined to support the Marine Corps and more likely to back its counterpart in the upper house. That fall, Lejeune shared several of his concerns in an essay in the U.S. Naval Institute *Proceedings*. He reminded readers of the sizable commitment of marines overseas: the residual force in Haiti, a brigade in Nicaragua, and a regiment in China. Meanwhile, traditional obligations to support the fleet remained. Despite a steady increase in requirements, Congress continued to slash away at personnel; by the end of 1928, the Marine Corps counted only 1,020 officers, 155 warrant officers, and 18,000 enlisted men. Two-thirds of all leathernecks served overseas or at sea.[42]

Failure to pass legislation changing the personnel promotion system governing his officers added to Lejeune's frustration. The commandant pointed out to both naval affairs committees that he had too many senior officers; at the same time, he had low-ranking officers who would always remain junior officers. Lejeune argued that junior officers must be young and vigorous and sufficiently fit to march with their men. Lejeune's assistant, Brigadier General Ben H. Fuller, testified at the same hearing and noted that more than half of the corps' majors were too old and infirm to serve overseas with an expeditionary force. In the same session of Congress, Lejeune attempted to gain an increase in the number of major generals. He argued—once again, unsuccessfully—that the responsibilities of his general officers commanding brigades in the field (Butler in China and Feland in Nicaragua) were no less demanding or important than those of admirals commanding fleets. Lejeune summed up the officer personnel problem succinctly: "The lack of promotion tends to deaden ambition; and excessive age in grades lessens efficiency, especially in junior grades."[43]

In the Senate, Lejeune received an even less favorable response than in the House. He testified that second lieutenants should be

promoted to first lieutenant after three years, just as their counterparts in the other services were. The same selection board should
choose heads of various staff departments from among the officers
of the line, putting an end to the system of separation between
staff and line. Lejeune's proposed legislation promised to reduce
costs by easing out the collection of sinecures blocking the promotion paths of more talented and energetic officers: "[In the present
system] the result is that the good man gets the burden and he
does not get any more pay [or rank] than the slacker who does not
do the work."[44]

Stunning most observers of the Marine Corps, Lejeune
announced on 7 February 1929 that he intended to step down the
day after President Hoover's inauguration. The day following
Lejeune's press release, the Department of the Navy proclaimed
that Major General Wendell C. Neville would succeed Lejeune.
Apparently, Lejeune recommended Neville without hesitation.
Because he did not reach mandatory retirement age until 10
January 1931, he indicated a willingness to take up the post with
the Department of the Pacific in San Francisco. Lejeune discussed his plans with Butler long before the official announcement.
Perhaps fearful that his frenetic protégé might challenge Neville's
candidacy, Lejeune moved to thwart any such confrontation. The
previous July, Butler appeared to calm any fears that Lejeune
might have as he prepared to step down from the commandancy:
"I can do no good in the Marine Corps after you have gone . . . I
would never be any good as Commandant myself, as I simply
could not get along with politicians."[45]

Notes

1. JAL to AL, 9 December 1920, reel 2, Lejeune MSS, Library of Congress.
2. Gerald E. Wheeler, "Edwin H. Denby," in Paolo E. Coletta, ed. *American Secretaries of the Navy*, 2 vols. (Annapolis, Md.: Naval Institute Press, 1980), 2: 583–603. A
   copy of Denby's stirring lecture on patriotism to new Marine Corps recruits is in
   container 2, Denby MSS, Burton Collection, Detroit Public Library.
3. JAL to Commandant, [1935], reel 6, Lejeune MSS.
4. Edwin H. Denby to George Barnett, 15 March 1921, scrapbook, museum box,
   Barnett MSS, MCHC.

5. John A. Lejeune to the Chief of Naval Operations, 16 August 1920, file 11112–1644, RG 80, NA; and Kenneth W. Conduit, John H. Johnstone, and Ella W. Nargile, *A Brief History of Headquarters Marine Corps*, rev. ed. (Washington: Headquarters Marine Corps, 1970), pp. 2–4.

6. Herbert J. Seligman, "The Conquest of Haiti," *Nation*, 10 July 1920, pp. 35–36.

7. Quoted in Robert D. Heinl, Jr., and Nancy Heinl, *Written in Blood, 1492–1791* (Boston: Houghton-Mifflin, 1978), p. 465.

8. George Barnett to John H. Russell, 2 October 1919, container 2, Barnett MSS; and E. David Cronan, ed. *The Cabinet Diaries of Josephus Daniels, 1913–1921* (Lincoln: University of Nebraska Press, 1963), pp. 553–58. See also, "Guard Is Gradually Being Withdrawn from Haiti," *NYT*, 31 March 1923. The complete report of the investigation is in "Haiti and Dominican Republic Military Occupation and Administration by the U.S.," Senate documents S204-0-A and S204-0-B. For an interesting perspective, see Edwin H. Denby to Senator Medill McCormick, 1 October 1923, Barnett's officer qualification record. See also Barnett's notes, n.d., container 3, Denby MSS, and Barnett's statement, 17 October 1923, George Barnett 1921 file, container 64, Daniels MSS, Library of Congress. Barnett's version, perhaps penned by his wife, is in chapters 30–31, "Soldier and Sailor Too," unpublished memoir, Barnett MSS.

9. Quoted in Robert H. Williams, "Those Pesky Boards," *Marine Corps Gazette* 66 (November 1982): 92.

10. *Annual Report of the Secretary of the Navy, 1923* (Washington: GPO, 1923), pp. 949–50.

11. "The Promotion Bill Before Congress," Marine Corps *Gazette* 7 (December 1922): 365; see also John A. Lejeune to the Judge Advocate-General of the Navy, 15 September 1922, file 26509-479, RG 80.

12. U.S. Congress, House Naval Affairs Committee, Hearings on the Fiscal Year 1923 Budget, 20 November 1922; see also House Naval Affairs Committee hearings, 9 January 1923, as it considered HR 13556.

13. Hans Schmidt, *Maverick Marine: General Smedley D. Butler and the Contradictions of American Military History* (Lexington: University Press of Kentucky, 1987), pp. 129–43; Ralph S. Keyser, "The 1921 Rifle and Pistol Team," *Marine Corps Gazette* 7 (December 1922): 325–28; and *Annual Report of the Secretary of the Navy, 1921*, pp. 49–52.

14. John H. Craige, "The Wilderness Maneuvers," *Marine Corps Gazette* 6 (December 1921): 418–21; and JAL to AL, 17 October 1921, reel 2, Lejeune MSS. For the public response to these events, see *NYT*, 2 and 3 October 1920, 2 and 3 July 1922, 27 August 1922, 6 October 1923, 3 and 25 August 1924, 7 September 1924, and 9 August 1925.

15. Edwin H. Denby to the Marine Corps mail guards, 11 November 1921, container 2, Denby MSS; see also Robert H. Dunlap to the Commandant, 25 November 1921, mail guards file, reference section, MCHC. For the appreciative response, see Postmaster-General to the Commandant, 14 May 1922, Denby MSS; for the public's response, see "History, Duties, Guarding of the Mails," *NYT*, 21 November 1926.

16. Theodore Roosevelt, Jr., diary entry, 22 February 1922, Theodore Roosevelt, Jr. MSS.

17. Cf. U.S. Congress, House, Hearings Before the House Naval Affairs Committee, Appropriations for FY 1923, 20–21 November 1922; with U.S. Congress, Senate, Hearings Before the Senate Naval Affairs Committee, Appropriations for FY 1923, 9 December 1922. See also JAL to AL, 2 August 1921, reel 2, Lejeune MSS.

18. John A. Lejeune, "It's in Their Blood," *Marine Corps Gazette* 6 (December 1921): 417; for an example of a Lejeune address, see "Fleet," *The Enquirer* (Cincinnati), 28 October 1924.

19. John A. Lejeune, "Preparation," *Marine Corps Gazette* 7 (March 1922): 53.

20. U.S. Congress, Senate, Senate Naval Affairs Committee, 4 May 1922; see also *NYT*, 17 March 1922.

21. U.S. Congress, Senate, Senate Naval Affairs Committee, Hearings on the Fiscal Year 1923 Budget, 4 May 1922; and Edward C. Johnson, *Marine Corps Aviation: The Early Years, 1912–1940* (Washington: GPO, 1977), pp. 27–31.

22. Frances Neville Vest, oral history, MCHC, p. 36. For a glimpse of the social demands on Lejeune, see JAL to AL, 18 April 1922, reel 2, Lejeune MSS. See also General Lemuel C. Shepherd, Jr., oral history, MCHC.

23. Gerald E. Wheeler, "Edwin Denby," in Coletta, ed., *American Secretaries of the Navy*, 2:599–600; see also James W. Hammond, Jr., "When '88 Had the Helm," *Shipmate* 47 (July–August 1983): 16–18. For Lejeune's view of Denby's demise, see JAL to AL, 25 February 1924, reel 2, Lejeune MSS.

24. Smedley D. Butler to his mother, 12 September 1926, Butler MSS, NewTown Square, Pennsylvania.

25. JAL to George Barnett, 26 June 1923, container 2, Barnett MSS; see also, *NYT*, 22 July 1925.

26. W. Freeland Kendrick to Calvin Coolidge, [1923], reel 23, Coolidge MSS, Library of Congress; see also, Hans Schmidt, *Maverick Marine*, pp. 144–60.

27. *Annual Report of the Secretary of the Navy, 1924*, p. 663.

28. John A. Lejeune to the Secretary of the Navy, 13 October 1925, reel 3, Lejeune MSS; see also *Annual Report of the Secretary of the Navy, 1926*, pp. 1213–29.

29. Thomas S. Butler to Curtis D. Wilbur, 18 December 1925, reel 3, Lejeune MSS; see also JAL to AL, 18 January 1925, reel 2, Lejeune MSS.

30. *Annual Report of the Secretary of the Navy, 1925*, pp. 1215–16; and U.S. Congress, House, Hearings Before the House Naval Affairs Committee, 4 December 1924.

31. John A. Lejeune to Smedley D. Butler, 14 July 1924, reel 3, Lejeune MSS; see also JAL to AL, 29 September 1924, reel 2, Lejeune MSS and "Butler's Recall," *NYT*, 6 December 1924.

32. Smedley D. Butler to John A. Lejeune, 26 January 1925, reel 3, Lejeune MSS.

33. John A. Lejeune to Curtis D. Wilbur, 27 November 1926, reel 23, Coolidge MSS.

34. JAL to AL, 24 May 1921 and 9 May 1922, reel 2, Lejeune MSS.

35. Curtis D. Wilbur to President Coolidge, 23 June 1924, reel 24, Coolidge MSS; see also Secretary of State Philander C. Knox to President William H. Taft, 29 August 1912, quoted in Richard D. Challener, *Admirals, Generals, and American Foreign Policy* (Princeton: Princeton University Press, 1973), pp. 25–26; and U.S. Congress, Senate, Hearings Before the Senate Naval Affairs Committee, 10 January 1927.

36. "Guard Is Gradually Being Withdrawn from Haiti," *NYT*, 31 March 1923; "Marines Leaving Santo Domingo," *NYT*, 26 June 1924; and editorial, *NYT*, 28 June 1924.
37. *Annual Report of the Secretary of the Navy, 1925*, pp. 1213–29.
38. Bernard C. Nalty, *The United States Marines in Nicaragua* (Washington: Headquarters Marine Corps, 1958), pp. 5–16; see also Lejeune to Logan Feland, 26 January 1925, entry 38, RG 127. In the same file, see the Secretary of State to Wilbur, 20 January 1925 and Wilbur's response of 22 January 1925.
39. Hans Schmidt, *Maverick Marine*, pp. 173–201; and Robert B. Aspray, "The Court-Martial of Smedley Butler," *Marine Corps Gazette* 43 (December 1959): 28–34. See also, "Marines Go to China," *NYT*, 2 April 1927.
40. Lt. General Edward A. Craige, oral history, MCHC; *Annual Report of the Secretary of the Navy, 1927*, pp. 1185–88; and *Annual Report of the Secretary of the Navy, 1928*, pp. 1227–44.
41. Thomas S. Butler to Curtis D. Wilbur, 27 April 1928; and Wilbur to Butler, 21 May 1928, Records of the House Naval Affairs Committee; see also House Resolution 13341.
42. John A. Lejeune, "The U.S. Marine Corps—Present and Future," U.S. Naval Institute *Proceedings* 54 (October 1928): 859–61; and *Annual Report of the Secretary of the Navy, 1928*, pp. 1227–44.
43. U.S. Congress, House, Hearings Before the House Naval Affairs Committee, 30 November 1928. For examples of Lejeune's concern, see *NYT*, 13 July 1934, *NYT*, 17 April 1934, and *NYT*, 15 January 1934. These statements were apparently published in support of his successor's efforts to effect legislative change with regard to officer promotion and retention.
44. U.S. Congress, Senate. Hearings Before the Senate Naval Affairs Committee, 19 January 1929.
45. Smedley D. Butler to John A. Lejeune, 23 July 1928, Butler MSS, MCHC.

7

THE VMI YEARS AND FINAL ROLL CALL
1929–1942

> My life without his tender love is completely shattered and
> oh! how I miss his sweet companionship and loving care.
>
> *Ellie Lejeune to John J. Pershing*

Lejeune's announcement that he planned to leave the commandancy surprised almost everyone. With more than twenty-two months remaining before mandatory retirement, he considered the Marine Corps post in San Francisco a final duty station. To friends and reporters alike, he made the same statement: "I have had my full share of service in that office [commandant] on 5 March and I will relinquish it voluntarily and cheerfully."[1]

Following Lejeune's announcement, Butler appeared in Washington to attend a memorial service for his father. Rumors persisted that he hoped to succeed to the commandancy. At the time, the frenetic and mercurial campaigner ranked as the senior of the corps' brigadier generals. The lineal list counted only two major generals besides the commandant: Wendell C. Neville, an equally distinguished campaigner and winner of the Medal of Honor at Veracruz; and another graduate of the Naval Academy, Eli K. Cole. Brigadier General Logan Feland and Colonel William C. Harlee both made feeble attempts to gain the commandancy, but neither effort amounted to much.[2]

Although Josephus Daniels hoped for Butler to succeed Lejeune, he remained silent and did not offer public support for the controversial leatherneck. Most likely, Daniels—a Democrat—realized that his influence was meaningless to a newly elected Republican

president and his secretary of the navy, a Boston Brahmin. Given
Daniels's plea to reward "those who have been at the cannon's
mouth," he must have realized that any attempt to elevate Butler
at the expense of Neville would appear as partisan politics at its
worst. The year before, Butler had exclaimed to Lejeune: "It is
my firm intention to retire as soon as this Chinese show is over
and, at the latest, when you hand over the reins."[3]

In "whispering Buck," as Neville was known (some claimed
that in France his loud voice could be heard across the battlefield,
thus eliminating the need for a field telephone), Lejeune saw a
successor capable of keeping the Marine Corps alive in an era of
retrenchment, with leadership characterized by prudence and
moderation. Like Lejeune, Neville had a diploma from the Naval
Academy. Whatever Butler's qualities as a combat leader, his
eccentric behavior, outspoken manner, penchant for the hyperbole, and anti-Navy attitude overshadowed his professionalism
more and more. Hardly anyone took Butler's claim for the
commandancy seriously in 1929, but his promotion to major
general the following July foreshadowed bitter controversy when
Neville's tenure as commandant of the Marine Corps ended.[4]

While Lejeune counted Butler among his close friends, and
the feisty and colorful Quaker considered himself Lejeune's
protégé, the two officers remained poles apart from a professional perspective. Butler harbored a conviction that the future
of the Marine Corps lay in the bushwhacking campaigns characteristic of America's brief period of neocolonialism. Any reason
to remain tied to the navy and committed to supporting the fleet
slipped away with the end of the age of sail. Butler's record of
vituperative anti-Navy and anti-Naval Academy rhetoric made it
appear doubtful that he could accomplish anything at the helm
of the Marine Corps, except to invite controversy and possibly
threaten its survival as a separate armed service. Lejeune and all
of the commandants who followed him into the next war believed
strongly in the mission of the corps to defend or seize advance
bases in support of the fleet, a mission Butler appeared to scorn.

Lejeune's strong endorsement of Neville as his successor was in the best interests of the Marine Corps.[5]

Events in nearby Virginia presented Lejeune with the opportunity for a rewarding second career. On 11 March 1929, Brigadier General William H. Cooke, U.S. Army (Retired), notified the Board of Visitors of the Virginia Military Institute (VMI) in Lexington that he intended to retire as superintendent. When both announcements of impending retirements became public, several Marine Corps officers who were alumni of VMI urged Lejeune's appointment to the position of superintendent. On 16 March 1929, the board voted to offer the post to Lejeune pending an interview, and four days later it traveled to Washington to meet with him. Impressed, it voted unanimously to offer Lejeune the post of superintendent of VMI, with a salary of eight thousand dollars per annum and quarters and utilities provided. In its deliberations, the Board of Visitors resolved to reiterate its policies should Lejeune accept the position (1) there should be no overemphasis on military training at the expense of academics; (2) the importance of VMI's contribution to the state of Virginia should be emphasized; and (3) further contribution by the Assembly of Virginia must continue to be pursued.[6]

With his future employment decided, Lejeune attended to the various details incident with relinquishing the commandancy. He notified both his successor and the secretary of the navy that he would be on terminal leave until 12 November 1929. He requested that on that date, his name appear on the list of retired officers. Neville received speedy confirmation as his successor. Apparently, Hoover and his secretary of the navy–designate, Charles F. Adams, considered no one else. A handful of Butler's supporters clamored briefly for his candidacy, but hardly anyone took them seriously. Although Neville wore the hated stripe of the Naval Academy, his credentials as a tropical campaigner and proven combat leader made him eminently acceptable to Butler and his coterie.[7]

While marines everywhere expressed surprise at the news of Lejeune's retirement, the announcement of his new position at VMI eased the shock of the disclosure. Numerous positive responses from friends and admirers survive; one note especially deserves mention because it came from Lemuel C. Shepherd, Jr., Lejeune's onetime aide-de-camp who became a commandant himself: "Nothing could please me more than to have you at the head of my old school."[8]

During the following April, the alumni of VMI honored Major General and Mrs. Lejeune with a dinner in Richmond. That evening, Governor and Mrs. Harry F. Bird hosted them. The following day, VMI held a reception in their honor and the Lejeunes met the faculty and the First Classmen. The entire arrangement could not have been more suitable to the aging warrior. After more than forty years in uniform and serving honorably with the highest ideals, Lejeune found the excesses of the Roaring Twenties and the jazz age disturbing. Lexington and VMI provided a brief respite from the troublesome era—honor codes, young men choosing to wear a uniform, and a military system accepted without question. Founded in 1839, the school possessed a proud tradition tailor-made for an idealist like Lejeune. All visitors came away with fresh reminders of the school's heroic legacy, especially the part the cadets played with Confederate forces at New Market on 15 May 1864. The superintendency of an institution with such a poignant and proud past may have been more of a demanding job than Lejeune wanted in retirement, however.[9]

On the campus of VMI, a seemingly tireless Lejeune continued to demonstrate the leadership that made him famous throughout the naval services. He appeared at cadet functions, occasionally in their mess hall, and at athletic events, and he spoke to them in large groups. The other side of his official duties had to do with the Board of Visitors to the institution. Lejeune met with it often, either in Richmond or when it came to Lexington, the trips to the former becoming increasingly onerous over the years as Lejeune drove himself. Lejeune made a significant contribution to VMI through a major program of expansion to the physical plant. Through his friendship with President Franklin D. Roosevelt, Lejeune brought a considerable amount of federal funds to Lexington. With grants totaling $222,411, four new buildings appeared on the campus, four others were rebuilt, and "VMI Hill" received a much-needed landscaping. VMI never experienced a more ambitious building program; Lejeune's original request to Roosevelt for funds from the Works Progress Administration (WPA) totaled more than $360,000!

In addition to an aggressive lobbying program to obtain funds for new construction, Lejeune took measures to correct the declining enrollment of VMI. In 1932–33, the number of cadets at VMI fell below the level that the institution could accommodate. Lejeune marshaled his forces throughout the region to encourage bright young men to apply for admission. By 1934, his efforts achieved tangible results and the downward trend in enrollment applications ceased. In that year, 146 cadets graduated. He pressed for earlier retirement of superannuated and disabled professors, recommended construction of a new library, and urged the establishment of an endowment fund. In addition, Lejeune directed the raising of entrance requirements, addition of new courses, an increase in faculty promotion standards coincident with improved scales of compensation, and the establishment of closer relationships between cadets and faculty. Finally, he insisted on an emphasis on cadet leadership in all matters related to cadet affairs.[10]

Finding suitable employment for VMI graduates remained a vexing problem for Lejeune. In June 1916, his predecessor as commandant visited VMI. Barnett told the faculty and cadets that he wished the Marine Corps could accept all of the graduating cadets as second lieutenants. Now, Lejeune pressed to obtain commissions in the corps for some of the graduates. During his first year in Lexington, the Marine Corps could accept only ten new officers from all sources, including the Naval Academy. Lejeune secured Neville's promise to save three of the vacancies for graduates of VMI. The following year, Lejeune obtained the approval of Neville's successor to accept what graduates he could from the institution. The new commandant seemed pleased with Lejeune's products: "I congratulate you and VMI for turning out such excellent men, and only regret that we could not commission more of them."[11]

Lejeune's love for the Marine Corps did not diminish even in retirement, and he shared his feelings when *Reminiscences of a Marine* appeared. The origins of Lejeune's memoirs are somewhat obscure. By his own account, Ellie and the children urged him to "tell his story." At first he demurred, insisting that few would be interested and no one would print it. Somehow, however, a World War One Marine Corps officer and Philadelphia publisher, Major Gordon Dorrance, pressed a contract into Lejeune's hand. For most of 1929 and into the spring of 1930, he wrote his autobiography, mailing handwritten pages to Quartermaster Sergeant Noble J. Wilson at Headquarters Marine Corps. Wilson returned typed pages to Lejeune, along with a bill for his services. Then, Lejeune mailed the chapters off to Philadelphia.

By May 1930, the manuscript had grown to 775 typed pages and Dorrance asked Lejeune to shorten it considerably, perhaps by 200 to 250 pages. Lejeune managed to cut 150 pages, and the autobiography went to press with considerable success. Dorrance advertised the book even before Lejeune completed the first draft of the manuscript, and orders began to arrive while the author continued to revise and edit. A first printing of sixteen hundred copies sold out almost immediately and Dorrance ordered another thousand printed. Meanwhile, the North American Newspaper Alliance agreed to publish the book as a serial. In print, the book brought success to both its author and publisher. Dorrance told Lejeune that it was the finest book that he had brought out. Lejeune basked in the glory of its publication, receiving numerous requests from strangers and friends alike for an autographed copy. Much of *The Reminiscences of a Marine* reminded fellow leathernecks of the pride and dedication characterizing his thirty-nine years of Marine Corps service.[12]

Senior Marine Corps officers and important civilian officials realized Lejeune's influence in the appointments of the commandants of the 1930s, first during consideration of a replacement for Lejeune's successor. Plagued by hypertension, Neville was told repeatedly by his physicians that he had to get his blood pressure down. On 27 March 1930, he suffered a stroke. Spokesmen for the Department of the Navy and Headquarters Marine Corps described his illness in mild terms, but those close to the scene knew that Neville would never use his paralyzed leg again. Neville suffered a second stroke and died on 8 June 1930. His untimely passing precipitated an intense flurry of political machinations over the selection of a successor.

Hoover and Adams considered two major generals, Butler and Logan Feland, and two brigadier generals, Ben H. Fuller and John H. Russell, for the post. Both Butler and Feland had distinguished records of expeditionary service, Fuller and Russell—both graduates of the Naval Academy—less so. To the scorn of some observers, Russell had served almost a decade on detached service with the Department of State as the U.S. High Commissioner in Haiti. At the time of Neville's illness, Fuller presided over Headquarters Marine Corps as assistant to the commandant and thus had been acting commandant of the Marine Corps since Neville became incapacitated.

Support for the ambitious Butler appeared to be tissue thin; most of the letters urging his appointment came from veterans groups or friends from the Philadelphia area. Butler realized at the outset of the controversy that he faced considerable opposition from within the Department of the Navy. To his brother, he declared: "Even the lowest ranking privates know that this is a showdown between the Naval Academy element and those from civil life and the ranks."[13]

When Butler asked Lejeune to assist him in his quest, the former commandant penned a remarkably oblique recommendation to Hoover's personal secretary. In the handwritten letter, he hardly mentioned Butler and claimed not to know the names of the other contenders for the commandancy! Most of Lejeune's letter contained information on the former commandant's activities since retirement and little material in support of his erstwhile friend and former protégé. Lejeune, like most senior officers, considered Butler more of a liability than an asset to the Marine Corps by 1930. Even Lejeune's lackluster support for Butler served to exacerbate further his strained relationship with Feland. The veteran campaigner concluded—probably correctly—that Lejeune's halfhearted support for Butler or himself resulted in the appointment of the least likely candidate for the commandancy.[14]

As had been the case since 1920, the machinations of civilian politicians came to influence the decision for a new commandant of the Marine Corps. Hoover's navy aide-de-camp gathered information on the various candidates. Commander Charles R. Train claimed to find no backing for Butler and dismissed Russell's candidacy because of his lengthy period of detached duty in Haiti under the aegis of the Department of State. He considered Feland to be only a second choice because the veteran leatherneck had not attended the Naval Academy. Train argued that both naval services favored Fuller because of his Naval Academy diploma—both Fuller and the new chief of naval operations, Admiral William Veazie Pratt, graduated with the class of 1889.[15]

When the choice of a successor to Neville became public, the losing candidates fumed and sulked. Feland expressed particular outrage in a letter to Harbord. In it, he took the opportunity to castigate Lejeune again and to malign Fuller's professional character: "I cannot help feeling deeply humiliated because it is true that I have been cast aside for one of the most worthless men we ever had in the Corps . . . I am very sorry that you wrote to Lejeune. . . . I know him like a book and there is nothing too low for him to do."[16]

Equally furious at the selection of Fuller, Butler vowed to remain in uniform until mandatory retirement age. In doing so, the controversial leatherneck hoped to block further accession of an Annapolitan to the corps' highest post. But his days as a Marine came to an end quickly. Following the delivery of inappropriate remarks concerning the Italian dictator Benito Mussolini in an after-dinner speech to a private audience, Butler faced a court-martial. Fuller asked Lejeune and Joseph H. Pendleton to return to active duty in order to sit on the judicial body, but both officers declined. Then, not willing to endure the political controversy any longer, President Hoover and his advisers found their way out of the dilemma with Butler's acceptance of a letter of reprimand. He retired shortly thereafter. Lejeune maintained his distance from the affair, only confiding to his sister that "I hope he [Butler] won't be punished severely."[17]

By then, Butler had become a serious embarrassment for both Lejeune and the Marine Corps. In a letter to the influential Claude A. Swanson of the Senate Naval Affairs Committee, former Secretary of the Navy Josephus Daniels attempted to ameliorate Butler's plight. Lejeune remained aloof from the controversy, and he declined his old friend's invitation to attend a retirement ceremony at Quantico, claiming to be pressed by his new duties at VMI.[18]

When Fuller approached mandatory retirement age in 1934, the political infighting over the choice of his successor began anew. From retirement, Butler telegraphed Lejeune excitedly to suggest that it might be possible to interject Hugh Matthews's name. Lejeune responded with the advice to support President Roosevelt's nomination of John H. Russell and wait for the next vacancy in the commandancy. Lejeune knew that Russell and Franklin D. Roosevelt had been close friends since the latter's tenure as assistant secretary of the navy during the World War One era. Butler followed up his initial telegram with an assertion that he thought might cause Lejeune to join the fray: "Believe we now have [the] chance [to] bring [the] Marine Corps back to the leadership approaching you and Neville."[19]

Meanwhile, Butler marshaled what political support he had remaining on Capitol Hill. Senator Hugo Black conducted a spirited campaign to prevent Russell's promotion to permanent major general. Their efforts failed and the veteran of Haiti took over as the sixteenth commandant, with the rank of permanent major general. With Russell's retirement in 1936, the issue was raised again. One candidate, a protégé of retired Major General Joseph H. Pendleton, came quickly to the top of the list. When many of the general officers of the Marine Corps gathered at Quantico on 10 November 1935 to celebrate the corps' birthday. Charles H. Lyman's position next to that of Russell suggested to some that as the senior general officer besides the commandant, he had the inside track. From Lexington, Lejeune urged the selection of his wartime comrade in the Second Division, AEF, Hugh Matthews. On Matthew's behalf, he wrote to Roosevelt's secretary extolling his friend's professional qualities. Lejeune even quoted from the published memoirs of his former division surgeon—Theodore Roosevelt's son-in-law—which praised Matthews further. Sadly for both Matthews and Lejeune, Russell considered Holcomb a protégé. Moreover, Russell enjoyed Roosevelt's confidence and friendship. Although Lyman and Holcomb had similar records—diplomas from both the Army and Navy War Colleges—Roosevelt accepted Russell's recommendation and nominated Holcomb to head the corps.[20]

At VMI, Lejeune performed his duties as superintendent with characteristic enthusiasm and professionalism. In the process, he almost lost his life. On 19 September 1932 while inspecting the construction of a new water tower, Lejeune fell and fractured his skull and arm. He was unconscious for nearly a week, and the accident kept him inactive for almost a year. Brain damage from the incident impaired Lejeune's ability to articulate completely. For the remainder of his days, he read his speeches from prepared scripts rather than deliver the stirring extemporaneous talks so admired by all who heard them. Except for the attack of appendicitis in 1902 and an occasional bout of malaria endemic to veterans of campaigns in the tropics, his health had been remarkably good. But the accident in 1932 may have worsened a medical problem that plagued him since his days as assistant to the commandant.

In 1917, doctors had diagnosed an enlarged prostate gland, a common problem in older men. In Lejeune's case, the condition seemed to be exacerbated by the long hours at a desk. Apparently, the problem abated, because he reported no sickness while in France during the war. After becoming commandant, Lejeune had begun horseback riding. Years later, he attributed his good health to exercise. Unable to continue riding while in Lexington, Lejeune played golf every afternoon. While at VMI, the nagging medical malady became increasingly bothersome. On 16 January 1937, Lejeune told the Board of Visitors that he planned to step down effective 1 October, informing it that "here he had found genuine enjoyment by reason of my assocation with the cadets, and it distresses me beyond measure to give this advance notice which involves the severance of the close ties that bind me to them."[21]

Even though he had elected to retire, Lejeune could not allow the Board of Visitors to select his successor by themselves. He sought the advice and counsel of a distinguished graduate, Brigadier General George C. Marshall, whom be believed interested in the selection of a new superintendent for his alma mater. In his first letter to Marshall, Lejeune even suggested that the future chief of staff of the army might consider applying for the position. Meanwhile, would-be candidates and their supporters besieged the popular and influential Marshall. In response to Lejeune's letter, Marshall came out strongly against the applications of Generals Boller and McCloskey, both of whom apparently lobbied strongly for the position: "To appoint either of these men . . . would be a fatal error. In personality and in methods they are completely disqualified . . . I dislike putting my oar in this matter, but my feelings for [VMI] are too strong to permit me to sit quite under these circumstances . . . Please treat this as most confidential."[22]

In any event, the Board of Visitors selected a VMI graduate from the class of 1894, General Charles E. Kilbourne, to succeed Lejeune. Even as the board deliberated, tributes to Lejeune's service to the school poured in. The VMI Alumni News trumpeted his contributions: "You have sent beams of greatness into the souls of 2,500 young Americans who have spent part of their lives under your guidance. Your name, sir, will live with those of [Stonewall] Jackson and many in our tradition."[23]

The year before his retirement from VMI, Lejeune gathered with his wartime comrades to participate in the dedication of a memorial statue to the Second Division, AEF. Located one-fourth of a mile from the White House and in the shadow of the Washington Monument, the marble edifice came into being through the efforts of the Second Division Association. Of the division's four commanding generals during World War I, only Lejeune and Harbord participated in the dedication. Charles A. Doyen died of influenza in 1918; Omar Bundy lay ill in Walter Reed Hospital.

Electing to move to Norfolk, Lejeune put off the advice of his physicians for surgery. They must have told him that in most cases involving removal of the prostate, impotence and incontinence resulted. From retirement at 518 Pembroke Avenue, Lejeune continued to maintain an active correspondence on both Marine Corps and VMI matters. Occasionally, he journeyed to Washington to join Kilbourne in meetings with President Roosevelt to press for additional building funds. Two years before his retirement, Lejeune's spinster sister died after a long illness, and he supervised the settlement of her estate. Lejeune and Augustine remained very devoted to one another, and he never shirked his responsibility for her welfare: "You are the best and dearest sister in the world. One of my greatest crosses is [how] little we see of each other."[24]

Meanwhile, his eldest daughter's son and daughter grew older. The boy, James B. Glennon, Jr., won an appointment to the U.S. Naval Academy. In 1937, Lejeune received the heartening news that his grandson planned to apply for a commission in the Marine Corps upon graduation with the class of 1939. As in Lejeune's day, Naval Academy officials established preference for service selection based on academic standing. With a position near the top of the class (82 out of 581), Lejeune's grandson assumed that he could obtain a commission in the Marine Corps without difficulty. However, in what must have been a case of déjà vu for Lejeune, he learned that navy officials hoped to correct the discouraging trend of a disproportionate number of graduates in the top half of the class choosing the Marine Corps rather than the navy. Admiral Wilson Brown, the superintendent, intended to have the midshipmen draw lots to determine service selection.

Brown's parochial decision was just the sort of bureaucratic malfeasance needed to bring an officer of Lejeune's decided character to the barricades. Immediately, the former commandant wrote to Lieutenant General Thomas Holcomb. The pungent comment of the seventeenth commandant of the Marine Corps reflected the opinion of most observers except those who wore navy blue: "I was astounded to hear that Wilson Brown would recommend anything so stupid as deciding who is to come into the Marine Corps by drawing lots from among the applicants."[25]

As the administrative dust settled, the secretary of the navy announced first an increase in the Marine Corps' quota of midshipmen. Brown's worst fears materialized, then: all of the new second lieutenants from the Naval Academy came from the top of the class of 1939. Gracious in defeat, the superintendent invited Lejeune to attend the graduation ceremonies, provided a place for him on the rostrum with the officials, and offered lunch at Buchanan House afterwards. Sadly, Marine Corps regulations of the era prevented a retired officer from administering the oath of office, and Holcomb had to turn down Lejeune's request to swear in his grandson.[26]

As Lejeune watched the class of 1939 march past to receive their diplomas and commissions, he must have noticed one graduate—Edward L. Beach, number two in his class, the commander of the midshipmen regiment, and the son of his former roommate from the class of 1888. Earlier, Midshipman Beach wrote to Lejeune to remind him of his father's fondness: "Pop has often spoken of you to me. He has very great admiration for you . . . the luckiest thing that happened to him at the Academy was getting you for a roommate."[27]

Lejeune shared the concern of his fellow citizens over the worsening situation in Europe. When Hitler's legions marched into Poland in September, the old warrior wrote to the commandant to volunteer for active service. Though it was a splendid example of Lejeune's patriotism, age precluded his acceptance back into uniform. Holcomb explained gently and officially to Lejeune that only officers with special qualifications—and below the rank of lieutenant colonel—would be called back to the colors. The following year, Lejeune donned his dress blues and Sam Browne belt one last time to join the marines at the Norfolk barracks to celebrate the Marine Corps' birthday.[28]

In 1942, Lejeune finally received promotion to lieutenant general. Attempts to elevate Barnett to that rank in 1918 had precipitated considerable controversy. A feeble try in the same direction in 1928 to benefit Lejeune went almost unnoticed and died at the hands of the House Naval Affairs Committee for lack of support. With the act of 23 June 1938, any officer commended could retire at the next higher rank. Lejeune learned to his dismay from Holcomb that the legislation did not apply to officers on the retired list. Lejeune wrote immediately to the chairmen of both the House and Senate Naval Affairs Committees seeking redress, while Holcomb pulled every political string at his disposal. On the eve of America's entry into World War II, Congress passed legislation granting tombstone promotions to retired officers with distinguished combat records. Lejeune became the second Marine Corps officer to hold the rank of lieutenant general, effective 8 April 1942. Earlier, President Roosevelt had elevated Holcomb to that rank.[29]

Even as Lejeune basked in this new and unexpected honor, he faced a life-threatening medical problem. He called it "chronic bladder trouble." Apparently, it had worsened in the past ten years. On 29 August 1942, Lejeune's doctors diagnosed the problem as an enlarged prostate gland and advised immediate surgery. Lejeune entered Baltimore's Union Hospital in early November. When his surgeons removed the prostate, they confirmed what had been suspected for some time. The gland had become malignant and metastasized, spreading deadly cancer cells throughout his body. Soon after the surgery, Lejeune's kidneys failed and he developed uremia. At 9:45 A.M. on 20 November 1942, he died.[30]

Except for his family and close friends, few knew of Lejeune's ill health. The announcement of his death shocked and saddened all who knew him or knew of his lifetime of service to corps and country. The news reached Pointe Coupee by radio, and the local newspaper devoted much of its front page to the event: "A pall is over the parish of Pointe Coupee since the news . . . Friday morning, that John Archer Lejeune had gone to meet his great commander."[31]

Messages of sympathy poured into the Lejeune home in Norfolk. Wartime comrades, especially, felt the loss of Lejeune. Pershing wrote a consoling note that spoke for the doughboys and leathernecks of the American Expeditionary Forces: "I shall ever cherish the memory of our association in France during the World War, and where his talents and force contributed so largely to the victory of our armies."[32]

At 11 A.M. on Monday, 23 November 1942, the Right Reverend James E. Freeman conducted a funeral service for Lejeune at the Church of the Epiphany at 1317 G Street N.W. in Washington. A funeral escort commanded by Holcomb and consisting of two battalions of marines, the Marine Corps band, a battery of field artillery, a company of sailors and another of soldiers, and a detachment of VMI cadets, met the body at the Second Division monument and escorted it past the Lincoln Memorial and over Memorial Bridge for burial in Arlington Cemetery. The thirteenth commandant of the Marine Corps was laid to rest at thirty minutes past noon. Ellie survived her husband by ten years, dying on 11 November 1953 after a short illness.[33]

Notes

1. Undated press clipping, Lejeune's biographical file, reference section, MCHC.
2. Wendell C. Neville to James G. Harbord, 24 August 1928, correspondence file ("N"), Harbord MSS, New York Historical Society; and [?], Senate Commerce Committee, to Secretary of the Navy Charles F. Adams, 21 September 1929, container 35, Herbert C. Hoover MSS, Herbert C. Hoover Presidential Library, West Branch, Iowa.
3. Smedley D. Butler to JAL, 23 July 1928, Butler MSS, MCHC, quoted in Hans Schmidt, *Maverick Marine: General Smedley D. Butler and the Contradictions of American Military History* (Lexington: University Press of Kentucky, 1987), p. 200; and Butler to JAL, 27 December 1927, Butler MSS, MCHC.
4. Editorials and reports in the *New York Times*, 7 February 1929, 9 February 1929, 24 February 1929, and 10 March 1929.
5. See Butler, as told to Lowell Thomas, *Old Gimlet Eye: The Adventures of Smedley D. Butler* (1933; reprint, Quantico: Marine Corps Association, 1981) for a variety of anti-navy and anti-Naval Academy comments (e.g., pp. 21, 32, and 36–37). See also Butler to his mother, 16 August 1915, Butler MSS, NewTown Square, Pennsylvania.
6. Records of the Board of Visitors, VMI Archives, Virginia Military Institute, 11 March 1929.
7. Candidates for Commandant of the Marine Corps 1929 file, container 38, Hoover MSS.
8. Lemuel C. Shepherd, Jr., to Lejeune, 25 February 1929, reel 13, Lejeune MSS, Library of Congress.
9. JAL to AL, 9 November 1924, reel 2, Lejeune MSS.
10. Lejeune to Franklin D. Roosevelt, 1 January 1934, folder 513, Roosevelt MSS; Roosevelt Library, Hyde Park, New York; Lejeune to VMI Alumni, 1 March 1931, reel 5, Lejeune MSS; William Couper, *One Hundred Years at VMI*, 4 vols. (Richmond, Va.: Garrett and Massie, 1939), 4: 268–271; and Henry A. Wise, *Drawing Out the Man: The VMI Story* (Charlottesville: University of Virginia Press, 1978), pp. 130–42.
11. Ben H. Fuller to Lejeune, 5 June 1931, reel 5, Lejeune MSS. See also Lejeune to Rufus H. Lane, 19 May 1932; and Lane to Lejeune, 20 May 1932, reel 5, Lejeune MSS; and Lejeune to Wendell C. Neville, 23 November 1929, reel 4, Lejeune MSS.
12. Gordon Dorrance to Lejeune, 23 May 1930, reel 4, Lejeune MSS. See also John N. W. Keeler to Dorrance, 21 May 1930; and John Craige to Lejeune, 14 May 1930, reel 4, Lejeune MSS.

13. Smedley D. Butler to Samuel Butler, 28 July 1930, Butler MSS, NewTown Square.
14. Logan Feland to James G. Harbord, 22 August 1930, correspondence file ("F"), Harbord MSS, New York Historical Society; and Harbord to the Secretary of the Navy, 4 August 1930, in the same file.
15. Lejeune to Walter H. Newton, 21 July 1930, and Commander Charles R. Train to Hoover, 21 July 1930, candidates for commandant, 1930 file, container 38, Hoover MSS. See also Maj. Gen. James G. Harbord to Hoover, 28 July 1930; "Legion to Protest Neglect of Butler," *Philadelphia Evening Bulletin*, 18 August 1930; and John Richard Meredith Wilson, "Herbert Hoover and the Armed Forces," (diss., Northwestern University, 1971), pp. 52–87.
16. Logan Feland to James G. Harbord, 22 August 1930, correspondence file ("F"), Harbord MSS, New York Historical Society. See also Harbord to Secretary of the Navy Charles F. Adams, 4 August 1930, in the same file.
17. JAL to AL, 3 February 1931, reel 2, Lejeune MSS; see also Ben H. Fuller to JAL, 29 January 1931, and JAL to Fuller, 29 January 1931, both letters in Lejeune's Officers Qualification Record, Headquarters Marine Corps.
18. JAL to Smedley D. Butler, 18 September 1931, reel 5, Lejeune MSS; and JAL to AL, 3 February 1931, reel 2, Lejeune MSS, for his terse comment on Butler's impending legal difficulties and his own subsequent refusal to attend the colorful marine's retirement ceremony. See also Josephus Daniels to Claude A. Swanson, 5 February 1931, container 102, reel 62, Daniels MSS.
19. Butler to Lejeune, 18 February 1935, reel 6, Lejeune MSS. See also Senator Hugo Black to Lejeune, 26 February 1935; and Lejeune to Black, 1 March 1935, on the same reel; see also Donald F. Bittner, "Conflict Under the Dome: Senator Hugo Black, General Smedley Butler, and the Challenged Appointment of John Russell as Commandant of the Marine Corps," a paper presented at the Annual Meeting of the American Historical Association, Chicago, 28 December 1984.
20. Lejeune to Roosevelt, 19 May 1935, file 18e, and Lejeune to Cordell Hull, 11 May 1936, file 18e, Roosevelt MSS; Lejeune to Harbord, 3 September 1936, and Hugh Matthews to Lejeune, 14 November 1936, reel 7, Lejeune MSS. See also Lejeune to John H. Russell, 26 June 1935, reel 6, Lejeune MSS. Apparently, Lyman and Lejeune were never close friends; see Charles H. Lyman to Joseph H. Pendleton, 18 August 1923, folder 60, Pendleton MSS, MCHC.
21. Lejeune to the Board of Visitors, Virginia Military Institute, 16 January 1937, Journal of the Board of Visitors, 1929–1937, VMI Archives.
22. George C. Marshall to Lejeune, 26 March and 5 April 1937; and Lejeune to Marshall, 31 March and 9 April 1937, Marshall MSS, George C. Marshall Institute, Lexington, Virginia.
23. *VMI Alumni News*, spring 1937, p. 3, file 513, Roosevelt MSS.
24. JAL to AL, 19 October 1899, reel 1, Lejeune MSS.
25. Holcomb to Lejeune, 17 February 1939, reel 7, Lejeune MSS. See also Lejeune to Secretary of the Navy Claude Swanson, 16 February 1939, reel 8, Lejeune MSS; and Bureau of Navigation to Brown, 25 February 1939, reel 7, Lejeune MSS.
26. *Register of Alumni* (Annapolis: United States Naval Academy Alumni Association, 1982), pp. 306–12; Wilson Brown to Lejeune, 11 May 1939; reel 7, Lejeune MSS; Lejeune to Thomas Holcomb, 25 May 1939, and Holcomb to Lejeune, 27 May 1939, Lejeune's Officer Qualification Record.
27. Edward L. Beach to Lejeune, 13 October 1937, reel 7, Lejeune MSS.
28. Lejeune to Commandant of the Marine Corps, 14 September 1939; and Holcomb to Lejeune, 16 September 1939, reel 8, Lejeune MSS.

29. Secretary of the Navy to the House Naval Affairs Committee, 26 December 1941, RG 80; Lejeune to Senator David I. Walsch and Representative Carl Vinson, 4 January 1941; and Holcomb to Lejeune, 3 and 5 June 1941, reel 9, Lejeune MSS. S. 1360 passed the Senate and went to the House on 11 December 1941. See also Holcomb to Lejeune, 11 April 1941, Lejeune's Officer Qualification Record.
30. Death certificate, Lejeune's Officer Qualification Record; and Adjutant and Inspector to Paymaster, Headquarters Marine Corps, 19 December 1942, Lejeune's Officer Qualification Record.
31. "Lieutenant General John Archer Lejeune Passes," *Pointe Coupee Banner*, 26 November 1942.
32. Pershing to Ellie Lejeune, 21 November 1942, box 116, Pershing MSS, Library of Congress. See also Ellie M. Lejeune to Pershing, 19 December 1942, box 116, Pershing MSS.
33. Press Release, Department of the Navy, 20 November 1942, Lejeune's biographical file, reference section, MCHC.

8

The Legacy of
John Archer Lejeune

Not since Brigadier General Archibald Henderson held the reins of the Marine Corps, 1820–1859, has a commandant had such an impact on the smaller of the naval services. And every institution that Lejeune touched honors him: a building at VMI, another at the Naval Academy, and one of the corps' largest installations all bear his name. His birthplace has been declared a national historic site. Yet Lejeune's yeoman contribution to the nation has been obscured by myth and his own penchant for circumspection. For the most part, historians—especially those with ties to the Marine Corps—have treated Lejeune kindly and with the same circumspection. His legend grows as the years pass, even though hardly anyone pronounces Lejeune's name correctly. Satisfied with legend, marines tend to be uncomfortable with iconoclasm. During the recent consecration of Butler Hall at Quantico, the dedication speaker suggested that Lejeune and Butler collaborated to mold a modern Marine Corps and its amphibious assault mission during the 1920s.[1]

Historical evidence intimates, instead, that the gist of any Lejeune-Butler conferences held in the post headquarters at Quantico dealt with Josephus Daniels's plan to oust Barnett from the commandancy and replace him with Lejeune. Although no proof exists to suggest that Lejeune was any more than a passive participant in the plot hatched by the wily and scheming secretary of the navy, his reticence suggested at least a submissive involvement. The unsavory affair threatened to besmirch the gallant record of the corps, earned by blood and sacrifice during the neo-colonial and World War One era. When the scheme became public, Barnett had every right to accuse Lejeune of being a false friend and an unprofessional officer. From the outset, Lejeune should have alerted Barnett of the plot. It was not until Barnett lay dying in 1929 that the two officers clasped hands and renewed their friendship.[2]

Lejeune's leadership of the Marine Corps represented a dramatic break from Barnett and the past. Selected largely on the basis of seniority or political influence, many commandants spent their tenures as undistinguished sinecures. In the early twentieth century, the corps' leaders devoted themselves to Capitol Hill politics and the social requirements of Washington, leaving the day-to-day management of leatherneck affairs to the staff at Headquarters Marine Corps. Planning for future wars and contingencies rarely took place. Emphasis remained focused on personnel end-strength, as successive commandants after 1898 found themselves meeting mounting requirements with increasing difficulty because of too few leathernecks.[3]

Despite leatherneck élan and bravery in World War One, the epic had ended, and participation in the upheaval could not promise a reason for further existence as a separate armed service. Lejeune recognized the fragility of his Marine Corps in the face of postwar retrenchment and public apathy. In the 1920s, the Marine Corps needed a new direction if it was to survive, a purpose consistent with America's definition of its military and naval future. At the same time, Lejeune realized that the corps' traditional mission in support of the fleet remained. During the interwar years, only the British Royal Marines survived as a separate service among foreign marine forces; even this proud organization lost its capability as a combined-arms body.

Lejeune's vision for the Marine Corps, and his planning to achieve it, occurred not at Quantico in collaboration with Butler but in conferences with the brightest senior officers at Headquarters Marine Corps during the discouraging decade of the 1920s; the frenetic and unpredictable Butler played little part in Lejeune's transformation of the Marine Corps from a rather quaint light-infantry constabulary into a modern amphibious force. Even before the end of the administration of President Woodrow Wilson, the American electorate had begun to display its disenchantment with the neocolonialism and altruism of the immediate post–Spanish-American War era. During Lejeune's tenure as commandant of the Marine Corps, his leathernecks returned from Santo Domingo and seemed likely to exit Haiti as soon as a reasonable withdrawal became politically feasible. Further imperialistic adventures in Nicaragua only forestalled the inevitable.

While some senior marines—notably Smedley D. Butler—appeared enamored with the colonial infantry role embraced by the Department of the Navy and the Marine Corps in the first two decades of this century, Lejeune realized all too well that the era had passed. The eclipse of the constabulary mission might result in a return to the Marine Corps that Lejeune joined in 1890—61 officers and 1,986 enlisted men performing only traditional duties in support of the fleet, characteristic of the age of sail. The commandant's discomfiture may be embodied in a laconic exchange during hearings before the House Naval Affairs Committee early in his tenure at the helm of the corps. In discussions of the employment of marines and personnel strenght, a frustrated congressman posed a droll question: "Will we ever get out of Haiti?" to which Lejeune replied, "That is for you to decide."[4]

An examination of roles and missions circa 1920 revealed few options for the thirteenth commandant of the Marine Corps. When Congress authorized the establishment of the corps with the act of 11 July 1798, it directed the new body to provide detachments of leathernecks for service in the ships of the fleet. The same legislation provided for duties ashore at the discretion of the president. Later, the act of 1834 allowed for detached service with the army. Following President Theodore Roosevelt's failed attempt to remove marines from the ships of the navy, Executive Order 969 added the mobile defense of naval bases and naval stations to the duties of the United States Marine Corps.

Because the army claimed it could not defend Subic Bay adequately, its forces were concentrated near Manila. A sizable contingent of leathernecks served subsequently in the Philippines to protect the huge naval complex.[5]

Following the disjointed combined operations that characterized the Spanish-American War a decade earlier, both of the armed services took measures to implement better planning. The army established a general staff while in March 1900, Secretary of the Navy John D. Long approved the formation of the General Board of the Navy. Beginning in 1911, both bodies cooperated with the Joint Army-Navy Board—established on 17 July 1903 by the secretary of war and the secretary of the navy—in preparing a series of contingency plans in the event of war. These plans—code named by color: Red (Great Britain), Green (Mexico), Black (Germany), and Orange (Japan)—served as the basis for war planning during Lejeune's commandancy. But of these contingencies, the only possible scenario in the 1920s foresaw war with Japan; Lejeune envisioned the role of his marines in an amphibious war in the Pacific and he ordered his staff to prepare accordingly.[6]

From the outset of his commandancy, Lejeune visualized the Division of Operations and Training at Headquarters Marine Corps as the springboard for leatherneck doctrine and planning. To it, he brought an unusual friend of long professional standing who would provide a major impact on the Marine Corps of the interwar era. Lieutenant Colonel Earl H. "Pete" Ellis, a morose individual and an unrepentant alcoholic, served to Lejeune's professional satisfaction during World War I as the adjutant of the Fourth Brigade (Marine), AEF. Upon his return home, Ellis received orders to the planning staff at the Naval War College. While there, he began a far-ranging study of the role of the United States Marine Corps in a possible naval war against Japan. Early in 1921, Lejeune ordered Ellis to Washington, where the mercurial leatherneck immersed himself fully in the development of amphibious strategy in the event of war in the Pacific.

Ellis foresaw the requirement to seize the islands in the central Pacific—given to Japan as a mandate by the League of Nations following the war—with the Marine Corps providing the amphibious forces in the prosecution of a naval campaign. Ellis predicted a requirement to mobilize four brigades of marines in Hawaii upon the beginning of hostilities. There, in the first phase of his plan, the force would train and equip for deployment to the central Pacific. In the second phase of Ellis's prophetic study, the marines would seize the Marshall Islands and hold them as an advance base. From there, amphibious forces would reduce the Carolines and Marianas to establish additional advance bases for a further prosecution of the naval war against the empire of Japan.

The result of Ellis's study, "Advanced Base Operations in Micronesia, 1921," appeared on Lejeune's desk coincident with a strange request from its author. Ellis asked for permission to visit the central Pacific to see for himself what fortifications the Japanese had erected in the islands. Lejeune gave his approval to the unusual venture, even accepting Ellis's undated letter of resignation and assisting his subordinate in the establishment of a covert identity. Ellis eventually traveled to Jaluit in the Caroline Islands, where he apparently died of chronic alcoholism on 12 May 1923. His presence in the region served to embarrass U.S. authorities and perplex Japanese officials—especially the latter, because Japan had not yet begun to fortify its island mandates.

Given the commandant's political acumen, observers wondered why Lejeune would risk a political maelstrom by allowing the unpredictable Ellis to undertake such a foolhardy mission. His controversial decision lay in the belief that revision of War Plan Orange—then under way by both the planning staff at the Naval War College and the planning division of the Joint Army-Navy Board—might reduce or eliminate the amphibious role of the Marine Corps. From the outset of his commandancy, Lejeune monitored the machinations of both bodies closely by assigning Colonel Ben H. Fuller to the former and Lieutenant Colonel

Holland M. Smith to the latter. Following receipt of Ellis's analysis, Lejeune ordered the Division of Operations and Training to formulate guidelines for leatherneck participation in a war against Japan. As for Ellis's embarrassing demise, Lejeune's prompt and forthright admission to having knowledge of Ellis's ill-conceived mission prevented the affair from becoming a cause célèbre.[7]

Even before Ellis completed his study, the General Board of the Navy recommended the maintenance of a force of six thousand to eight thousand marines stationed on the West Coast. Planners envisioned this sizable contingent of leathernecks as a spearhead to seize the Marshalls and Carolines in the event of hostilities against Japan. Admiral Robert E. Coontz, the chief of naval operations, also recommended that a similar force be organized and stationed on the East Coast for possible deployment to the Caribbean. Both units—renamed "expeditionary forces" after 1923, actually appeared. In 1931, revisions of War Plan Orange called for a thirty-day marine force: one division plus one reinforced brigade, one base defense force, one barracks, and one supply depot. Planners envisioned the requirement for an additional 8,123 leathernecks 90 days later, while 11,952 more would be required 120 days after the beginning of hostilities.[8]

The Fourth Marines, following its return from Santo Domingo in 1925, constituted the West Coast Expeditionary Force until it deployed to China in 1927 with the Sixth Marines. The Eighth and Eleventh Marines formed the backbone of the East Coast Expeditionary Force; both regiments deployed to Nicaragua in 1927. When the Eleventh Marines returned to Quantico a year later, the regiment was disbanded because of shortages in personnel and appropriations. The same fate befell the Sixth Marines following its return from China, but it only reverted to cadre status rather than casing its colors. Apparently in support of the corps' increased participation in the development of amphibious doctrine, Assistant Secretary of the Navy Theodore Roosevelt, Jr., requested that the secretary of war approve the attendance of several Marine Corps officers at army schools in

1922–23: War College, Infantry School, Field Officers Course, and Infantry Officers Course.[9]

Both Coontz and Lejeune, as well as their staffs, swam against the tide of conventional naval wisdom. Following the disaster of the Allied effort to force the Dardanelles in 1915, most naval planners concluded that major amphibious landings in the face of heavy opposition could not possibly succeed. Visionaries in Marine Corps green thought otherwise. While traditionalists, such as Butler at Quantico, looked to the past for a raison d'être for the Marine Corps, luminaries such as Colonel Robert H. Dunlap studied the abortive Gallipoli campaign in depth. Dunlap, among others at the Quantico schools, concluded that the flaws in the operation could have been corrected. This group of officers prophe-sied the "Golden Age of Amphibious Warfare" decades before its occurrence.[10]

In an influential essay published in the U.S. Naval Institute *Proceedings* in 1922, Colonel Dion Williams argued that the best support for the fleet lay in a Marine Corps defense of advance bases. In his essay, Williams noted the lack of coordination between the navy and the Marine Corps. He suggested that the sea services send officers to each others' schools and sponsor exchange tours to better understand the organization and opera-tions of their respective armed forces. In the early years of the interwar era, Lejeune and his marines found little enthusiasm for amphibious warfare. Instructors at the various army schools and at the Army War College suggested that opposed landings offered little chance of success. Unopposed landings, on the other hand, need not be naval in character, and army forces could absorb such missions easily.[11]

The fleet maneuvers of 1922, held at Guantanamo Bay and Culebra, differed little from the advance base exercises of 1913–14. As in the previous maneuvers, bluejackets ferried leathernecks to the beach, where the latter wrestled huge naval guns ashore and constructed emplacements. Even though the amphibious force was now called expeditionary force, the organization and mission remained the same. A decade before, a group of naval reformers—led by the articulate and outspoken Captain William F. Fullam—argued that marines should be employed in support of the fleet by defending advance bases. Although Fullam and his supporters had insisted on a new role for the Marine Corps—coincident with outright removal of leathernecks from the warships of the fleet—it was not until 1913 that this proposal was taken seriously by the General Board of the Navy. In documents presented by Fullam in that year, he stated: "It is necessary to make a complete breach with the past as regards the organization, employment, and training of the Marine Corps. The advance base duty and expeditionary work of that Corps should be considered as its true field, the one most useful and important purpose to which it can possibly be assigned."[12]

When the fleet put to sea for the next set of maneuvers, December 1923–February 1924, the amphibious play increased markedly. This time, the entire East Coast Expeditionary Force from Quantico—totalling more than thirty-three hundred Marines—embarked under the command of Brigadier General Eli K. Cole and Colonel Dion Williams. Both officers represented a class of senior officers with intelligence and vision. But the landings in the Caribbean continued to underscore major problems for the practice of amphibious warfare that had plagued senior officers and planning staffs since the abortive Dardanelles Campaign of 1915. Forces still landed on the wrong beaches, naval gunfire support remained sporadic and inadequate, supplies that had been loaded improperly were unloaded in similar fashion, and the navy's landing craft proved to be wholly unsuitable. Cole and Williams returned to Quantico determined to improve, encouraged by Lejeune's support for their pioneering effort.[13]

In 1925, the navy conducted fleet maneuvers in the Hawaiian Islands. In a major escalation of U.S. forces, a Marine Corps contingent of twenty-five hundred men—assembled from Quantico, Mare Island, and the ships of the fleet—formed a constructive force of two divisions. As part of the "blue" force, the marines assaulted the "black" defenders in the islands, mostly from the army garrison on Oahu. This time, the fleet provided adequate naval gunfire support with eleven battleships, six light cruisers, and fifty-six destroyers. Major General Wendell C. Neville commanded the expeditionary force with Brigadier General Logan Feland and Brigadier General Dion Williams, each commanding a constructive division. In an innovative move, Colonel Robert H. Dunlap brought the staff and students from Quantico to operate as an ad hoc staff during the exercise.[14]

Although a radical improvement over the clumsy attempt in the Caribbean the year before, the exercises identified further problems. Ordinary ship's boats did not appear suitable for amphibious operations. Naval air and shore-based air support remained inadequate to support a major amphibious operation, and troops required extensive training in at-sea transfer to facilitate ship-to-shore movement. Effective communications equipment required development; existing technology proved unsuitable for amphibious operations.[15]

Increasing commitments for Lejeune's marines precluded significant participation in fleet maneuvers after 1925. The following year, the press of developments in China and Nicaragua resulted in only a small detachment from Quantico joining the navy at sea. Full-scale participation in fleet exercises by marines did not resume again until 1934. Despite the lack of interest in amphibious warfare by senior officers in both the army and navy during Lejeune's commandancy, he continued to press for official sanction and a codified mission for the Marine Corps in this specialized aspect of naval warfare. The result of Lejeune's efforts during the era—direction and emphasis from the office of the commandant, doctrine from the Division of Operations and Training at Headquarters Marine Corps, indoctrination by the schools at Quantico, and practice with the fleet in maneuvers—resulted in the publication of the most important document to date related to amphibious warfare. In *Joint Actions of the Army and Navy* (1927), the joint board specified that naval forces would "seize, establish, and defend until relieved by Army forces, advance naval bases and to conduct such related auxiliary land operations as are necessary to the prosecution of the naval campaign . . . Marines organized as a landing force perform the same functions as for the Army, whether operating with the Navy alone or in conjunction with the Army and Navy."[16]

Some of Lejeune's officers, typified by Joseph H. Pendleton, John T. Myers, Smedley D. Butler, Logan Feland, and Frederic M. Wise, looked to the past for the Marine Corps' raison d'être. Visionaries and luminaries such as Ellis, Neville, Dunlap, Cole, Williams, Ben H. Fuller, and John Russell embraced Lejeune's concept of the seizure of hostile shores as a logical and important prosecution of a naval campaign. Their collective thinking and efforts on this subject were consistent with the view of a promising young captain, George Barnett, as put forth in a letter to Brigadier General Commandant Charles Heywood in 1897: "Marines on shore or at sea must be considered an expeditionary force for use in any part of the world and not merely a collection of watchmen."[17]

An unequivocal embrace of the amphibious assault mission as a logical successor to the advance base role, made possible only by Lejeune's determined leadership and ability to deflect the destructive views of anti-navy officers such as Butler, meant a future for the U.S. Marine Corps. Significant leatherneck participation in the naval war against Japan remains Lejeune's most important legacy to the Marine Corps. By redirecting the focus of the corps away from colonial infantry duties and small-unit deployment toward major amphibious operations in support of naval campaigns, he ensured significant marine participation in the world war to follow. To his credit, Lejeune conducted this major shift in focus while maintaining the loyalties, energies, and friendships of the officers of the Marine Corps—even though many of them believed the future of the corps lay in a refinement and continuation of traditional shipboard or expeditionary duties, led by officers commissioned from civil life or from the ranks.

Lejeune's persistence and unwavering belief in the amphibious assault mission for his marines is codified by a decision of the Joint Army-Navy Board: "Marine forces organized as a landing force perform the same functions as above stated for the Army and because of the constant association with naval units will be given special training in the conduct of landing operations."[18]

Lejeune's impact on the Marine Corps is perhaps best embodied in the landing of the First Marine Division in the Solomon Islands during the year of his death. By planning and preparing for large-scale marine involvement in the event of war with Japan, Lejeune set the stage for the genesis of amphibious doctrine in the years after his commandancy. Although the *Tentative Manual for Landing Operations* did not appear until after Lejeune relinquished the helm of the corps, his vision and leadership established the basis for the most important era in leatherneck history. Without his foresight and persistence, Lejeune's marines might have spent the golden age of amphibious warfare manning detachments in the warships of the fleet and providing forces for defense battalions on lonely island outposts—missions rapidly becoming antiquated and redundant.[19]

Despite the unflagging support of Congressman Thomas S. Butler and three successive secretaries of the navy—Josephus Daniels, Edwin H. Denby, and Curtis Wilbur—Lejeune never succeeded in using political allegiance as adroitly as his predecessor. He never demonstrated the same skill in steering personnel and budgetary legislation through Congress that had marked Barnett's tenure at the helm of the corps. Attempts to establish an efficient system of officer retention and promotion eluded him. But in changing the direction of the Marine Corps from colonial infantry duties toward an amphibious assault mission in support of the fleet, Lejeune skillfully marshaled the talents, energies, and loyalties of his fellow Marines.

Notes

1. The letter "j" next to the diphthong creates a sound in French for which there is no English equivalent; thus, the Lejeune family Americanized the name to "Le-Zhurn" which is easier to pronounce. See Gary Fridell, "Pronouncing Lejeune Correctly is an Accomplishment to Treasure," *Richmond News Leader,* 5 March 1984. See also Maj. Gen. Matthew Caufield, "Butler Hall Dedicated," *Marine Corps Gazette* 74 (March 1990): 10–11. For examples of the hagiographic material that has obscured Lejeune, see Frank O. Hough, "Personalities of Men Who Differed," *Marine Corps Gazette* 34 (November 1950): 30–35; Joseph O. Dodd, "The Vision of John A. Lejeune," *Marine Corps Gazette* 51 (November 1967): 35–40; James W. Hammond, Jr., "Lejeune of the Naval Service," *U.S. Naval Institute Proceedings* 107 (November 1981): 42–46; and Rolfe L. Hilman, "Second to None: The Indianheads," *U.S. Naval Institute Proceedings* 113 (November 1987): 57–62.

2. Lejeune to the Commandant of the Marine Corps, [1935], reel 6, Lejeune MSS, Library of Congress.

3. *Annual Report of the Secretary of the Navy, 1914* (Washington: GPO, 1914) pp. 527–28.

4. U.S. Congress, House, 66th Cong., 3rd sess., Hearings Before the Naval Appropriations Committee, 21 January 1922. See also General Board Study 432, 11 February 1922, Records of the General Board, RG 80, NA; and Joint Board Serial 280, 21 July 1928, Records of the Joint Army-Navy Board, RG 225, microfilm series 1421, reel 18, NA.

5. Theodore Roosevelt to the Joint Army-Navy Board, 26 October 1907, file 305, Records of the Joint Board, RG 225, microfilm reel 6, MF 1421, NA.

6. Thomas G. Roe, et al., *A History of Marine Corps Roles and Missions.* (Washington: Headquarters Marine Corps, 1962), pp. 6–8.

7. For the most recent study on Ellis, see Dirk Anthony Ballendorf, "LtCol. Earl Hancock Ellis," a paper presented at the Ninth Naval History Symposium, 20 October 1989, Annapolis, Maryland. See also, Hirama Touichi, "The Death of LCOL E. H. Ellis, USMC, and Why the Japanese Navy Was Suspected of Poisoning Him," *Journal of the Pacific Society* 39 (July 1988): 21–33. Other published accounts that may be useful include: Dirk Anthony Ballendorf, "Earl Hancock Ellis: The Man and the Mission," *U.S. Naval Institute Proceedings* 109 (November 1983): 53–60; Ballendorf, "The Micronesian Ellis Mystery," *Guam Recorder* 5 (1975): 35–48; and John J. Reber, "Pete Ellis: Amphibious Warfare Prophet," *U.S. Naval Institute Proceedings* 103 (November 1977): 53–64.

8. Director, War Plans Division, to the General Board of the Navy, 10 August 1931, General Board Study 432, Records of the General Board, RG 80.

9. Theodore Roosevelt, Jr., Acting Secretary of the Navy, to the Secretary of War, 29 June 1922, file 6000-1288.3, RG 80, NA.

10. For the most recent study of the Marine Corps' role in the genesis of amphibious doctrine, see Karen L. Corbett, "The Influence of Gallipoli Studies on Amphibious Warfare Development at Quantico in the 1930s," a paper presented at the Annual Meeting of the American Military Institute, Arlington, Virginia, 31 March 1990. See also Kenneth J. Clifford, *Progress and Purpose: A Developmental History of the Marine Corps* (Washington: Headquarters Marine Corps, 1963), pp. 25–59.

11. Dion Williams, "Coordination in Army and Navy Training," *U.S. Naval Institute Proceedings* 48 (April 1922): 593–620.

12. William F. Fullam to the Secretary of the Navy, 1 May 1913, General Board Study 432, Records of the General Board, RG 80, NA. See also Josephus Daniels to George Barnett, 23 June 1913, in the same study.

13. Dion Williams, "The Fall Exercises of 1924," *Marine Corps Gazette* 10 (June 1925): 30–35.

14. Dion Williams, "Blue Marine Corps Expeditionary Force," *Marine Corps Gazette* 10 (September 1925): 76–88.

15. "History of Advance Base Training in the Marine Corps," 28 August 1931, General Board Study 432, Records of the General Board, RG 80, NA; for a complete study of the fleet problems of the 1920s, see Records Relating to United States Navy Fleet Problems I to XXII, 1923–41, microfilm series 964, reels 1–8, NA. See also Chief Umpire's Report, 6 May 1925, Records of the Joint Army-Navy Board, RG 225, reel 15, microfilm series 1421, NA.

16. *Joint Action of the Army and Navy* (Washington: GPO, 1927), sections IV and VII.

17. George Barnett to the Commandant, 16 November 1897, entry 5, letters received, RG 127, NA.

18. Joint Board to the Secretary of the Navy, 5 April 1927, JB 350, reel 15, microfilm series 1421, Records of the Joint Army-Navy Board, RG 225, NA.

19. Ben H. Fuller to Director, Division of Operations and Training (War Plans Section) and Commandant, Marine Corps Schools, 29 November 1932, confidential correspondence of the Secretary of the Navy, container 184, KG-KV file, RG 80, NA.

NOTES ON SOURCES

John Archer Lejeune left a better trail of paper than most public figures. His autobiography, *The Reminiscences of a Marine* (Philadelphia: Dorrance, 1930; reprint, Quantico: Marine Corps Association, 1979), is useful in identifying the key junctures in his career. Sadly, the longer and more detailed first draft of this manuscript is not extant. Lejeune's personal papers are resident in the Manuscripts Division, Library of Congress. Before his family donated the papers, a microfilm set was kept by Louisiana State University. In 1979, the Naval Academy Research Council (NARC) and Nimitz Library funded the microfilming of the Lejeune papers held by the Manuscripts Division, Library of Congress. This request precipitated a major reorganization of the Lejeune MSS. Subsequently, paper copies of this collection were prepared for the Personal Papers Section, Marine Corps Historical Center (MCHC); a register of this last collection is available for researchers.

Like most prominent people, Lejeune saved few papers before he was well known; then, he retained almost everything—including correspondence from fawning admirers and others seeking favors. But for most of his life, he maintained a prolific correspondence with his sister, Augustine. Apparently without his knowledge, she saved these valuable letters and they, too, were donated to the Library of Congress. Unfortunately, however, this portion of the Lejeune MSS bears evidence of tampering. Significant and unexplained gaps occur in his correspondence with Augustine, especially when periods of turmoil occur; portions of other letters appear to be missing.

Several published records are useful for any study of Lejeune's career. The *Annual Reports of the Secretary of the Navy, 1884–1930* (Washington: GPO) all contain sections on both the Marine

Corps and the U.S. Naval Academy. The *Register of Commissioned Officers of the Navy and Marine Corps*, published annually by the Government Printing Office, was consulted. Both the *Army-Navy Journal* and the *New York Times* provided relevant materials on the Marine Corps during Lejeune's career. The subject files and personality files in the reference section, Marine Corps Historical Center (MCHC), Washington, proved to be invaluable.

Of the personal papers of Lejeune's fellow Marine Corps officers, the Major General Smedley D. Butler MSS are the most important. A small collection held by the MCHC, Washington, contains a few interesting items, but by far the most useful body of Butler papers are held by General Butler's son, Tom, in the family home at Newtown Square, Pennsylvania. Congressman Butler's personal papers were destroyed by the family following his death in 1928. General Butler's published memoir, written with Lowell Thomas, *Old Gimlet Eye: The Adventures of Smedley D. Butler* (New York: Farrar & Rinehart, 1933; reprint, Quantico: Marine Corps Association, 1981) is useful chiefly for vignettes, anti-navy and anti-Naval Academy rhetoric, and an appreciation of Butler's worldview.

Also at the MCHC, I researched the personal papers of Major General George Barnett; his unpublished autobiography in the collection "Soldier and Sailor Too" contains a wealth of information on the Marine Corps of Lejeune's era. Because General Barnett was gravely ill during much of the writing of this memoir, a careful researcher may conclude that the latter portions were penned by Mrs. Barnett. A register of this collection was published by the GPO in 1980. Other collections of personal papers consulted at the MCHC included: Major General Joseph H. Pendleton, Major General Wendell C. Neville, and Major General Ben H. Fuller. The Pendleton MSS is supported by a register (GPO, 1975).

For an appreciation of Lejeune's Naval Academy experience, I referred first to the Records of the U.S. Naval Academy, Record

Group 405, National Archives. In this collection, the most valuable documents proved to be the Records of the Academic Board
and the Conduct Roll of Cadets. The former documentation is
also contained on microfilm. Since I researched these documents,
they have been moved to the archives of the Naval Academy in
Nimitz Library. During Lejeune's era in Annapolis, annual reports
on the Naval Academy were published by the Government Printing Office and contain such items as academic scores, number of
demerits, and rosters of naval cadets as his class dwindled in size.
The log of the *Vandalia* is, obviously, not extant, but the logs of
the *Mohican* and *Adams,* located in Record Group 24 at the
National Archives, were consulted.

The unpublished memoir of Lejeune's roommate, Captain
Edward C. Beach ("From Annapolis to Scapa Flow")—privately
held—added to the special insight into Lejeune's Naval Academy
days. Published memoirs of naval cadets of that era added to my
understanding of the Annapolis experience: Cyrus Townsend
Brady, *Under Top'sl and Tents* (New York: Scribner's Sons, 1901),
and Robert E. Coontz, *From the Mississippi to the Sea* (Philadelphia: Dorrance, 1930). For Lejeune's career as a junior officer,
1890–1915, I referred to the Records of the U.S. Marine Corps,
Record Group 127, at the National Archives. In the same
repository in Record Group 24, I found the logs of the ships in
which Lejeune served. Record Group 94 contains a few materials
related to Lejeune's studies at the Army War College.

In studying Lejeune's tour with the American Expeditionary
Forces (AEF) in World War One, I referred first to the Records of
the AEF, Record Group 120, National Archives. In addition,
both the Records of the Department of the Navy in Record
Group 80 and Records of the Secretary of War in Record Group
124 were consulted. Published memoirs from this era that proved
useful included: Richard Derby, *Wade in Sanitary* (New York:
Putnam's Sons, 1919)—Derby, the son-in-law of President Theodore Roosevelt, was the Division Surgeon, Second Division,
AEF; Hunter Liggett, *Ten Years Ago in France* (New York: Dodd,

Mead, 1925); Liggett, *Commanding an American Army: Recollections of the World War* (Boston: Houghton-Mifflin, 1925); John J. Pershing, *My Experiences in the World War*, 2 vols. (New York: Stokes, 1931); Peyton March, *The Nation at War* (Garden City, New York: Doubleday, 1932); William S. Sims, as told to Burton J. Hedrick, *Victory at Sea* (New York: Doubleday, 1920); John Thomason, *Fix Bayonets and Other Stories* (New York: Scribner's Sons, 1925; reprint, Quantico: Marine Corps Association, 1978); and Frederick M. "Fritz" Wise with Megs O. Frost, *A Marine Tells It To You* (New York: Sears, 1929).

Three published records of the Second Division, AEF were helpful: *Record of the Second Division, AEF*, 9 vols. (Washington and San Antonio: Second Division Association, 1930–32); *Second Division: Summary of Operations in World War Two* (Washington: GPO, 1944); and *The Second Division, AEF* (Coblenz, Germany: Coblenzer Volkszeitung, 1919). For Marine Corps participation in the AEF, Edwin N. McClellan, *The United States Marines in the World War*, rev. ed. (Washington: Headquarters Marine Corps, 1968), proved to be invaluable. The Manuscripts Division, Library of Congress, holds small collections of the personal papers of Major General Hunter Liggett and Major General Charles P. Summerall but neither MSS proved particulary helpful or useful. A larger collection of World War One–era correspondence saved by Major General James G. Harbord proved to be valuable. The Army War College, Carlisle Barracks, Pennsylvania, holds copies of several addresses delivered by General Harbord that added to my understanding of the AEF.

For the Marine Corps during the administration of President Woodrow Wilson, the huge collection of papers of Josephus Daniels in the Manuscripts Division, Library of Congress, was the most useful. Careful researchers may note, however, that while carbon copies of some correspondence are carefully filed in the Daniels MSS, not all orginal letters can be located in the MSS of the intended recipient. Daniels's two-volume autobiography, *The Wilson Years: Years of Peace, 1910–1917* (Chapel Hill, North

Carolina: University of North Carolina Press, 1944), and *The Wilson Years: Years of War and After, 1917–1923* (Chapel Hill, N.C.: University of North Carolina Press, 1947), buttressed the evidence found in Daniels's correspondence.

Besides the George Barnett MSS and his unpublished autobiography, "Soldier and Sailor Too," I had access to the personal papers and unpublished autobiography of Lelia Montague Barnett (privately held). Some materials related to the Marine Corps during the World War One era may be found in the Franklin D. Roosevelt MSS, Hyde Park, New York. With regard to the abrupt dismissal of Major General Barnett, the author interviewed Lelia Gordon Lucas, General Barnett's stepdaughter; Vice Admiral Lloyd R. Mustin, Mrs. Barnett's nephew; Lieutenant Colonel R. Frederick Roy, a close family friend; Brigadier General Lester A. Dessez, another Barnett confidant; and Thomas Butler, General Butler's son.

The commandancy of John Archer Lejeune offered the most elusive records. The papers of Secretary of the Navy Edwin H. Denby are held in the Burton Collection, Detroit Public Library; for the most part, important documents from this era reside in Record Group 80 at the National Archives. The diary of Assistant Secretary of the Navy Theodore Roosevelt, Jr., in the Theodore Roosevelt, Jr., MSS, Manuscripts Division, Library of Congress, provided an insider's view of the tenure of Secretary of the Navy Denby during the presidency of William G. Harding. Secretary of the Navy Curtis D. Wilbur retained only documents related to his legal career and political aspirations, and these are found in two collections: Stanford University and the Manuscripts Division of the Library of Congress. Correspondence pertaining to the Department of the Navy during Wilbur's tenure are located among the papers of President Calvin Coolidge, Manuscripts Division, Library of Congress. The records of the Marine Corps during this period are contained in a quaint and elusive filing system, "ELLS-DRAN," in Record Group 127 at the National Archives. While file numbers and topics are listed in profusion, researchers may be disappointed in finding empty file folders and unexplained gaps in these materials; many times, letters are misfiled.

At the MCHC, I read the oral histories of two of Lejeune's aides-de-camp for the period of his commandancy: General Lemuel C. Shepherd and Lieutenant General Edward A. Craig. Other oral histories containing information on Lejeune were: General Gerald C. Thomas, Mrs. Francis Neville Vest, General Clifton B. Cates, Lieutenant Colonel R. Frederick Roy, Major General Ray A. Robinson, and Major General William A. Worton. I also had access to not only Lejeune's Officer Qualification Record (OQR), but to the OQRs of George Barnett, Wendell C. Neville, and Ben H. Fuller. These OQRs contained not only fitness reports—in Lejeune's case, some had been removed—but correspondence that should have been filed in Record Group 127 at the National Archives. The OQRs of former commandants are kept at Headquarters Marine Corps, while similar files of other officers are maintained at the Military Records Center, St. Louis.

Correspondence and records germane to Lejeune's retirement years are found in the Franklin D. Roosevelt MSS; Records of the Board of Visitors, Virginia Military Institute, Lexington, Virginia; and the George C. Marshall MSS, Marshall Institute, Lexington, Virginia. Lejeune's participation in the selection process for successive commandants can be observed in the correspondence files related to the Department of the Navy and Marine Corps in both the Herbert C. Hoover MSS, Hoover Presidential Library, West Branch, Iowa; and in the Franklin D. Roosevelt MSS, Roosevelt Presidential Library, Hyde Park, New York. In the papers of Major General James G. Harbord, New York Historical Society, researchers will find an unusual assortment of correspondence relative to the selection process for commandant during the 1930s; many of these letters are critical of Lejeune for his unwillingness to support a particular candidate for the Marine Corps' highest post. Unlike Lejeune and most of his contemporaries who kept controversial and damaging correspondence out of their collections of personal papers, Harbord appears to have had no such compunction.

INDEX

FEB -- 1992

B
LEJEUNE   Bartlett, Merrill L.
            Lejeune.

$24.95

DATE			